George P. (George Putnam) Upton

The Standard Cantatas

Their Stories, their Music, and their Composers

George P. (George Putnam) Upton

The Standard Cantatas
Their Stories, their Music, and their Composers

ISBN/EAN: 9783744750868

Printed in Europe, USA, Canada, Australia, Japan

Cover: Foto ©Thomas Meinert / pixelio.de

More available books at **www.hansebooks.com**

THE

STANDARD CANTATAS

THEIR STORIES, THEIR MUSIC, AND
THEIR COMPOSERS

A Handbook

By GEORGE P. UPTON

AUTHOR OF
"THE STANDARD OPERAS," "THE STANDARD ORATORIOS,"
"WOMAN IN MUSIC," ETC.

CHICAGO
A. C. McCLURG AND COMPANY
1888

PREFACE.

THE "Standard Cantatas" is the third of the series in which the "Standard Operas" and "Standard Oratorios" have been its predecessors. Of necessity, therefore, the same method has been followed in the arrangement and presentation of the author's scheme. As in the works above mentioned, short sketches of the music and stories of the cantatas are presented, together with biographies of their composers, some of which are reproduced from the other volumes with slight changes, the repetitions being necessary for the sake of uniformity. The sketches are prefaced by a comprehensive study of the cantata in its various forms, from its early simple recitative or aria style down to its present elaborate construction, which sometimes verges closely upon that of the opera or oratorio.

The word "cantata" is so flexible and covers such a wide area in music, that it has been a work of some difficulty to decide upon the compositions that properly come within the scheme of this volume. During the past two centuries it has been variously applied to songs, like those of the early Italian school; to ballads, like those of the early English composers; to concert arias, like those of Mozart, Beethoven, and Mendelssohn; to short operettas, dramatic scenas, cycles of ballads, and even to oratorios, whose subjects are more or less dramatic. It is believed, however, that the most important of the modern cantatas are included in the volume, and with them will be found several works, such as the "Damnation of Faust" and the "Romeo and Juliet" vocal symphony and others, which, though not in the strict cantata form, are nevertheless compositions belonging to the concert-stage, for voices and orchestra, performed without scenery, costumes, or stage accessories.

The author has paid particular attention to cantatas by American composers, and has selected for description and analysis those which in his estimation rank the highest in musical merit. It would be manifestly impossible to include in a volume of the present size all the compositions by Americans which have been called cantatas, for their number is well-nigh "legion." Those have been selected which are creditable to American musical scholarship and are making a name for American music. It is possible some have been omitted which fulfil these conditions; if so, it is only because they have not come within the author's observation. The

Appendix has been a work of great care, labor, and research, and wherever it was practicable the date of each cantata was verified.

Like its two predecessors, the "Standard Cantatas" has been prepared for the general public, which has not the time or opportunity to investigate such matters, rather than for musicians, who are presumed to be familiar with them. On this account the text is made as untechnical as possible, and description takes the place of criticism   The work is intended to answer the purpose of a handbook and guide which shall acquaint the reader with the principal facts and accomplishments in this very interesting form of composition. The favor so generously accorded to the "Standard Operas" and "Standard Oratorios" leads the author to hope that this volume will also be welcome to music-lovers, and will find a place by the side of its companions in their libraries.

G. P. U.

CHICAGO, September, 1887.

CONTENTS.

	PAGE
PREFACE	3
THE CANTATA	13
BACH	29
Ich hatte viel Bekümmerniss	31
Gottes Zeit	33
Festa Ascensionis Christi	37
Ein' Feste Burg	38
BALFE	44
Mazeppa	45
BEETHOVEN	48
The Ruins of Athens	49
The Glorious Moment	53
BENEDICT	56
St. Cecilia	57
BENNETT	62
The May Queen	64
The Exhibition Ode	66

	PAGE
BERLIOZ	68
Romeo and Juliet	70
The Damnation of Faust	74
BRAHMS	82
Triumphlied	83
BRUCH	86
Frithjof	87
Salamis	92
Fair Ellen	93
Odysseus	95
BUCK	101
Don Munio	103
Centennial Meditation of Columbia	106
The Golden Legend	109
The Voyage of Columbus	114
The Light of Asia	117
CORDER	123
The Bridal of Triermain	124
COWEN	128
The Sleeping Beauty	129
DVOŘÁK	134
The Spectre's Bride	136
FOOTE	140
Hiawatha	141
GADE	143
Comala	144
Spring Fantasie	146
The Erl King's Daughter	147
The Crusaders	149

	PAGE
GILCHRIST	153
THE FORTY-SIXTH PSALM	154
GLEASON	156
THE CULPRIT FAY	157
THE PRAISE SONG TO HARMONY	161
HANDEL	163
ACIS AND GALATEA	166
ALEXANDER'S FEAST	173
L' ALLEGRO	178
HATTON	186
ROBIN HOOD	187
HAYDN	191
THE SEVEN WORDS	194
ARIADNE	198
HILLER	201
SONG OF VICTORY	203
HOFMANN	205
MELUSINA	206
LESLIE	209
HOLYROOD	210
LISZT	215
PROMETHEUS	217
THE BELLS OF STRASBURG	221
MACFARREN	226
CHRISTMAS	228
MACKENZIE	232
THE STORY OF SAYID	233
JUBILEE ODE	237

	PAGE
MASSENET	241
Mary Magdalen	242
MENDELSSOHN	246
The Walpurgis Night	248
Antigone	254
Œdipus at Colonos	259
As the Hart Pants	262
The Gutenberg Fest-Cantata	263
Lauda Sion	265
MOZART	268
King Thamos	270
Davidde Penitente	274
The Masonic Cantatas	276
PAINE	280
Œdipus Tyrannus	281
The Nativity	286
The Realm of Fancy	288
Phœbus, Arise	289
PARKER, H. W.	291
King Trojan	292
PARKER, J. C. D.	295
The Redemption Hymn	296
RANDEGGER	298
Fridolin	299
RHEINBERGER	303
Christophorus	304
Toggenburg	306
ROMBERG	308
Lay of the Bell	309

CONTENTS.

	PAGE
SCHUBERT	313
Miriam's War Song	314
SCHUMANN	317
Advent Hymn	319
The Pilgrimage of the Rose	321
The Minstrel's Curse	322
SINGER	324
The Landing of the Pilgrims	325
SMART	327
The Bride of Dunkerron	328
King René's Daughter	330
SULLIVAN	332
On Shore and Sea	334
The Golden Legend	335
WAGNER	338
Love Feast of the Apostles	340
WEBER	342
Jubilee Cantata	344
Kampf und Sieg	346
WHITING	348
The Tale of the Viking	349
APPENDIX	353
INDEX	365

THE STANDARD CANTATAS.

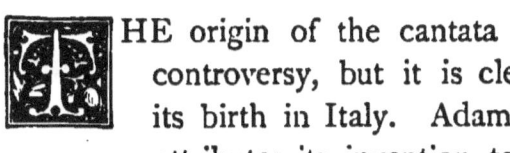

THE CANTATA.

THE origin of the cantata is a matter of controversy, but it is clear that it had its birth in Italy. Adami, an old writer, attributes its invention to Giovanni Domenico Poliaschi Romano, a papal chapel-singer, who, it is claimed, wrote several cantatas as early as 1618. The same writer also asserts that the Cavalier da Spoleto, a singer in the same service, published cantatas in 1620. Hawkins asserts in one chapter of his "History of Music" that the invention is due to Carissimi, chapel-master of the Church of St. Apollinare in Rome, who unquestionably did an important service for dramatic music by perfecting recitative and introducing stringed accompaniments; but in a subsequent chapter the historian states that Barbara Strozzi, a Venetian lady contemporary with Carissimi, was the inventor, and assigns the year 1653 as the date when she published certain vocal compositions with the title "Cantate, Ariette e Duetti," prefixed by an advertisement setting forth that having invented this form of music, she had published them as an experiment. Burney takes notice of the claim made for Romano and Da Spoleto, but does not think it valid, and says: "The first time that I have found the term 'cantata' used for a short narrative lyric poem was in the *Musiche varie a voce sola del Signor Benedetto Ferrari da Reggio*, printed at Venice, 1638." This, as will be observed, disposes of the Venetian lady's claim, as it is antedated twenty years, and Burney states his facts from personal investigation. He mentions several cantatas written about this period, among them a burlesque one describing the leap of Marcus Curtius into the gulf. He concedes to Carissimi, however, the transfer of the cantata from the chamber to the church, and on this point nearly all the early writers are agreed.

The cantata in its earliest form was a recitative, which speedily developed into a mixture of recitative and melody for a single voice, and was suggested by the lyric opera. Burney says: —

"The chief events were related in recitative. In like manner they received several progressive changes during the last century previous to their perfection. First, they consisted, like opera scenes, of little more than recitative, with frequent formal closes, at which the singer, either accompanied by himself or another performer on a single instrument, was left at liberty to show his taste and talents."

The form then changed to a single air in triple time, independent of the recitative, and repeated to the different verses as in a ballad, the melody being written every time, as the *Da Capo* was not then in use.[1] Choron defines the cantata as follows :—

"It is a little poem, which, considered in a literary sense, has no very determinate character, though it is usually the recital of a simple and interesting fact interspersed with reflections or the expression of some particular sentiment. It may be in all styles and all characters, sacred, profane, heroic, comic, and even ludicrous, representing the action or feeling of either a single or several persons. It even sometimes assumes the character of the oratorio."

As applied to recitative, the new form was variously called "recitativo," "musica parlante," or "stilo rappresentativo," one of the first works in which style was "The Complaint of Dido," by the Cavalier Sigismondo d' India, printed in Venice in 1623. The mixture of recitative and air was eventually called "ariose cantate;" and with this title several melodies were printed by Sebastian Enno at Venice, 1655.[2]

[1] Its first use is to be found in the opera of "Enea," performed at Genoa in 1676. Before 1680 it was universally adopted.

[2] It is noteworthy that in this volume occur for the first time the musical terms "adagio," "piu adagio," "affetuoso," "presto," and "allegro." In the "Cantate da Camera a voce sola," published at Bologna (1677) by Gio. Bat. Mazzaferrata, the terms "vivace," "largo," and "ardito" are also found for the first time.

The seventeenth century witnessed the rapid perfecting of the cantata in its early forms by the Italian composers. The best examples are said to have been those of Carissimi, of whom mention has already been made. Several of them are preserved in the British Museum and at Oxford; among them, one written on the death of Mary Queen of Scots. Burney says: —

"Of twenty-two of his cantatas preserved in the Christ Church collection, Oxon., there is not one which does not offer something that is still new, curious, and pleasing; but most particularly in the recitatives, many of which seem the most expressive, affecting, and perfect that I have seen. In the airs there are frequently sweet and graceful passages, which more than a hundred years have not impaired."

Of the thirteenth in this collection the same authority says: —

"This single air, without recitative, seems the archetype of almost all the *arie di cantabile*, the adagios, and pathetic songs, as well as instrumental, slow movements, that have since been made."

Fra Marc Antonio Cesti, in his later life a monk in the monastery of Arezzo, and chapel-master of the Emperor Ferdinand III., was a pupil of Carissimi, and devoted much attention to the cantata, the recitative of which he greatly improved. One of his most celebrated compositions of this kind was entitled, "O cara Liberta," and selections from it are given both by Burney and Hawkins. He must have been one of the jolly monks of old, for all his cantatas are secular in character, and he was frequently censured for devoting so much time to theatrical instead of church music. Luigi Rossi was contemporary with Cesti, and has left several cantatas which are conspicuous for length and pedantry rather than for elegance or melodious charm. Giovanni Legrenzi of Bergamo, the master of Lotti and Gasparini, published twenty-four cantatas in Venice between 1674 and 1679, which were great favorites in his time. The celebrated painter Salvator Rosa not only wrote the words for many cantatas by his musical friends, but it is known that he composed both words and music to eight. The texts of these works have preserved for posterity pictures more graphic than any he could paint of his misanthropical character; for when he is not railing against his mistress he is launching satires against Nature and mankind in general. In one of these he complains that the earth is barren and the sun is dark. If he goes out to see a friend, it always rains. If he goes on shipboard, it always storms. If he buys provisions at the market, the bones outweigh the flesh. If he goes to court —

> " The attendants at my dress make sport;
> Point at my garb, threadbare and shabby,
> And shun me, like a leper scabby."

His only wealth is hope, which points to nothing better than " workhouse or a rope." In the heat of summer he has to trudge in winter clothes. He cannot even run away from misfortune. In a word, nothing pleases the poor painter, as is evident from the gloomy moral which "adorns the tale":—

> " Then learn from me, ye students all,
> Whose wants are great and hopes are small,
> That better 't is at once to die
> Than linger thus in penury;
> For 'mongst the ills with which we 're curst,
> To live a beggar is the worst."

In 1703 Giambatista Bassani, of Bologna, published twelve cantatas devoted to the tender passion, and all of them set to a violin accompaniment,—a practice first introduced by Scarlatti, of Naples, who was one of the most prolific writers of his day. The cantata was Scarlatti's favorite form of composition, and hundreds of them came from his busy pen, which were noted for their beauty and originality. The accompaniments were written for the violoncello as well as for the violin; those for the first-named instrument were so difficult and yet so excellent that those who could perform them were often thought to have supernatural assistance.[1] Contemporary with Scarlatti was Francesco Gasparini, a Roman composer and harpsichord player of such eminence that Scarlatti sent his son Domenico, who afterwards became famous by his musical

[1] Geminiani used to relate that Franceschelli, a celebrated performer on the violoncello at the beginning of this century, accompanied one of these cantatas at Rome so admirably, while Scarlatti was at the harpsichord, that the company, being good Catholics, and living in a country where miraculous powers have not yet ceased, were firmly persuaded it was not Franceschelli who had played the violoncello, but an angel that had descended and assumed his shape.—*Burney's History*, vol. iv. p. 169 (1789).

THE CANTATA.   19

achievements, to study with him. Gasparini wrote twelve cantatas, — not so scholarly but quite as popular as those by Scarlatti. As a return for the compliment which Scarlatti had paid him, Gasparini sent him a cantata, which was the signal for a lively cantata-correspondence between them, each trying to outdo the other. Following Gasparini came Bononcini, whose contentions with Handel in England are familiar to all musical readers. He was the most prolific cantata-writer of all the Italians next to Scarlatti, and dedicated a volume of them, in 1721, to the King of England. He also published in Germany a large number which show great knowledge of instrumentation, according to the musical historians of his time. Antonio Lotti, his contemporary, wrote several which are particularly noticeable for their harmony. His pupil Benedetto Marcello, the illustrious psalm-composer, excelled his master in this form of music. Two of his cantatas, "Il Timoteo" (after Dryden's ode) and "Cassandra," were very celebrated. He was of noble family, and is famous even to this day by his masses, serenades, and sonnets, and by his beautiful poetical and musical paraphrase of the Psalms, which was translated into English, German, and Russian. The Baron d'Astorga, whose "Stabat Mater" is famous, wrote many cantatas, but they do not reach the high standard of that work. Antonio Caldara, for many years composer to the Emperor at Vienna, published a volume of them at Venice in 1699. Porpora, who was a rival of

Handel in England as an opera composer, published and dedicated twelve to the Prince of Wales in 1735 as a mark of gratitude for the support which he had given him in his disputes with the testy German.[1] After Pergolesi, who made himself famous by his "Stabat Mater," and published several cantatas at Rome, and Handel, who wrote many, which were eclipsed by his operas and oratorios, and are now hardly known, this style of the cantata languished, and gradually passed into the form of the concert aria, of which fine examples are to be found in the music of Mozart, Beethoven, and Mendelssohn. After the death of Pergolesi, Sarti and Paisiello made an attempt to revive it, and in so doing prepared the way for the cantata in its beautiful modern form. In the latter's "Guinone Lucina," written for the churching of Caroline of Austria, Queen of Naples, and in his "Dafne ed Alceo" and "Retour de Persée" the melody is intermixed with choruses for the first time.

Thus far the Italian cantatas have alone been considered; but it must not be supposed that this form of composition was confined to Italy. In France it was also a favorite style in the early part of the eighteenth century. Montclair, Campra, Mouret, Batistin, Clerambault, and Rousseau excelled in it. M. Ginguené, in the "Encyclopædia Methodique," says of these composers and their works: —

[1] Doctor Arbuthnot, in a humorous pamphlet called out by the operatic war, entitled " Harmony in an Uproar," calls Handel the Nightingale, and Porpora the Cuckoo.

"They have left collections in which may be discovered among all the faults of the age, when Italian music was unknown in France, much art and knowledge of harmony, happy traits of melody, well-worked basses, and above all recitatives in which the accent of declamation and the character of the language are strictly observed."

In Germany, however, the cantata at this time was approximating to its present form. Koch, a celebrated musical scholar of the early part of the present century, says : —

"The cantata is a lyrical poem set to music in different, alternating compositions, and sung with the accompaniment of instrumental music. The various melodies of which the whole is composed are the aria, with its subordinate species, the recitative or accompaniment, and the arioso, frequently also intermixed with choruses."

Heydenreich, another writer of the same period, says : —

"The cantata is always lyrical. Its distinctive character lies in the aptitude of the passions and feelings which it contains to be rendered by music. The cantata ought to be a harmonious whole of ideas poetically expressed, concurring to paint a main passion or feeling, susceptible of various kinds and degrees of musical expression. It sometimes may have the character of the hymn or ode, sometimes that of the elegy, or of a mixture of these, in which, however, one particular emotion must predominate."

The church cantata, according to Du Cange, dates back to 1314; but subsequent writers have shown that the term prior to the seventeenth century was used indiscriminately and without reference to any well-defined style of vocal music, and that as applied to church compositions it meant the anthem such as we now have, although not as elaborate. The noblest examples of the sacred cantata are those by Sebastian Bach, three hundred and eighty in all, over a hundred of which have been published under the auspices of the Bach-Gesellschaft. They are written in from four to seven movements for four voices and full orchestra, usually opening with chorus and closing with a chorale, the intermediate movements being in the form of recitatives, arias, and duets. The text of these cantatas is either a literal transcription of the Gospel or of portions of it. In the latter case the Gospel of the Sunday for which the cantata was written is introduced entire in the body of the work as the nucleus around which the great composer grouped the remaining parts. For instance, the cantata for Sexagesima Sunday turns upon the parable of the sower, and this being the Gospel for the day is made its central point. In like manner the cantata for the fourteenth Sunday after Trinity has for its subject the story of the ten lepers, which is introduced in recitative form in the middle of the work. The astonishing industry of Bach is shown by the fact that for nearly five years he produced a new cantata for each Sunday, in addition to his numerous fugues, chorales, motets, magnificats, masses, sanctuses, glorias, and other church music. The artistic sincerity and true genius of the old master also reveal themselves in the skill with which he finished these works for the congregation of St. Thomas, — few of whom, it is to be feared, had any conception of their real merit, — and in the untiring regularity with which he produced them, unrewarded by the world's applause, and little dreaming that long years after he had passed away they would be brought to light again, be published to the world, and command its admiration and astonishment on account of their beauty and scholarship.[1] Before passing to the consideration of the cantata in its present form, the following abridged description of those written by Bach, taken from Bitter's Life of the composer, will be of interest : —

" The directors who preceded Bach at Leipsic used to choose the cantatas or motets to be sung in the churches quite arbitrarily, without any regard to their connection with the rest of the service. But Bach felt that unless these elaborate pieces of music were really made a means of edification, they were mere intellectual pastimes suitable for a concert, but an interruption to divine worship ; and he thought that they could best edify the congregation if their subjects were the themes to which attention was specially directed in the service and sermon of the day. He therefore made it a rule to ascertain from the clergymen of the four

[1] It is curious to remember that the sacred cantatas were not composed for universal fame or for a musical public, but for the use of congregations who probably looked on them as a necessary part of the service, and thought little about the merits of their composition. In those days art-criticism was in its infancy, and they were scarcely noticed beyond the walls of Leipsic till after the composer's death. — *Bitter's Life of Bach.*

churches the texts of the sermons for the following Sunday, and to choose cantatas on the same or corresponding texts. As most of the clergy were in the habit of preaching on the Gospel of the day, the service thus became a harmonious whole, and the attention of the congregation was not divided between a variety of subjects. The clergyman of highest standing at Leipsic, Superintendent Deyling, a preacher of great eloquence and theological learning, co-operated heartily with Bach in this scheme. A series of cantatas for every Sunday and festival for five years — about three hundred and eighty in all — was composed by Bach, chiefly during the first years of his stay at Leipsic. Unfortunately many of these are lost; but one hundred and eighty-six for particular days, and thirty-two without any days specified, still remain. Their music is so completely in character with the subject of the words as to form a perfect exposition of the text. In some the orchestral introductions and accompaniments are made illustrative of the scene of the text; as for instance in one on Christ's appearing to His disciples in the evening after His resurrection, the introduction is of a soft, calming character, representing the peacefulness of evening and of the whole scene. Another, on the text 'Like as the rain and snow fall from heaven,' is introduced by a symphony in which the sound of gently-falling rain is imitated. In others the instrumental parts and some of the voices express the feelings excited by meditation on the words. Sometimes, in the midst of a chorus in which the words of the text are repeated, and, as it were, commented on, a single voice, with the accompaniment of a few instruments, breaks off into some well-known hymn in a similar strain of thought or feeling."

THE CANTATA. 25

Handel in his younger days wrote many cantatas for the church, though they are now but little known. The entire list numbers one hundred and fifty. On his return from England to his post of chapel-master at Hanover in 1711 he composed twelve, known as the Hanover cantatas, for the Princess Caroline, the words written by the Abbé Hortentio Mauro, to which no objection was offered by Handel's master and patron, notwithstanding he was a Lutheran prince. Several written in England are still preserved in the royal collections. On Holy Week of the year 1704, the same week in which Reinhardt Kaiser brought out his famous Passion oratorio, "The Bleeding and Dying Jesus," Handel's Passion cantata was first produced. Kaiser's work had been denounced as secular by the pastors, because it did not contain the words of Holy Scripture. Handel's was founded on the nineteenth chapter of St. John, and thus escaped the pulpit denunciation. This cantata is sometimes called the First Passion Oratorio, the second having been written at Hamburg in 1716.[1] In 1707 Handel was in Florence, where he wrote several cantatas, and thence went to Rome, where he produced some church music in the same form, notably the "Dixit

[1] Handel's Second German Passion, as it is now generally called, differs entirely from the earlier Passion according to St. John, and bears no analogy at all to the Passion Music of Sebastian Bach. The choruses are expressive or vigorous in accordance with the nature of the words; but none exhibit any very striking form of contrapuntal development; nor do they ever rise to the grandeur of the Utrecht Te Deum or Jubilate. — *Rockstro's Life of Handel.*

Dominus," for five voices and orchestra; "Nisi Dominus," also for five voices; and "Laudate pueri," for solos and full orchestral accompaniment. The famous anthems written for the private chapel of James Brydges, Duke of Chandos, familiarly known as the Chandos Anthems, are in reality cantatas, as each one is preceded by an overture and in its structural form comprises solos, choruses, and instrumentation for full band and choir. It is also noteworthy that it was during Handel's residence at the Duke's palace at Cannons that he wrote his first English oratorio, the legitimate successor of the Chandos Anthems, and the precursor of the great works destined to immortalize his name.

The cantatas left by Haydn are mainly secular in character; but it may well be imagined that during the days of his early married life, when his fanatical and termagant spouse was forcing him to write so much music for the priests and monks whom she entertained so sumptuously below-stairs while he was laboring above, more than one cantata must have come from his pen, which would have been preserved had he not reluctantly parted company with them to pacify his wife.

The term "cantata," as it is now used, is very elastic, and covers a range of compositions which are too large to be considered as dramatic arias or ballads, — though ballads are sometimes written for various voices and orchestra, — and too small to be called operas or oratorios. It can best be defined, perhaps, as a lyric narrative, sacred, didactic, or dramatic in character, set to music for the concert stage only, being without *dramatis personæ* in the theatrical acceptation of those words. Its general form is that of the oratorio, being for solo voices, usually the quartet, full chorus, and orchestra, though its shortness as compared with the oratorio adapts it to performance by a small chorus, and sometimes with only piano accompaniment. Among the most perfect forms of the modern cantatas are such works as Mendelssohn's "Walpurgis Night," Sterndale Bennett's "May Queen," Max Bruch's "Odysseus" and "Frithjof's Saga," Cowen's "Sleeping Beauty," Gade's "Comala," Hiller's "Song of Victory," Romberg's somewhat antiquated "Song of the Bell," Sullivan's "Golden Legend," Randegger's "Fridolin," and Dudley Buck's "Don Munio" and "Light of Asia." But besides such as these there are numerous other works, not usually classed as cantatas, which clearly belong to the same musical family; such as Berlioz's "Damnation of Faust," Brahms's "Triumphlied," Mendelssohn's settings of various Psalms, Handel's "Acis and Galatea" and "Alexander's Feast," Hofmann's "Melusina," Liszt's "Prometheus," Rheinberger's "Toggenberg," Schubert's "Song of Miriam," Schumann's ballads and "Advent Hymn," and Weber's "Kampf und Sieg." These and others of the same kin are drawn upon as illustrations and for analysis in the pages which follow.

Considering the possibilities of the cantata, its adaptability to every form of narrative, and the musical inducements it holds out, particularly in these days, when a new opera or oratorio must be of extraordinary merit to suit the public, it is somewhat remarkable that no more of them are written. Mr. Charles Barnard has made this point very aptly and forcibly in a short article printed in the "Century" for January, 1886, in which he urges the cantata form of composition upon our writers, and makes many excellent suggestions.[1] It is certainly an inviting field, especially to American composers, among whom but three or four have as yet produced works of this kind possessing real merit.

[1] The following list of cantatas by Americans hardly sustains Mr. Barnard in his assertion that there are but a few of them: BAKER, B. F., "Burning Ship;" "Storm King." — BECHEL, J. C., "Pilgrim's Progress;" "The Nativity;" "Ruth." — BRADBURY, W. B., "Esther." — BRANDEIS, F., "The Ring." — BRISTOW, G. F., "The Pioneers;" "No More." — BUCK, DUDLEY, "Don Munio;" "Centennial;" "Easter Cantatas;" "The Golden Legend;" "Light of Asia;" "Voyage of Columbus." — BUTTERFIELD, J.A., "Belshazzar;" "Ruth." — CHADWICK, G.W., "The Viking's Last Voyage." — DAMROSCH, LEOPOLD, "Ruth and Naomi;" "Sulamith." — FOOTE, A., "Hiawatha." — GILCHRIST, W. W., "Forty-sixth Psalm;" "The Rose." — GLEASON, F. G., "God our Deliverer;" "Culprit Fay;" "Praise of Harmony." — HAMERIK, A., "Christmas Cantata." — LEAVITT, W. J. D., "The Lord of the Sea;" "Cambyses; or, the Pearl of Persia." — MARSH, S. B., "The Saviour;" "King of the Forest." — PAINE, J. K., "Œdipus Tyrannus;" "The Nativity;" "Phœbus, Arise;" "Realm of Fancy." — PARKER, J. G., "Redemption Hymn." — PARKER, H. W., "King Trojan." — PRATT, S. G., "Inca's Downfall." — ROOT, G. F., "Flower Queen;" "Daniel;" "Pilgrim Fathers;" "Belshazzar's Feast;" "Haymakers;" "Song Tournament;" "David." — SINGER, OTTO, "Landing of the Pilgrim Fathers;" "Festival Ode." — TRAJETTA, PHILIP, "The Christian's Joy;" "Prophecy;" "The Nativity;" "Day of Rest." — WHITING, G. E., "Dream Pictures;" "Tale of the Viking;" "Lenora;" and many others.

BACH.

OHANN SEBASTIAN BACH, the most eminent of the world's organ-players and contrapuntists, was born at Eisenach, March 21, 1685, and was the most illustrious member of a long line of musicians, the Bach family having been famous almost from time immemorial for its skill in music. He first studied the piano with his brother, Johann Christoph, and the organ with Reinecke in Hamburg, and Buxtehude in Lübeck. In 1703 he was court musician in Weimar, and afterwards was engaged as organist in Arnstadt and Mühlhausen. In 1708 he was court organist, and in 1714 concert-master in Weimar. In 1718 he was chapel-master to the Prince von Köthen, and in 1723 was appointed music-director and cantor at the St. Thomas School in Leipsic, — a position which he held during the remainder of his life. He has left for the admiration of posterity an almost endless list of vocal and instrumental works, including cantatas, chorales, motets, magnificats, masses, fugues, sonatas, and fantasies, the "Christmas Oratorio," and several settings of the Passion, of which the most famous are the "St. John" and "St. Matthew," the latter of which Mendelssohn re-introduced to the world in 1829, after it had slumbered an entire century. His most famous instrumental work is the "Well-tempered Clavichord," — a collection of forty-eight fugues and preludes, which was written for his second wife, Anna Magdalena Bach, to whom he also dedicated a large number of piano pieces and songs. His first wife was his cousin, Maria Barbara Bach, the youngest daughter of Johann Michael Bach, a composer of no common ability. By these two wives he had twenty-one children, of whom the most celebrated were Carl Phillipp Emanuel, born in 1714, known as the "Berlin Bach;" Johann Christoph Friedrich, born in 1732, the "Bücheburger Bach;" and Johann Christian, born in 1735, who became famous as the "London Bach." Large as the family was, it is now extinct. Bach was industrious, simple, honest, and God-fearing, like all his family. He was an incessant and laborious writer from necessity, as his compensation was hardly sufficient to maintain his large family, and nearly all his music was prepared for the service of the church by contract. The prominent characteristics of his work are profound knowledge, the clearest statements of form, strength of logical sequences, imposing breadth, and deep religious sentiment. The latter quality was the outcome of his intense religious nature. Upon every one of his principal compositions he inscribed "S. D. G.," "to the glory of God alone." He died July 28, 1750, and was buried at Leipsic; but no cross or stone marks the spot where he lies. His last composition was the beautiful chorale, "Wenn wir in höchsten Nöthen sein," freely translated, "When my last hour is close at hand," as it was written in his last illness. The only record of his death is contained in the official register: "A man, aged sixty-seven, M. Johann Sebastian Bach, musical director and singing-master at the St. Thomas School, was carried to his grave in the hearse, July 30, 1750."

Ich hatte viel Bekümmerniss.

The cantata with the above title, best known in English as "My Heart was full of Heaviness," was the first sacred piece in this form which Bach wrote. Its date is 1714, in which year he was living at Weimar, and its composition grew out of a difficulty which he had with the elders of the Liebfrauenkirche at Halle, touching his application for the position of organist. It occasioned him great sorrow, and it was while in this sad plight that he wrote the cantata. It was composed for the third Sunday after Trinity, June 17, and consists of eleven numbers, — an instrumental prelude, four choruses, three arias, a duet, and two recitatives.

The prelude, which is brief and quiet in character, introduces the opening chorus ("Deep within my Heart was Sorrowing and great Affliction"), which in turn leads to the first aria ("Sighing, Mourning, Sorrow, Tears waste away my troubled Heart"), a tender and beautiful number for soprano, with oboe and string accompaniment. It is followed by the tenor recitative and aria, "Why hast Thou, O my God, in my sore Need so turned Thy Face from me?" in which the feeling of sorrow is intensified in utterance. The chorus, "Why, my Soul, art thou vexed?" a very pathetic number, closes the mournful but beautiful first part of the cantata.

The second part is more tranquil and hopeful. It opens with a duet for soprano and bass, the two parts representing the soul and Christ, and sustaining a most expressive dialogue, leading up to a richly harmonized chorus ("O my Soul, be content and be thou peaceful") in which a chorale is introduced with consummate skill. A graceful tenor aria with a delightful and smoothly flowing accompaniment ("Rejoice, O my Soul, change Weeping to Smiling") follows and leads to the final number, which is based on the same subject as that of the "Hallelujah" in Handel's "Messiah." All the voices give out the words, "The Lamb that for us is slain, to Him will we render Power and Glory," with majestic effect; after which the solo bass utters the theme, "Power and Glory and Praise be unto Him forevermore," introducing the "Hallelujah," which closes the work in a burst of tremendous power, by voices and instruments.

Gottes Zeit.

During the first half of the period in which Bach resided at Weimar, occupying the position of court and chamber musician to Duke Wilhelm Ernst, he wrote three cantatas in the old church form which are notable as being the last he composed before adopting the newer style, and as the most perfect of that kind extant. The first of these, " Nach dir, Herr, verlanget mich," is based upon the first two verses of the Twenty-fifth Psalm. The second, "Aus der Tiefe rufe ich," includes the whole of the One hundred and thirtieth Psalm and two verses of the hymn " Herr Jesu Christ, du höchstes Gut." The third and most famous of the trio, " Gottes Zeit ist die allerbeste Zeit " ("God's time is the best of all "), is generally known as the " Actus Tragicus," and sometimes as the " Mourning Cantata." Of its origin Spitta says : —

"Judging by its contents it was designed for the mourning for some man, probably of advanced age, to whom the song of Simeon could be suitably applied. No such death took place in the ducal house at this time, for Prince Johann Ernst died when a youth, and also when Bach's style of composition had reached a different stage. Possibly the cantata has reference to Magister Philipp Grossgebauer, the rector of the Weimar school before its reorganization, who died in 1711 ; at least, I can find no other suitable occasion. The contrast between the spirit of the Old and New Testaments, — between the wrath of an avenging God and the atoning love of Christ, — which had already appeared in the One hundred and thirtieth Psalm, is the germ and root of this cantata to such a degree that it is evident that Bach had fully realized by this time how fertile a subject for treatment it was. It contains no chorus of such depth and force as those of the One hundred and thirtieth Psalm. Its character is much more entirely individual and personal, and so it has a depth and intensity of expression which reach the extreme limits of possibility of representation by music. The arrangement of the poetic material is most excellent; it does not wholly consist of Scripture texts and verses of hymns; and in several fit and expressive thoughts, which are freely interspersed, we can almost recognize Bach's own hand. If such be the case, the whole arrangement of the poetry may with reason be ascribed to him."

The introduction to the work is a quiet, tender movement in sonata form, written for two flutes, two viol-da-gambas and figured bass, which gives out some of the themes in the middle of the cantata. The opening chorus ("God's own Time is the best, ever best of all. In Him we live, move, and have our Being, as long as He wills. And in Him we die at His good Time") is very descriptive in character, opening with a slow and solemn movement, then passing to a quick fugue, and closing with phrases of mournful beauty to suit the last sentence of the text. A tenor solo follows, set to the words, "O Lord, incline us to consider that our Days are numbered; make us apply our Hearts unto Wisdom," and accompanied by the flutes, leading into a mournful aria for the bass, which forms the second part of the tenor solo ("Set in order thine House, for thou shalt die and not live"). The choir resumes with a new theme ("It is the old Decree, Man, thou art mortal"), in which the lower voices carry a double fugue, the soprano sings alone ("Yea, come, Lord Jesus"), and the instruments have the melody of the old hymn: —

> "I have cast all my care on God,
> E'en let Him do what seems Him good;
> Whether I die, or whether live,
>   No more I'll strive,
> But all my will to Him will give."

Of this effective movement and its successor Spitta says: —

"The design is clear. The curse of death has been changed into blessing by the coming of Christ, and that which mankind dreaded before, they now stretch out entreating hands to; the bliss of the new condition of things shines out in supernatural glory against the dark background of a dispensation that has been done away. This is the idea of the concerted vocal parts; and the fact that thousands upon thousands have agreed in the joy of this faith is shown by the chorale tune now introduced; for to the understanding listener its worldless sounds convey the whole import of the hymn which speaks so sweetly of comfort in the hour of death, sounds which must recall to every pious heart all the feelings they had stirred when, among the chances and changes of life, this hymn had been heard, — feelings of sympathy with another's grief or of balm to the heart's own anxiety."

The alto voice follows with the words spoken on the cross ("Into Thy Hands my Spirit I commend"), to which the bass replies in an arioso ("Thou shalt be with Me to-day in Paradise"). The next number is a chorale ("In Joy and Peace I pass away whenever God willeth") sung by the alto, the bass continuing its solo at the same time through a portion of the chorale. The final chorus is the so-called fifth Gloria : —

> "All glory, praise, and majesty
> To Father, Son, and Spirit be,
> The holy, blessed Trinity;
> Whose power to us
> Gives victory
> Through Jesus Christ. Amen."

The "Actus Tragicus" was one of the youthful compositions of Bach, but it has always attracted the notice of the best musical critics. It was a great favorite with Mendelssohn. Spitta says : —

"It is a work of art well rounded off and firm in its formation, and warmed by the deepest intensity of feeling even in the smallest details."

Hauptmann writes to Jahn : —

"Yesterday, at the Euterpe concert, Bach's 'Gottes Zeit' was given. What a marvellous intensity pervades it, without a bar of conventionality! Of the cantatas known to me, I know none in which such design and regard are had to the musical import and its expression."

Festa Ascensionis Christi.

The cantata beginning with the words, "Wer da glaubet und getauft wird" ("Whoso believeth and is baptized"), commonly known as the Ascension cantata, was written for four voices, with accompaniment of two oboes, two violins, viola, and "continuo,"— the latter word implying a bass part, the harmonies indicated by figures from which the organist built up his own accompaniment. The original score has been lost; but it has been reconstructed from the parts, which are preserved in the Royal Library at Berlin.

The cantata is in five numbers. A short prelude of a quiet and cheerful character introduces the stately opening chorus ("Who believeth and obeyeth will be blest forever"). Another brief prelude prepares the way for the brilliant tenor aria ("Of Love, Faith is the Pledge and Token"), which leads up to the chorale, "Lord God, my Father, holy One," based upon the old chorale, "Wie schön leucht uns der Morgenstern" ("How brightly shines the Morning Star"), which has always been a favorite in the church service, and which more than one composer has chosen for the embellishment of his themes. The chorale is not employed in its original form, but is elaborated with all the contrapuntal skill for which Bach was so famous. The next number is a short recitative for the bass voice ("Ye Mortals, hear, all ye who would behold the Face of God"), and leads to a stately bass aria ("Through Faith the Soul has Eagle's Pinions"). The cantata closes, after the customary manner of Bach, with a strong, earnest chorale ("Oh, give me Faith, my Father!"), in plain, solid harmony, for the use of the congregation, thus forming an effective devotional climax to the work.

Ein' Feste Burg.

"A safe stronghold our God is still,
  A trusty shield and weapon;
He'll help us clear from all the ill
  That hath us now o'ertaken.
The ancient Prince of Hell
Hath risen with purpose fell;
Strong mail of craft and power
He weareth in this hour.
  On Earth is not his fellow.

. . . . .

"And were this world all devils o'er,
  And watching to devour us,
We lay it not to heart so sore,
  Not they can overpower us.
And let the Prince of Ill
Look grim as e'er he will,
He harms us not a whit;
For why? His doom is writ,
  A word shall quickly slay him."

There is now but little question that Martin Luther not only wrote the words but the music of the grand old hymn, the first and third stanzas of which, taken from Carlyle's free and rugged translation, are given above. Sleidan, a contemporary historian, indeed says that "Luther made a tune for it singularly suited to the words and adapted to stir the heart." The date of its composition is a matter of controversy; but it is clear that it must have been either in 1529 or 1530, and most writers agree that it was just before the Diet at Augsburg, where it was sung. Niederer, in a work published at Nuremberg, 1759, fixes the date as 1530, and finds it in Preussen's psalm-book, printed in 1537. Winterfeld observes it for the first time in the "Gesangbuch" of the composer Walther, a friend of Luther. Its usual title is, " Der XLVI. Psalm : Deus noster Refugium et virtus, pp. D., Martin Luther." It matters little, however, the exact year in which the sturdy old Reformer wrote the hymn which has stirred the human heart more than any other. It is indissolubly connected with his name, and every line of it is a reflex of his indomitable and God-fearing nature. Heine and Carlyle have paid it noble tributes. The German poet says : —

" The hymn which he composed on his way to Worms,[1] and which he and his companions chanted as they entered that city, is a regular war-song. The old cathedral trembled when it heard these novel sounds. The very rooks flew from their nests in the towers. That hymn, the Marseillaise of the Reforma-

[1] This assumption, repeated by others, grows out of the similarity of sentiment in the third stanza to that of Luther's famous reply when he was urged not to attend the Diet of Worms.

tion, has preserved to this day its potent spell over German hearts."

Carlyle still more forcibly says: —

"With words he had now learned to make music; it was by deeds of love or heroic valor that he spoke freely. Nevertheless, though in imperfect articulation, the same voice, if we listen well, is to be heard also in his writings, in his poems. The one entitled 'Ein' feste Burg,' universally regarded as the best, jars upon our ears; yet there is something in it like the sound of Alpine avalanches, or the first murmur of earthquakes, in the very vastness of which dissonance a higher unison is revealed to us. Luther wrote this song in times of blackest threatenings, which, however, could in no sense become a time of despair. In these tones, rugged and broken as they are, do we hear the accents of that summoned man, who answered his friends' warning not to enter Worms, in this wise: 'Were there as many devils in Worms as these tile roofs, I would on.'"

It was the battle-song of the Reformation, stirring men to valiant deeds; and it did equal service in sustaining and consoling the Reformers in their darkest hours. "Come, Philip, let us sing the Forty-sixth Psalm," was Luther's customary greeting to Melanchthon, when the gentler spirit quailed before approaching danger, or success seemed doubtful. In music it has frequently served an important purpose. Not only Bach, but other composers of his time arranged it. Mendelssohn uses it with powerful effect in his Reformation symphony. Nicolai employs it in his Fest overture. Meyerbeer more than once puts it in the mouth of Marcel the Huguenot, when dangers gather about his master, though the Huguenots were not Lutherans but Calvinists; and Wagner introduces it with overwhelming power in his triumphal Kaiser March.

Bitter, in his Life of Bach, says: —

"The bicentenary Reformation Festival was celebrated in October and November, 1717, and at Weimar especially it was, as an old chronicle tells us, a great jubilee. Bach composed his cantata, 'Ein' feste Burg,' for the occasion. In this piece it is clear that he had passed through his first phase of development and reached a higher stage of perfection."

Winterfeld is inclined to the same belief; but Spitta, in his exhaustive biography of Bach, argues that it must have been written either for the Reformation Festival of 1730, or for the two hundredth anniversary of Protestantism in Saxony, May 17, 1739. The former date would bring its composition a year after the completion of his great Passions music, and four years before his still more famous "Christmas Oratorio," — a period when he was at the height of his productive power; which favors the argument of Spitta, that in 1717 a chorus like the opening one in the cantata was beyond his capacity.[1] In the year 1730 Bach wrote three

[1] There is yet a fourth rearrangement, which we may assign to 1730. The assertion is no doubt well founded that in this year the celebration of the Reformation Festival was considered of spe-

Jubilee cantatas, rearranged from earlier works, and Spitta claims that it was only about this period that he resorted to this practice. Further, he adds that "the Chorale Chorus [the opening number], in its grand proportions and vigorous flow, is the natural and highest outcome of Bach's progressive development, and he never wrote anything more stupendous."

The cantata has eight numbers, three choruses and five solos. The solo numbers are rearranged from an earlier cantata, "Alles was von Gott geboren" ("All that is of God's creation"), written for the third Sunday in Lent, March 15, 1716. The opening number is a colossal fugue based upon a variation on the old melody and set to the first verse of the Luther hymn. It is followed by a duet for soprano and bass, including the second verse of the hymn and an interpolated verse by Franck,[1] who prepared the text. The third and fourth numbers are a bass recitative and soprano aria, the words

cial importance, and kept accordingly; and it is evident that the cantata "Ein' feste Burg" must have been intended for some such extraordinary solemnity. — *Spitta*, vol. ii. p. 470.

The Reformation Festival had no doubt a very distinct poetical sentiment of its own; and when any special occasion took the precedence, as in 1730 and 1739, the years of Jubilee, it would be misleading to seek for any close connection between the sermon and the cantata. Thus the cantata, "Ein' feste Burg," may very well have been connected with the sermon in 1730; still, it is possible that it was not written till 1739. — *Ibid.*, vol. iii. p. 283.

[1] Salomo Franck, a poet of more than ordinary ability, was born at Weimar, March 6, 1759. He published several volumes of sacred lyrics.

also by Franck, leading up to the second great chorale chorus set to the words of the third stanza of the hymn,

"And were the world all devils o'er,"

of which Spitta says: —

"The whole chorus sings the *Cantus firmus* in unison, while the orchestra plays a whirl of grotesque and wildly leaping figures, through which the chorus makes its way undistracted and never misled, an illustration of the third verse, as grandiose and characteristic as it is possible to conceive."

The sixth number is a recitative for tenor followed by a duet for alto and tenor ("How blessed then are they who still on God are calling"). The work closes with a repetition of the chorale, set to the last verse of the hymn, sung without accompaniment. The cantata is colossal in its proportions, and is characterized throughout by the stirring spirit and bold vigorous feeling of the Reformation days whose memories it celebrated.

BALFE.

MICHAEL WILLIAM BALFE was born at Dublin, Ireland, May 15, 1808. Of all the English opera-composers, his career was the most versatile, as his success, for a time at least, was the most remarkable. At seven years of age he scored a polacca of his own for a band. In his eighth year he appeared as a violinist, and in his tenth was composing ballads. At sixteen he was playing in the Drury Lane orchestra, and about this time began taking lessons in composition. In 1825, aided by the generosity of a patron, he went to Italy, where for three years he studied singing and counterpoint. In his twentieth year he met Rossini, who offered him an engagement as first barytone at the Italian opera in Paris. He made his début with success in 1828, and at the close of his engagement returned to Italy, where he appeared again on the stage. About this time (1829–1830) he began writing Italian operas, and before he left the country had produced three which met with considerable success. In 1835 he returned to England; and it was in this year that his first English opera,

"The Siege of Rochelle," was brought out. It was played continuously at Drury Lane for over three months. In 1835 appeared his "Maid of Artois;" in 1837, "Catharine Grey" and "Joan of Arc;" and in 1838, "Falstaff." During these years he was still singing in concerts and opera, and in 1840 undertook the management of the Lyceum. His finest works were produced after this date, — "The Bohemian Girl," in 1843; "The Enchantress," in 1844; "The Rose of Castile," "La Zingara," and "Satanella," in 1858; and "The Puritan's Daughter" in 1861. His last opera was "The Knight of the Leopard," known in Italian as "Il Talismano," which has also been performed in English as "The Talisman." He married Mademoiselle Rosen, a German singer, whom he met in Italy in 1835. His daughter Victoire, who subsequently married Sir John Crampton, and afterwards the Duc de Frias, also appeared as a singer in 1856. Balfe died Oct. 20, 1870, upon his own estate in Hertfordshire.

Mazeppa.

The cantata of "Mazeppa," the words written by Jessica Rankin, was one of the last productions of Balfe, having been produced in 1862, a year after "The Puritan's Daughter," and several years after he had passed his musical prime. The text is based upon the familiar story as told by Byron in his poem of the wild ride of the page of King Casimir, " The Ukraine's hetman, calm and bold," and of the

> "noble steed,
> A Tartar of the Ukraine breed,
> Who looked as though the speed of thought
> Was in his limbs."

The main incidents in the story — the guilty love of the page Mazeppa for the Count Palatine's Theresa, his surprise and seizure by the spies, her mysterious fate, the wild flight of the steed with his wretched load through forest and over desert, and the final rescue by the Cossack maid — are preserved, but liberties of every description are taken in the recital of the narrative. It is but a feeble transcript of Byron's glowing verse, and in its diluted form is but a vulgar story of ordinary love, jealousy, and revenge.

The cantata comprises twelve numbers. The first is a prelude in triplets intended to picture the gallop of the steed, a common enough device since the days when Virgil did it much better without the aid of musical notation, in his well-known line, —

> " Quadrupedante putrem sonitu quatit ungula campum."

It leads to a stirring chorus which is followed by still another, based upon a very pleasant melody. The third number is a solo for barytone, in which the Count gives expression to his jealousy, which brings us to the heroine, who makes her appearance in a florid number. The next is a duet for Theresa and

Mazeppa, followed by a solo for the tenor (Mazeppa) which is very effective. The chorus then re-enter and indicate the madness of the Count in words, the following sample of which will show their unsingableness : —

> "Revenge fires his turbulent soul;
> No power his boundless rage can control."

The eighth number is another duet for the Countess and Mazeppa in the conventional Italian style. It is followed by a graceful aria for tenor, which leads up to the best number in the work, a trio in canon form. A final aria by the Count leads to the last chorus, in which the repetition of the triplet gallop forebodes the ride into the desert and the punishment of the page. As might be inferred from the description, the cantata is like Hamlet with *Hamlet* left out. There is very little of Mazeppa and his Tartar steed in the work, but very much of the jealousy and revenge which lead up to the penalty.

BEETHOVEN.

LUDWIG VON BEETHOVEN was born Dec. 16, 1770, at Bonn, Germany. His father was a court-singer in the Chapel of the Elector of Cologne. The great composer studied in Vienna with Haydn, with whom he did not always agree, however, and afterwards with Albrechtsberger. His first symphony appeared in 1801, — his earlier symphonies, in what is called his first period, being written in the Mozart style. His only opera, "Fidelio," for which he wrote four overtures, was first brought out in Vienna, in 1805; his oratorio, "Christ on the Mount of Olives," in 1812; and his colossal Ninth Symphony, with its choral setting of Schiller's "Ode to Joy," in 1824. In addition to his symphonies, his opera, oratorios, and masses, and the immortal series of piano sonatas, which were almost revelations in music, he developed chamber music to an extent far beyond that reached by his predecessors, Mozart and Haydn. His symphonies exhibit surprising power, a marvellous comprehension of the deeper feelings in life, and the influences of nature, both human and physical. He wrote with the deepest earnestness, alike in the passion and the repose of his music, and he invested it also with a genial humor as well as with the highest expression of pathos. His works are epic in style. He was the great tone-poet of music. His subjects were always lofty and dignified, and to their treatment he brought not only a profound knowledge of musical technicality, but intense sympathy with the innermost feelings of human nature, for he was a humanitarian in the broadest sense. By the common consent of the musical world he stands at the head of all composers since his time, and has always been their guide and inspiration. He died March 26, 1827, in the midst of a raging thunder-storm, — one of his latest utterances being a recognition of the "divine spark" in Schubert's music.

The Ruins of Athens.

The most important compositions by Beethoven in 1811 were the music to two dramatic works written by the poet Kotzebue to celebrate the opening of the new theatre at Pesth, Hungary. One of these was a prologue in one act with overture and choruses, entitled "König Stephan,[1] Ungarn's erster Wohlthäter" ("King Stephen, Hungary's first Benefactor"); the other, an alle-

[1] Born in the year 977 at Gran, and known in Austrian and Hungarian history as Saint Stephen.

gorical sketch, called "The Ruins of Athens," the subject of which is thus concisely stated by Macfarren:—

"Minerva has been since the golden age of Grecian art, the glorious epoch of Grecian liberty, for some or other important offence against the Olympian tribunal, the particulars of which I am unable to furnish, fettered with chains of heaven-wrought adamant by the omnipotent thunderer within a rock impenetrable alike to the aspirations of man and to the intelligence of the goddess, a rock through which neither his spirit of inquiry could approach, nor her wisdom diffuse itself upon the world. The period of vengeance is past; Jove relents, and the captive deity is enfranchised. The first steps of her freedom naturally lead Minerva to the scene of her ancient greatness. She finds Athens, her Athens, her especially beloved and most carefully cherished city, in ruins, the descendants of her fostered people enslaved to a barbarous and fanatic race; the trophies of her former splendor, the wrecks of that art which is the example and the regret of all time, appropriated to the most degrading purposes of vulgar householdry; and the frenzied worshippers of a faith that knows not the divine presence in its most marvellous manifestation, the intellect of man. Here is no longer the home of wisdom and the arts; so the liberated goddess proceeds to Pesth, where she establishes anew her temple in the new theatre, and presides over a triumphal procession in honor of the Emperor, its patron, under whose auspices the golden age is to prevail again."

After the opening performances the music to "King Stephen" was laid aside until 1841, when it was given in Vienna; but the after-piece, "The Ruins of Athens," was presented again during Beethoven's lifetime upon the occasion of the opening of a theatre in that city. The new text, which was prepared for it by Carl Meisl, was entitled "Die Weihe des Hauses" ("The Dedication of the House"), and Beethoven wrote for it the overture which is now so famous, solos for soprano and violin, and a final chorus with dances.

The music to the "Ruins of Athens" comprises eight numbers. The overture is very light and unpretentious, and by many critics, among them Ferdinand Ries, Beethoven's pupil, has been deemed unworthy of the composer. Thayer says:—

"When the overture was first played at Leipsic, people could hardly trust their ears, could hardly believe it to be the work of the author of the symphonies, of the overtures to 'Coriolan,' 'Egmont,' and 'Leonore' (Fidelio)."

The opening number is a chorus ("Daughter of mighty Jove, awake!"), which is followed by a beautiful duet ("Faultless, yet hated"), voicing the lament of two Greek slaves for the destruction of their temples and the degradation of their land. The duet is very pathetic in character, and the melody, carried by the two voices, leaves an impression of sadness which cannot be resisted. The third number is the well-known chorus of Dervishes sung in unison by tenors and basses, thus forming a kind of choral chant. The melody is a weird one, and full of local color, but its powerful effect is gained by the manner of treatment. It begins pianissimo and is gradually worked to the extreme pitch of true Dervish delirium, culminating in the exclamation, "Great Prophet, hail!" and then gradually subsiding until it dies away, apparently from the exhaustion of such fervor. It is followed by the familiar Turkish march, founded on the theme of the Variations in D, op. 76, very simple in construction, Oriental in its character throughout, and peculiarly picturesque in effect. After an instrumental movement behind the scenes, a triumphal march and chorus ("Twine ye a Garland") is introduced. The seventh number is a recitative and aria by the high priest with chorus, which lead to a beautifully melodious chorus ("Susceptible Hearts"). An adagio aria for bass ("Deign, great Apollo") and a vigorous chorus ("Hail, our King") bring the work to a close. The piece was first brought out in England by Mendelssohn in 1844 at one of the Philharmonic Society's concerts; and ten or twelve years later an English version of it was performed at the Prince's Theatre, when the Royal Exchange and statue of Wellington were substituted for the Pesth Theatre, and Shakspeare took the place of the Emperor of Austria, concerning the good taste of which Macfarren pithily says: —

"Modifications admirably adapted to the commercial character and the blind vainglory that so eminently mark the British nation."

The Glorious Moment.

In September, 1814, the same year in which the Allies entered Paris, the Vienna Congress met to adjust the relations of the various European States. It was an occasion of great moment in the ancient city, — this gathering of sovereigns and distinguished statesmen, — and the magistracy prepared themselves to celebrate it with befitting pomp and ceremony. Beethoven was requested to set a poem, written by Dr. Aloys Weissenbach, of Salzburg, in cantata form, which was to be sung as a greeting to the royal visitors. It was "Der glorreiche Augenblick," sometimes written "Der heilige Augenblick" ("The Glorious Moment"). The time for its composition was very brief, and was made still shorter by the quarrels the composer had with the poet in trying to reduce the barbarous text to a more inspiring and musical form. He began the composition in September, and it was first performed on the 29th of the following November, together with the "Battle of Vittoria," and the A major (Seventh) symphony, written in the previous year. The concert took place in the presence of the sovereigns and an immense audience which received his works with every demonstration of enthusiasm, particularly "The Glorious Moment," — a moment which all hailed as the precursor of a happier epoch for Europe, soon to be freed from Napoleonic oppression. The occasion was one of great benefit to the composer at a time when he was sorely in need of assistance. The distinguished foreign visitors thronged the salon of the Archduke Rudolph to pay him homage. Handsome gifts were lavished upon him so that he was enabled to make a permanent investment of 20,000 marks in shares of the bank of Austria. Brilliant entertainments were given by the Russian ambassador, Prince Rasoumowsky,[1] in his palace, at one of which Beethoven was presented to the sovereigns. The Empress of Russia also gave him a reception and made him magnificent presents. Schindler says:

"Not without feeling did the great master afterwards recall those days in the Imperial Palace and that of the Russian Prince; and once with a certain pride remarked that he had allowed the crowned heads to pay court to him, and that he had carried himself thereby proudly."

The stern old republican, however, who could rebuke Goethe for taking off his hat in the presence of royalty, spoke such sentiments jocosely. He expresses his real feelings in a letter written to the attorney, Herr J. Kauka, of Prague: —

"I write nothing about our monarchs and monarchies, for the newspapers give you every information on these subjects. The intellectual realm is the most precious in my eyes, and far above all temporal and spiritual monarchies."

[1] Prince Rasoumowsky, who was the Russian ambassador at the Austrian Court for twenty years, was himself a thorough musician, and ranked as one of the best players in Vienna, of the Haydn and Beethoven quartets. His instrument was the second violin.

THE GLORIOUS MOMENT. 55

The cantata itself, while not one of the most meritorious of the composer's works, for reasons which are sufficiently apparent, still is very effective in its choruses. The detailed parts do not need special description; they are six in number, as follows: No. 1, chorus ("Europa steht"); No. 2, recitative and chorus ("O, seht sie nah und näher treten"); No. 3, grand scena, soprano, with violin obligato and chorus ("O Himmel, welch' Entzücken"); No. 4, soprano solo and chorus ("Das Auge schaut"); No. 5, recitative and quartet for two sopranos, tenor, and bass ("Der den Bund im Sturme festgehalten"); No. 6, chorus and fugue ("Es treten hervor die Scharen der Frauen"), closing with a stirring "Heil und Gluck" to Vindobona, the ancient name of the city. In 1836, nine years after the composer's death, the cantata appeared with a new poetical setting by Friedrich Rochlitz, under the title of "Preis der Tonkunst" ("Praise of Music"), in which form it was better adapted for general performance.

Among other compositions of Beethoven which assimilate to the cantata form, are op. 112, "Meeresstille und glückliche Fahrt," for four voices, with orchestra accompaniment; op. 121, "Opferlied," for soprano solo, with chorus and orchestra accompaniment; and op. 122, "Bundeslied," for two solo voices, three-part chorus, and accompaniment of two clarinets, two bassoons, and two horns.

BENEDICT.

SIR JULIUS BENEDICT, whose name is so intimately connected with music in England, was born at Stuttgart, Nov. 27, 1804. After a short period of study with Hummel at Weimar he became a pupil of Weber. He progressed so rapidly that at the age of nineteen he conducted operatic performances in Vienna, and a few years afterwards was leader at the San Carlo in Naples, where he produced his first opera, "Giacinta ed Ernesto." In 1835 he went to Paris and thence to London, where he remained until his death. In 1836 he led the orchestra at the Lyceum Theatre, and was also conductor at Drury Lane during the memorable seasons in which the best of Balfe's operas were brought out. It was during this period also that he produced two of his own operas, — "The Brides of Venice" and "The Crusaders," which are ranked among his best works of this class. In 1850 he accompanied Jenny Lind on her memorable tour through this country. On his return to England he was engaged as conductor at Her Majesty's Theatre, and afterwards at Drury Lane.

In 1860 he produced the cantata of "Undine;" in 1862 the opera "Lily of Killarney;" in 1863 the cantata "Richard Cœur de Leon;" in 1864 the operetta "Bride of Song;" in 1866 the cantata "St. Cecilia;" and in 1870 the oratorio "St. Peter." In 1871 he received the honor of knighthood, and in 1873 brought out a symphony which met with great success. In 1874, the occasion of his seventieth birthday, he was made Knight Commander of the orders of Francis and Joseph and of Frederic, Austrian and Wurtembergian decorations. Nearly every sovereign in Europe had thus honored him. He was also conductor of the London Monday Popular Concerts for many years, and directed many chamber concerts. He died full of honors in June, 1885.

St. Cecilia.

The legend of St. Cecilia for two centuries has inspired the poet and composer, and the custom of celebrating her festival has obtained in nearly all European countries during the same period. The earliest observance was at Evreux, France, in 1571. The first celebration in England of which any record remains was that of 1683; though it is clear from the accounts of musical writers in the seventeenth century that the custom had been practised many years prior to that date. From 1683 to 1750 St. Cecilia festivals were given annually in London, and for these occasions an ode was written and set to music.[1] In the latter year the distinctive name of the festival fell into disuse, though large musical festivals were frequently held after that year on the saint's day. In France regular entertainments were given on St. Cecilia's Day from 1573 to 1601, when the record terminates. In Italy the anniversary of the saint has not been celebrated except as a church festival. In Germany the custom prevailed as early as the sixteenth century; and in the next century Cecilia festivals were quite common in Spain. Prior to Benedict's work the most modern composition having the legend for its basis was a cantata by Van Bree, of Amsterdam, written in 1845.

These preliminaries will enable the reader the better to understand the introduction which Mr. Chorley has written to the text of the cantata by Benedict, composed for the Norwich Festival of 1866. Mr. Chorley says: —

"It has long been a favorite fancy of mine to treat the legend of St. Cecilia for music with a view to the possible revival of such celebrations as were held

---

[1] The Ode for St. Cecilia's Day in 1683 was written by Christopher Fishburn and set to music by Purcell. The most famous odes of the next hundred years were as follows: "A song for St. Cecilia's Day, 1687," by John Dryden, originally composed by Draghi, afterwards by Handel; ode by Thomas d'Urfrey, music by Dr. Blow, 1691; "Alexander's Feast," by Dryden, original music by Jeremiah Clark, afterwards composed by Handel, 1697; ode by Joseph Addison, composed by Purcell, 1699; "Hymn to Harmony," by Congreve, composed by John Eccles, 1701; ode by Pope in 1708, set to music in 1757 by William Walond; an ode by Christopher Smart, composed by William Russell, 1800.

in gone-by years, when English sympathy for the art was more limited in every respect than at the present time. It is true that the names of Dryden and Addison among the poets, and of Handel among the musicians, who have made 'divine Cecilia's' praise immortal, might be thought to deter any one from dealing with the subject. But theirs were merely votive odes indirectly bearing on the power of the art of which Cecilia is patron saint. This cantata of mine sets forth her story, which, so far as I am aware, has not been done before in any of the works produced for the Cecilian festivals in England. All who are familiar with the accepted legend, as told in the 'Legenda Aurea' of Jacobus Januensis, Archbishop of Genoa, will perceive that I have treated it with a certain liberty. Some of the minor incidents —such as the conversion and martyrdom of Tiburtius, the brother of Valerianus—have been omitted with a view of avoiding the introduction of secondary persons, and of concentrating the main interest in the martyr heroine. Further, the catastrophe which (to cite Dryden's known line in defiance of its original import)

"Raised a mortal to the skies,"

has been simplified. The legend narrates that after the agony of slow fire, which failed to kill the Christian bride, the sword ended her days. A literal adherence to this tradition might have weakened the closing scene by presenting two situations of the same character. Others must judge how far I have been indiscreet, or the reverse, in its omission."

The story of the cantata is strikingly similar to that which forms the theme of Donizetti's opera "Il Poliuto," though the manner of the conversions differs. In the former it is Valerianus, the lover of Cecilia, who is turned from heathenism by the angelic vision. In the latter it is Paulina, the wife of the Roman convert Polyutus, who witnesses the divine illumination and hears the celestial harps, which induce her to abjure the worship of the gods and join her husband in martyrdom. It is in fact the old, old story of the persecutions of a new faith by the old. Cecilia, though married to Valerianus, hears the divine call summoning the bride away from her lover until he shall have been converted. She appeals to Heaven in his behalf. A vision of angels appears to him and their songs win his soul. The infuriated prefect, who has but just performed the rites of their marriage, orders their death, — Valerianus to be beheaded, and Cecilia to die by the slow martyrdom of fire. The tragedy of the former is left to the imagination. Cecilia dies surrounded by the angels and hears their voices : —

> "Before mine eyes, already dim,
>   Doth heaven unclose the gate;
> I hear the choiring seraphim
>   Around the throne that wait.
> To join the song of that bright choir
>   Thy mercy sets me free;
> And so I triumph o'er the fire,
>   And rise, O Lord, to Thee."

The work contains thirteen numbers, and the solos are divided as follows : Cecilia, soprano ; Valerianus, tenor ; the Prefect of Rome, bass ; a Christian woman, contralto. The remaining numbers are assigned to choruses of Roman citizens, Christians, and angels.

A tender and sorrowful prelude, foreshadowing the tragedy, introduces a bright and joyous wedding chorus ("Let the Lutes play their loudest"), which in its middle part is divided between male and female choir, returning to four-part harmony in the close. The next number is an ecstatic love-song for Valerianus ("The Love too deep for Words to speak"), which leads up to a scena and duet for Valerianus and Cecilia ("O my Lord, if I must grieve you"), which is very dramatic in its texture. The conversion music, including an obligato soprano solo with chorus of angels ("Praise the Lord"), recitative and air for tenor with choral responses ("Cease not, I pray you"), and an animated chorus of angels ("From our Home"), follows, and closes the first part.

The second part opens with the curse of the prefect, a very passionate aria for bass ("What mean these Zealots vile?"), following which in marked contrast is a lovely aria for contralto ("Father, whose Blessing we entreat"). The next number, a quartet with full choral accompaniment ("God is our Hope and Strength"), is one of the most effective in the work, and is followed by the trial scene, a duet between Valerianus and the prefect, the latter accompanied by chorus. A short funeral march intervenes. Valerianus and Cecilia bid each other farewell; the former is borne away, and Cecilia sings her dying song ("Those whom the Highest One befriends") amid the triumphant hallelujahs of the angels.

BENNETT.

ILLIAM STERNDALE BENNETT, one of the most gifted and individual of English composers, was born at Sheffield, April 13, 1816. His musical genius displayed itself early, and in his tenth year he was placed in the Royal Academy of Music, of which in his later years he became principal. He received his early instruction in composition from Lucas and Dr. Crotch, and studied the piano with Cipriani Potter, who had been a pupil of Mozart. The first composition which gained him distinction was the Concerto in D minor, written in 1832, which was followed by the Capriccio in D minor. During the next three years he produced the overture to "Parisina," the F minor Concerto, and the "Naïades" overture, the success of which was so great that a prominent musical house in London offered to send him to Leipsic for a year. He went there, and soon won his way to the friendship of Schumann and Mendelssohn. With the latter he was on very intimate terms, which has led to the erroneous statement that he was his pupil. In 1840 he made a

second visit to Leipsic, where he composed his Caprice in E, and the "Wood Nymphs" overture. In 1842 he returned to England, and for several years was busily engaged with chamber concerts. In 1849 he founded the Bach Society, arranged the "Matthew Passion" music of that composer, as well as his "Christmas Oratorio," and brought out the former work in 1854. The previous year he was offered the distinguished honor of the conductorship of the Gewandhaus concerts at Leipsic, but did not accept. In 1856 he was appointed conductor of the Philharmonic Society, and filled the position for ten years, resigning it to take the head of the Royal Academy of Music. In the same year he was elected musical professor at Cambridge, where he received the degree of Doctor of Music and other honors. In 1858 his beautiful cantata "The May Queen" was produced at the Leeds Festival, and in 1862 the "Paradise and the Peri" overture, written for the Philharmonic Society. In 1867 his oratorio, or, as he modestly terms it, "sacred cantata," "The Woman of Samaria," was produced with great success at the Birmingham Festival. In 1870 he was honored with a degree by the University of Oxford, and a year later received the empty distinction of knighthood. His last public appearance was at a festival in Brighton in 1874, where he conducted his "Woman of Samaria." He died Feb. 1, 1875, and was buried in Westminster Abbey with distinguished honors.

The May Queen.

"The May Queen," a pastoral cantata, the libretto by Henry F. Chorley, was first performed at the Leeds Festival of 1858. The solo parts are written for the May Queen (soprano); the Queen (contralto); the Lover (tenor); and the Captain of the Foresters, as Robin Hood (bass). The opening scene pictures the dressing of the tree for the spring festivity on the banks of the Thames, and the preparations for the reception of the May Queen. A despondent lover enters and sings his melancholy plight as he reflects upon the fickleness of the May Queen, interrupted at intervals by the merry shouts of the chorus: —

> "With a laugh as we go round
> To the merry, merry sound
> Of the tabor and the pipe,
>   We will frolic on the green;
> For since the world began,
> And our royal river ran,
> Was never such a May Day,
>   And never such a Queen."

The lover continues his doleful lamenting, which is at last interrupted by the entrance of the May Queen herself, who chides him for his complaints and argues her right to coquet on such a day. As their interview closes, a band of foresters enter with their greenwood king, Robin Hood, at their head, who after a rollicking hunting-song makes open love to the May Queen. The enraged lover resents his impertinence, and at last strikes him a blow, which by the laws exposes him to the loss of his hand. Before he can make his escape there is a flourish of trumpets, and the Queen enters and demands the reason for the brawl. The revellers inform her that the lover has struck the forester. She orders his arrest, whereupon the May Queen intercedes with her for her lover's release and declares her affection for him. Her appeal for mercy is granted. The forester is banished from the royal presence for lowering himself to the level of a peasant girl, the May Queen is ordered to wed her lover on the coming morn, and all ends happily with the joyous chorus: —

> "And the cloud hath passed away,
>   That was heavy on the May;
> And the river floweth fair,
>   And the meadow bloometh green.
> They embrace, no more to part,
> While we sing from every heart,
>   A blessing on the bridal!
>   A blessing on the Queen!"

The music of the cantata is divided into ten numbers, which are characterized by exquisite refinement and artistic taste. The solos, particularly No. 2, for tenor ("O Meadow, clad in early Green"), No. 4, the obligato soprano ("With the Carol in the Tree"), and No. 6, the forester's lusty greenwood song ("'T is jolly to hunt in the bright Moonlight"), are very melodious, and well adapted to the individual characters. The concerted music is written in the most scholarly manner, the choruses are full of life and spirit, and the instrumentation is always effective. There are few more beautiful cantatas than "The May Queen," though the composer was hampered by a dull and not very inspiring libretto. Poor words, however, could not affect his delightful grace and fancy, which manifest themselves in every number of this little pastoral. It is surprising that so excellent a work, and one which is so well adapted to chorus singing and solo display, without making very severe demands upon the singers, is not more frequently given in this country.

The Exhibition Ode.

The music for the opening of the International Exhibition at London, which occurred in May, 1862, was of unusual excellence. Auber sent a composition which, though called a march, was in reality a brilliant overture. Meyerbeer contributed an overture in march form, in which three marches were blended in one, the whole culminating in "Rule Britannia." Verdi wrote a cantata, which was rejected by the Commissioners because by the side of the national anthem he had introduced the revolutionary Marseillaise and the Italian war-song called "Garibaldienne." Its rejection not only caused great indignation in the musical world, but at once made it famous; and it was afterwards publicly performed, Mademoiselle Titiens taking the soprano solos, Sir Julius Benedict conducting.

The prominent feature of the musical programme, however, was the Ode which the poet laureate and Bennett conjointly furnished. Never before were Mr. Tennyson's verses more completely united with music. The work is divided into three parts, all choral, linked by recitatives. The first number is a hymn to the Deity ("Uplift a thousand Voices full and sweet"), written as a four-part chorale, which is very jubilant in style. The next movement, —

> "O silent father of our kings to be,
> Mourned in this golden hour of jubilee,
> For this, for all, we weep our thanks to thee,"

eloquently referring to the Prince Consort, is set in the minor key, and is one of the most pathetic musical passages ever written. Then follows a descriptive catalogue of the industries represented, — "harvest tool and husbandry," "loom and wheel and engin'ry," and so on, through which the music labors some, as might have been expected; but in the close it once more resumes its melodious flow, leading up to the final chorus, in which the theme of the opening chorale is borrowed and developed with peculiar originality and artistic skill into a movement of great richness in effects and beauty in expression. It is unfortunate for the popularity of such an excellent work that it was composed for a special occasion.

BERLIOZ.

HECTOR BERLIOZ, one of the most renowned of modern French composers, and an acute critic and skilful conductor as well, was born, Dec. 11, 1803, at La Côte St. André, in France. His father was a physician, and intended him for the same profession. He reluctantly went to Paris and began the study of medicine; but music became his engrossing passion, and medicine was abandoned. He entered the Conservatory as a pupil of Lesueur, and soon showed himself superior to all his masters except Cherubini, which aroused a strong opposition to him and his compositions. It was only after repeated trials that he took the first prize, which entitled him to go to Italy for three years. On his return to Paris he encountered renewed antipathy. His music was not well received, and he was obliged to support himself by conducting at concerts and writing articles for the press. As a final resort he organized a concert-tour through Germany and Russia, the details of which are contained in his extremely interesting Autobiography. At these concerts his own music was the staple of the programmes, and it met with great success, though not always played by the best of orchestras, and not always well by the best, as his own testimony shows; for his compositions are very exacting, and call for every resource known to the modern orchestra. The Germans were quick in appreciating his music; but it was not until after his death that his ability was conceded in France. In 1839 he was appointed librarian of the Conservatory, and in 1856 was made a member of the French Academy. These were the only honors he received, though he long sought to obtain a professorship in the Conservatory. A romantic but sad incident in his life was his violent passion for Miss Smithson, an Irish actress, whom he saw upon the Paris stage in the *rôle* of Ophelia, at a time when Victor Hugo had revived an admiration for Shakspeare among the French. He married her, but did not live with her long, owing to her bad temper and ungovernable jealousy; though after the separation he honorably contributed to her support out of the pittance he was earning. Among his great works are the opera, "Benvenuto Cellini;" the symphony with chorus, "Romeo and Juliet;" "Beatrice and Benedict;" "Les Troyens," the text from Virgil's "Æneid;" the symphony, "Harold in Italy;" the symphony, "Funèbre et Triomphe;" the "Damnation of Faust;" a double-chorused "Te Deum;" the "Symphony Fantastique;" the "Requiem;" and the sacred trilogy, "L'Enfance du Christ." Berlioz stands among all other composers as the foremost representative of "programme music," and has left explicit and very detailed explanations of the meaning of his works, so that the hearer may listen intelligently by seeing the external objects his music is intended to picture. In the knowledge of individual instruments and the grouping of them for effect, in warmth of imagination and brilliancy of color, and in his daring combinations and fantastic moods, which are sometimes carried to the very verge of eccentricity, he is a colossus among modern musicians. He died in Paris, March 8, 1869.

Romeo and Juliet.

"Dramatic symphony, with choruses, solos, chant, and prologue in choral recitative" is the title which Berlioz gives to his "Romeo and Juliet." It was written in 1839, and its composition commemorates an interesting episode in his career. In the previous year he had written his symphony "Harold in Italy," the subject inspired by Byron's "Childe Harold." Paganini, the wonder of the musical world at that time, was present at its performance, and was so pleased with the work that he sent Berlioz an enthusiastic tribute of applause as well as of substantial remembrance.[1] The composer at that

[1] MY DEAR FRIEND, — Beethoven is dead, and Berlioz alone can revive him. I have heard your divine composition, so worthy of your genius, and beg you to accept, in token of my homage, twenty thousand francs, which will be handed to you by the Baron de Rothschild on presentation of the enclosed. — Your most affectionate friend, NICOLO PAGANINI.
PARIS, Dec. 18, 1838.

time was in straitened circumstances, and in his gratitude for this timely relief he resolved to write a work which should be worthy of dedication to the great violinist. His Autobiography bears ample testimony to the enthusiasm with which he worked. He says : —

"At last, after much indecision, I hit upon the idea of a symphony, with choruses, vocal solos, and choral recitatives, on the sublime and ever novel theme of Shakspeare's 'Romeo and Juliet.' I wrote in prose all the text intended for the vocal pieces which came between the instrumental selections. Émile Deschamps, with his usual delightful good-nature and marvellous facility, set it to verse for me, and I began. . . .

"During all that time how ardently did I live! How vigorously I struck out on that grand sea of poetry caressed by the playful breeze of fancy, beneath the hot rays of that sun of love which Shakspeare kindled, always confident of my power to reach the marvellous island where stands the temple of true art! Whether I succeeded or not it is not for me to decide."

The work opens with a fiery introduction representing the combats and tumults of the two rival houses of Capulet and Montague, and the intervention of the Prince. It is followed by a choral recitative for four altos, tenors, and basses ("Long smouldering Hatreds"), with which is interwoven a contralto solo ("Romeo too is there"), the number closing with a passionate chorus ("The Revels now are o'er"). A beautiful effect is made at this point by assigning to the alto voice two couplets ("Joys of first Love ") which are serious in style but very rich in melody. A brief bit of choral recitative and a few measures for tenor — Mercutio's raillery — lead up to a dainty scherzetto for tenor solo and small chorus ("Mab! bright Elf of Dreamland"), and a short choral passage brings this scene to a close.

The second scene, which is for orchestra only, an impressive declamatory phrase developing into a tender melody, representing the sadness of Romeo, set in tones against the brilliant dance music in the distance accompanying the revel of the Capulets, is one of the most striking effects Berlioz has accomplished, and illustrates his astonishing command of instrumentation. The third scene represents Capulet's garden in the stillness of night, the young Capulets passing through it, bidding each other adieu and repeating snatches of the dance music. As their strains die away in the distance the balcony scene between Romeo and Juliet is given by the orchestra alone in a genuine love-poem full of passion and sensuousness. No words could rival the impassioned beauty of this melodious number. The fourth scene is also given to the orchestra, and is a setting of Mercutio's description of Queen Mab. It is a scherzo intensely swift in its movement and almost ethereal in its dainty, graceful rhythm. The instrumentation is full of subtle effects, particularly in the romantic passages for the horns.

In the fifth scene we pass from the tripping music of the fairies to the notes of woe. It describes the funeral procession of Juliet, beginning with a solemn march in fugue style, at first instrumental, with occasional entrances of the voices in monotone, and then vocal ("O mourn, O mourn, strew choicest Flowers"), the monotone being assigned to the instruments. It preludes a powerful orchestral scene representing Romeo's invocation, Juliet's awakening, and the despair and death of the lovers.[1] The finale is mainly for double chorus, representing the quarrel between the Montagues and Capulets in the cemetery, which is written with great dramatic power and conceived on the large scale of an operatic *ensemble* both in the voice parts and instrumentation, and the final reconciliation through the intercession of Friar Laurence, whose declamatory solos are very striking, particularly the air, "Poor Children mine, let me mourn you." The work is one of almost colossal difficulty, and requires great artists, singers and players, to give expression to its daring realism. Among all of Berlioz's programme-music, this tone-picture of the principal episodes in Shakspeare's

---

[1] COMPOSER'S NOTE. The public has no imagination; therefore pieces which are addressed solely to the imagination have no public. The following instrumental scene is in this case, and I think it should be omitted whenever this symphony is given before an audience not having a feeling for poetry, and not familiar with the fifth act of Shakspeare's tragedy. This implies its omission ninety-nine times out of a hundred. It presents, moreover, immense difficulties of execution. Consequently, after Juliet's funeral procession a moment of silence should be observed, then the finale should be taken up.

tragedy stands out clear and sharp by virtue of its astonishing dramatic power.

The Damnation of Faust.

The "Damnation of Faust," dramatic legend, as Berlioz calls it, was written in 1846. It is divided in four parts, the first containing three, the second four, the third six, and the fourth five scenes, the last concluding with an epilogue and the apotheosis of Marguerite. It was first produced in Paris in November, 1846, and had its first hearing in this country Feb. 12, 1880, when the late Dr. Leopold Damrosch brought it out with the assistance of the New York Symphony, Oratorio, and Arion Societies.

Berlioz has left in his Autobiography an extremely interesting account of the manner in which he composed it. Though he had had the plan of the work in his mind for many years, it was not until 1846 that he began the legend. During this year he was travelling on a concert-tour through Austria, Hungary, Bohemia, and Silesia, and the different numbers were written at intervals of leisure. He says: —

"I wrote when I could and where I could; in the coach, on the railroad, in steamboats, and even in towns, notwithstanding the various cares entailed by my concerts."

He began with Faust's invocation to Nature, which was finished "in my old German post-chaise." The introduction was written in an inn at Passau, and at Vienna he finished up the Elbe scene, Mephistopheles' song, and the exquisite Sylph's ballet. As to the introduction of the Rákóczy march, his words deserve quoting in this connection, as they throw some light on the general character of the work. He says:—

"I have already mentioned my writing a march at Vienna, in one night, on the Hungarian air of Rákóczy. The extraordinary effect it produced at Pesth made me resolve to introduce it in Faust, by taking the liberty of placing my hero in Hungary at the opening of the act, and making him present at the march of a Hungarian army across the plain. A German critic considered it most extraordinary in me to have made Faust travel in such a place. I do not see why, and I should not have hesitated in the least to bring him in in any other direction if it would have benefited the piece. I had not bound myself to follow Goethe's plot, and the most eccentric travels may be attributed to such a personage as Faust without transgressing the bounds of possibility. Other German critics took up the same thesis, and attacked me with even greater violence about my modifications of Goethe's text and plot; just as though there were no other Faust but Goethe's, and as if it were possible to set the whole of such a poem to music without altering its arrangement. I was stupid enough to answer them in the preface to the 'Damnation of Faust.' I have often wondered why I was never reproached about the book of 'Romeo and Juliet,' which is not very like the immortal tragedy. No doubt because Shakspeare was not a German. Patriotism! Fetichism! Idiotcy!"

One night when he had lost his way in Pesth he wrote the choral refrain of the "Ronde des Paysans" by the gaslight in a shop; and at Prague he arose in the middle of the night to write down the Angels' Chorus in Marguerite's apotheosis. At Breslau he wrote the Students' Latin Song, "Jam nox stellata velamina pandit;" and on his return to France he composed the grand trio in the work while visiting a friend near Rouen. He concludes:

"The rest was written in Paris, but always improvised, either at my own house, or at the café, or in the Tuileries gardens, and even on a stone in the Boulevard du Temple. I did not search for ideas, I let them come; and they presented themselves in a most unforeseen manner. When at last the whole outline was sketched, I set to work to re-do the whole, touch up the different parts, unite and blend them together with all the patience and determination of which I am capable, and to finish off the instrumentation, which had only been indicated here and there. I look upon this as one of my best works, and hitherto the public seems to be of the same opinion."

This opinion, however, was of slow growth, for of the first performance of the work he says:—

"It was the end of November, 1846; snow was falling; the weather was dreadful. I had no fashionable cantatrice to sing the part of Marguerite. As for Roger, who did Faust, and Herman Léon, who took the part of Mephistopheles, they might be heard any day in this same theatre; moreover, they were no longer the fashion. The result was that Faust was twice performed to a half-empty room. The concert-going Parisian public, supposed to be fond of music, stayed quietly at home, caring as little about my new work as if I had been an obscure student at the Conservatoire; and these two performances at the Opéra Comique were no better attended than if they had been the most wretched operas on the list."

The opening scene introduces Faust alone in the fields at sunrise on the Hungarian plains. He gives expression to his delight in a tender, placid strain ("The Winter has departed, Spring is here"). It is followed by an instrumental prelude of a pastoral character, in which are heard fragments of the roundelay of the peasants and of the fanfare in the Hungarian march, leading up to the "Dance of Peasants," a brisk, vivacious chorus ("The Shepherd donned his best Array"), beginning with the altos, who are finally joined by the sopranos, tenors, and basses in constantly accelerating time. The scene then changes to another part of the plain and discloses the advance of an army to the brilliant and stirring music of the Rákóczy march.[1]

[1] This march, though the best known of all Hungarian airs, is liable to be confounded with others bearing the same name. It forms one of the group of national patriotic melodies called into existence by the heroism of the Transylvanian prince Franz Rákótzy, who at the beginning of the last century fought with rare valor, though little success, against the dominating power of Austria. Who composed it remains as unknown as the authorship of its less familiar companions; but though the origin of the tune, like that of so many others which nations cherish, is veiled in mystery, the march has enjoyed an enviable prominence. It was proscribed by the Austrian Government in the bad days when Hungary was treated as a conquered appanage of the Hapsburgs; its performance was a criminal act, and the possession of printed or written copies, if suspected, brought down domiciliary visits from the police. — *Albert Hall Programmes*, 1874.

The second part (Scene IV.) opens in north Germany and discloses Faust alone in his chamber, as in Gounod's opera; he sings a soliloquy, setting forth his discontent with worldly happiness, and is about to drown his sorrow with poison, when he is interrupted by the Easter Hymn ("Christ is risen from the Dead"), a stately and jubilant six-part chorus, in the close of which he joins. As it comes to an end he continues his song ("Heavenly Tones, why seek me in the Dust?"), but is again interrupted by the sudden apparition of Mephistopheles, who mockingly sings, "Oh, pious Frame of Mind," and entraps him in the compact. They disappear, and we next find them in Auerbach's cellar in Leipsic, where the carousing students are singing a rollicking drinking-song ("O what Delight when Storm is crashing"). The drunken Brander is called upon for a song, and responds with a characteristic one ("There was a Rat in the Cellar Nest"), to which the irreverent students improvise a fugue on the word "Amen," using a motive of the song. Mephistopheles compliments them on the fugue, and being challenged to give them an air trolls out the lusty *lied*, "There was a King once reigning, who had a big black Flea," in the accompaniment of which Berlioz makes some very realistic effects. Amid the bravas of the drunken students they disappear again, and are next found in the flowery meadows of the Elbe, where Mephistopheles sings a most enchanting melody ("In this fair Bower"). Faust is lulled to slumber, and in his vision hears the chorus of the gnomes and sylphs ("Sleep, happy Faust"), a number of extraordinary beauty and fascinating charm. Its effect is still further heightened by the sylphs' ballet in waltz time. As they gradually disappear, Faust wakes and relates to Mephistopheles his vision of the "angel in human form." The latter promises to conduct him to her chamber, and they join a party of soldiers and students who will pass "before thy beauty's dwelling." The finale of the scene is composed of a stirring soldiers' chorus ("Stoutly-walled Cities we fain would win") and a characteristic students' song in Latin ("Jam nox stellata"), at first sung separately and then combined with great skill.

The third part begins with a brief instrumental prelude, in which the drums and trumpets sound the tattoo, introducing a scene in Marguerite's chamber, where Faust sings a passionate love-song ("Thou sweet Twilight, be welcome"), corresponding with the well-known "Salve dimora" in Gounod's garden scene. At its close Mephistopheles warns him of the approach of Marguerite and conceals him behind a curtain. She enters, and in brief recitative tells her dream, in which she has seen the image of Faust, and discloses her love for him. Then while disrobing she sings the ballad "There was a King in Thule." As its pathetic strains come to a close, the music suddenly changes and Mephistopheles in a characteristic strain summons the will-o'-the-wisps to bewilder the maiden. It is followed by their lovely and graceful minuet, in which Berlioz again displays his wonderful command of orchestral realism. It is followed by Mephistopheles' serenade ("Why dost thou wait at the Door of thy Lover?"), with a choral accompaniment by the will-o'-the-wisps, interspersed with demoniac laughter. The last number is a trio ("Angel adored") for Marguerite, Faust, and Mephistopheles, wonderfully expressive in its utterances of passion, and closing with a chorus of mockery which indicates the coming tragedy.

The fourth part opens with a very touching romance ("My Heart with Grief is heavy"), the familiar "Meine Ruh' ist hin" of Goethe, sung by Marguerite, and the scene closes with the songs of the soldiers and students heard in the distance. In the next scene Faust sings a sombre and powerful invocation to Nature ("O boundless Nature, Spirit sublime"). Mephistopheles is seen scaling the rocks and in agitated recitative tells his companion the story of Marguerite's crime and imprisonment. He bids him sign a scroll which will save him from the consequences of the deed, and Faust thus delivers himself over to the Evil One. Then begins the wild "Ride to Hell," past the peasants praying at the cross, who flee in terror as they behold the riders, followed by horrible beasts, monstrous birds, and grinning, dancing skeletons, until at last they disappear in an abyss and are greeted by the chorus of the spirits of hell in a tempest of sound, which is literally a musical pandemonium ("Has! Irimiru Karabras," etc.) in its discordant vocal strains and in the mighty dissonances and supernatural effects in the accompaniment. A brief epilogue, "On Earth," follows, in which Faust's doom is told, succeeded by a correspondingly brief one, "In Heaven," in which the seraphim plead for Marguerite. The legend closes with "Marguerite's Glorification," a jubilant double chorus announcing her pardon and acceptance among the blest.

BRAHMS.

JOHANNES BRAHMS, one of the most eminent of living German composers, was born at Hamburg, May 7, 1833. His father was a double-bass player in the orchestra in that city, and devoted his son at a very early age to his own profession. His first piano teacher was Cossell; but to Edward Marxsen, the royal music director, he owes his real success as a composer. Brahms remained in Hamburg until 1853, when he went upon a concert-tour with Reményi, the eccentric and somewhat sensational Hungarian, who has been a familiar figure upon the American concert-stage. He remained with him however but a very short time, for in October of that year they parted company. Brahms had attracted the notice of Liszt and Joachim, and it may have been through their advice that the musical partnership was dissolved. In any event, soon after leaving Reményi he went to Düsseldorf and visited Schumann, who announced him to the musical world in a very enthusiastic manner. The next year (1854) appeared his first works, — three sonatas, a trio and scherzo for piano, and three books of songs. After a visit to Liszt at Weimar he settled down as chorus-conductor and music-teacher at the court of Lippe-Detmold, where he remained a few years. After leaving Detmold he successively resided in Hamburg, Zürich, and Baden-Baden, though most of his time has been spent in Vienna, where he has directed the Singakademie and the concerts of the Gesellschaft der Musikfreunde. Among his most famous compositions are a funeral hymn for chorus and wind-band; the "German Requiem;" "Triumphlied," for double chorus and orchestra; "Schicksalslied," for chorus and orchestra; six symphonies; variations on a theme of Haydn, for orchestra; the "Tragic" and "Academic" overtures; besides several trios, quartets, quintets, sextets, concertos, and sonatas.

Triumphlied.

"Triumphlied" ("Song of Triumph") was written by Brahms in commemoration of the victories of German arms and the re-establishment of the Empire, and is dedicated to "the German Emperor Wilhelm I." It was first performed at the fifty-first festival of the Lower Rhine at Cologne in 1873. The text is a paraphrase of certain verses in the nineteenth chapter of Revelation, and reads as follows : —

"Hallelujah, praise the Lord! Honor and power and glory to God!

"For in righteousness and truth the Lord giveth judgment.

"Glory be to God, all ye His servants, and ye that fear Him, all both humble and mighty.

"Hallelujah, for the omnipotent God hath exalted His kingdom.

"O, be joyful, let all be glad, to Him alone give honor.

"Behold, the heavens opened wide, and yonder a snow-white horse, and on him sat one called Steadfast and Faithful, who warreth and judgeth all with righteousness.

"And he treads the wine-press of wrath of the Lord God Almighty.

"Lo! a great name hath he written upon his vesture and upon his girdle.

"A King of kings and Lord of lords! Hallelujah! Amen!"

The scriptural selections are divided into three movements, written for double chorus (with the exception of two short barytone solos), orchestra, and organ, and are introduced by a brief instrumental prelude of a solemn but animated and exultant character, in the closing measures of which both choirs break in with jubilant shouts of "Hallelujah! praise the Lord!" The theme of the movement is the stirring old German song "Heil dir im Siegerkranz,"[1] which is worked up with consummate skill. The first part closes with a climax of

---

[1] A German national song, written by Heinrich Harries, a Holstein clergyman, for the birthday of Christian VII. of Denmark. It was originally in eight stanzas, but was reduced to five and otherwise slightly modified for Prussian use by B. G. Schumacher, and in this form appeared as a "Berliner Volkslied" in the *Spenersche Zeitung* of Dec. 17, 1793. — *Grove's Dictionary.*

power and contrapuntal effect hardly to be found elsewhere outside the choruses of Handel.

The second movement ("Glory be to God!") is of the same general character as the first. After the opening ascription, a short fugue intervenes, leading to a fresh melody alternately sung by both choruses.

The third movement, after a very brief but spirited orchestral flourish, opens with an exultant barytone solo ("And behold then the Heavens opened wide"). The choruses respond with animation ("And yonder a snow-white Horse"). Again the barytone intervenes ("And lo! a great Name hath He written"), and then the choruses take up the majestic theme, "King of Kings and Lord of Lords," each answering the other with triumphant shouts that gather force and fire as they proceed, and closing with a mighty hallelujah in which voices, orchestra, and organ join with fullest power to produce one of the grandest harmonies ever written. The work is one of extreme difficulty, as the two choirs are treated independently and their harmonies are complicated, though blended in general effect. Neither choir receives assistance from the other. In fact, each rank of voices is required to perform music of the most exacting kind, so that a perfect performance of this great jubilee hymn requires singers of trained skill and more than ordinary intelligence. When thus given, few choruses of modern times reveal such artistic richness and symmetrical proportions.

BRUCH.

MAX BRUCH, one of the most successful choral composers of the present time, was born at Cologne, Jan. 6, 1838. His father was a government official, and his mother a singer of more than ordinary ability. He received his early instructions, under her watchful supervision, from Professor Breidenstein, at Bonn. In 1852 he continued his studies with Hiller, Reinecke, and Breuning, at Cologne; and at this time began to produce compositions which gave unusual promise. In 1865 he was musical director at Coblenz, and subsequently at Berlin, where he conducted the Singakademie. In 1867 he was appointed chapelmaster to the Prince of Schwarzburg-Sondershausen, — a post which he held until 1870. Since that time he has also been honored with a call to the directorship of the Liverpool Philharmonic Society. For some years past he has lived at Bonn and Berlin, and devoted himself exclusively to composition. His first public appearance as a composer was in connection with the performance of his operetta, "Scherz, List und Rache," set to Goethe's words;

following which he produced several chamber compositions, among them a trio (op. 5), two string quartets (op. 9, 10), Capriccio (op. 2) for four hands, Fantasie (op. 11) for two pianos, the G minor and D minor violin concertos, besides two symphonies. He has also written an oratorio, "Arminius," and two operas, "Loreley," to the text which the poet Geibel wrote for Mendelssohn, and "Hermione," an adaptation of Shakspeare's "Winter's Tale." His greatest successes, however, have been made with his works in the cantata form, as he is a recognized master in writing for large masses of voices and instruments, though many of his solo melodies possess great beauty. In this class of his compositions the most conspicuous are "Scenes from the Frithjof-Saga," familiarly known as "Frithjof," "Flight of the Holy Family," "Roman Triumph Song," "Roman Obsequies," "Salamis," "Fair Ellen," "Odysseus," and "Rorate Coeli."

Frithjof.

The story of the old Norse hero Frithjof is told with exceeding spirit and beauty in the "Frithjof's Saga" of Esaias Tegnér, Bishop of Wexiö, Sweden, which has been translated into almost every European language, and to which music has been adapted by Crusell, Hedda Wrangel, Boman, Sandberg, Zanders, Caroline Ridderstolpe, Panny, Silcher, and other Scandinavian and German composers. It was Bishop Tegnér's Saga from which Bruch derived the incidents of his musical setting of this stirring Norse theme.[1]

To make the text of the libretto intelligible, the incidents leading up to it must be briefly told. Frithjof was the son of Thorstein, a friend of King Bele of Baldershage, and was in love with Ingeborg, the king's daughter and his foster sister. Bele died, and left his kingdom to his two sons. When Thorstein passed away, he bequeathed to his son his ship "Ellida" and his gold ring. Soon thereafter Frithjof sailed across the fiord to demand the hand of Ingeborg. Her brothers Helge and Halfdan scorned his suit, whereupon Frithjof swore they should never have help from him. King Ring, a neighboring monarch, hearing of the trouble between them, improved the opportunity to menace their kingdom. The brothers appealed to Frithjof for aid, but he turned a deaf ear; and when they took the field against Bele, he returned to Baldershage and made love to Ingeborg, with whom he exchanged rings. Helge and Halfdan were defeated by Ring, and as part of the indemnity he demanded Ingeborg's hand. Finding upon their return that Frithjof had been there without their permission, they required him as a penalty to go to the Orkneys and collect the tribute which the

---

[1] An admirable translation of the Saga was made by George Stephens, published in London and Stockholm in 1839. It includes besides the Saga, a life of Tegnér, by Bishop Franzén of Hernösand, Sweden; the Frithjof literature; description of Ingeborg's Arm Ring, by Hildebrand, the Royal Antiquarian of Sweden; Crusell's songs; and numerous notes and illustrations.

islanders had neglected to pay since the death of Bele. Frithjof sailed away in "Ellida." Meanwhile the brothers resorted to witchcraft to raise a storm that should destroy his vessel, burned his barrow, and married the lamenting Ingeborg to Ring.

It is at this point that the text of the cantata begins. The first scene pictures the return of Frithjof and his joy at the prospect of seeing Ingeborg, whose hand the false brothers had promised him if he were successful. Learning what had occurred in his absence, Frithjof goes to the temple where the kings are sacrificing, hurls the tribute in Helge's face, fires the edifice, and hurries to the sea, pursued by his enemies. The hero sails away again in "Ellida," and becomes a sea-rover. The text closes with this incident. In the Saga, after gaining great fame, Frithjof returns and goes disguised as a salt-burner to Ring's palace. The king recognized him, and moved by his sad story became his friend and appointed him guardian of his heir. Ring died soon after, and Frithjof married Ingeborg. Helge and Halfdan made war against him. Helge was killed, and Halfdan became his vassal.

The cantata opens with an animated instrumental introduction, "Frithjof's Return," leading to the barytone recitative and aria ("How bravely o'er the Flood so bright"), — a very expressive song, interspersed with the tender, graceful chorus of his companions ("O, 't is Delight when the Land far appeareth"). The second scene is preluded with a wedding march, whose blithe measures are in marked contrast with the bridal chorus ("Sadly the Skald walks before the Train"), and Ingeborg's song ("My Heart with Sorrow overflowing"), which describes her grief over her unhappy destiny. The third scene ("Frithjof's Revenge"), for barytone, chorus, and orchestra, is one of great power in its dramatic and descriptive character, as well as in its masterly instrumentation. It begins with a chorus of priests ("Midnight Sun on the Mountain burns"), gradually accelerating until it is interrupted by Frithjof's cry ("Go to Helas' dark Abode"). Three bars of chorus intervene ("Woe! O wicked Deed"), when Frithjof, after a short recitative, sings a spirited aria ("Where my Father rests"). At its close, as he rescues Ingeborg's ring and fires the temple, the chorus resumes ("Woe! he tugs with all his Might at the Ring"). The choral finale of this scene, with its effective instrumentation, is a masterpiece of dramatic music, worthy to rank with the highest work of its kind in opera. After the storm, the calm. In that calm occurs a melodical episode of an extraordinary character. The melody itself is so unlike anything which precedes or follows it that it must have been interpolated. In grateful contrast with the revenge of Frithjof, the burning of the temple, and the curses of the infuriated priests, comes the fourth scene, "Frithjof's Departure from the Northland,"— a solo quartet for male voices ("Sun in the Sky now mounteth high"), of exquisite harmony, leading up to and accompanying a barytone solo which has rarely been surpassed in the tender beauty of its melody or the majestic sonority of its style : [1] —

> " World's grandest region, thou mighty North!
> From thy dominions I am driven forth ;
> Within thy border I lov'd to dwell ;
> Midsummer sun, farewell, farewell.
> Thou mighty North, farewell.
> My love is foiled, my roof-tree rent,
> Mine honor soiled, I in exile sent!
> Cheerless is my soul within me,
> Hopeless I must bear my lot.
> Ye rugged mountains, where heroes dwell,
> And Thor commandeth clouds and winds ;
> Ye azure lakes, that I love so well,
> Ye woods and brakes, farewell."

[1] In the original Saga the "Farewell" has six verses, the first, second, and sixth of which are thus literally translated: —

> " Heimskringla's forehead,
> Thou lofty North !
> Away I'm hurried
> From this thine earth.
> My race from thee goes,
> I boasting tell ;
> Now, nurse of heroes,
> Farewell! Farewell!

> " Farewell, high-gleaming
> Walhalla's throne,
> Night's eye, bright-beaming,
> Midsummer's sun !
> Sky! where, as in hero's
> Soul, pure depths dwell,
> And thronging star-rows,
> Farewell ! Farewell!
> . . . . . .

> " My love insulted,
> My palace brent,
> My honor tarnished,
> In exile sent,
> From land in sadness
> To the sea we appeal,
> But life's young gladness,
> Farewell! Farewell!"

The fifth scene is Ingeborg's lament for her lost lover ("Storms wildly roar"), — a soprano solo, which, if not as dramatic as the music assigned to Frithjof, is nevertheless full of beautiful sentiment. The work closes with a delightful chorus, with short phrases for Frithjof ("Now he crosseth the Floods of the salt desert Waste"), supposed to be sung on board the hero's good ship "Ellida" as they sail off for conquest and the enjoyment of the booty he has promised his companions.

Salamis.

"Salamis, Triumphal Hymn of the Greeks" was written in 1862. It is a composition mostly for male chorus, and is admirably adapted for festival purposes. The poem, which celebrates the defeat of Xerxes, is by H. Lingg, and runs as follows: —

> "Adorn the ships with Persian trophies!
> Let the purple sails be swelled!
> Joy floats about the masts!
> Evoe, the mighty foe, is vanquished!
> We broke, O sea, we broke the bond,
> Which the Persian Prince threw around thy neck.
> Thou rollest now unfettered, no longer embittered
> By the hateful trampling of the horses,
> Which thy waving surface,
> Thy bridge-fettered wrath, bore reluctantly.
> Fate overtook Xerxes
> And achieved a Hellenic victory on the waves.
> To the tyrant, to the arbitrary master,
> Did not succumb the people that dwell by the sea,
> For the old ruler of the sea filled his beloved race
> With boundless courage for the sea-fight.

All around, the waves with delight
Hear many an Ionic song;
They roar and join the pæan
After the splendid struggle
There arise dithyrambic days of liberty!"

The instrumental introduction to the work is written in massive style, its grand chorus being elegantly interwoven with runs by the wood instruments, preparing the way for the festive adorning of the ships,—a very beautiful allegro movement. This is followed by a slower movement which pictures the breaking of the bond, the rolling of the sea, and the trampling of the horses with all that vividness for which the composer is famous. It is succeeded by a passage which is very stately, particularly in the basses ("Fate overtook Xerxes"), leading up to the grand climax ("All around, the Waves with Delight"), when the orchestra and voices are in splendid accord. After a short repetition of the opening allegro the hymn closes. It would be hard to find a more admirable musical setting of a poem than this, whether in the strength and beauty of its vocal parts, or in the color, vigor, and general effectiveness of the instrumentation.

Fair Ellen.

The heroic defence of Lucknow by its British garrison in 1857, during the Sepoy rebellion, is one of the most memorable events in the English administration of India. The world is familiar with the story of the disaffection of the native troops, the failure of Sir Henry Lawrence, who was in command, to overcome the mutiny, the stubborn defence which the brave little garrison made against the repeated assaults of the native troops, their temporary assistance from Outram and Havelock, who cut their way into the city, and the final relief which was brought to them by Sir Colin Campbell. Of all the stirring incidents of the siege, however, not one has made such a strong impression as the fanciful story of the Scotch girl who heard the slogan of the MacGregors far away and knew the Highlanders were coming to their rescue.

It is this incident which Bruch has used as the theme of his cantata "Schön Ellen" ("Fair Ellen"). The story is identical with the one so often told in prose and poetry, but the *dramatis personæ* differ. Instead of General Lawrence we have Lord Edward, and instead of familiar Jessie Brown we have "Fair Ellen." The text of the libretto is weak and spiritless as compared with that of the poetical versions. The salient point of the story is thus versified in the former: —

> "The Campbells are coming, I told you true;
> I hear the bugle blowing:
> The pibroch is borne adown the wind,
> The tones on the breezes quiver;
> 'Neath the tread of battalions that hurry along
> Afar the plains do shiver."

Compare the above with the corresponding verses from Robert Lowell's fine poem: —

"The Highlanders! O dinna ye hear
  The slogan far awa?
The MacGregors? Ah! I ken it weel;
  It's the grandest of them a'.

. . . .

"Then Jessie said, 'The slogan's dune,
  But can ye no hear them noo?
The Campbells are comin'! It's nae a dream;
  Our succors hae broken through."

Weak as the text may be, the strong healthy music of the cantata makes ample compensation. It is quite brief, there being but two solo parts, "Fair Ellen" (soprano) and Lord Edward (barytone), and five short chorus numbers. The former are vigorous and somewhat declamatory in style, but the choruses are very melodious and stirring. The instrumentation is unusually effective, and a fine point is made in the climax by the interweaving of the familiar air, "The Campbells are Coming," with the orchestral score. It lends spirit and color to the finale, and closes up the work with a fine burst of powerful effect. Short as it is, "Fair Ellen" will always be a favorite with popular audiences.

Odysseus.

The cantata of "Odysseus," like that of "Frithjof," is made up of detached scenes, in this case selected from the Odyssey and arranged by William Paul Graff. The work was first produced in 1872, and has met with great success in Germany, England, and the United States. It is divided into two parts, the first containing four, and the second, six scenes. The characters are as numerous as those of a grand opera, and include Odysseus, barytone; Penelope, alto; Alcinoos, King of the Pheaces, bass; Arete, his consort, alto; Nausicaa, their daughter, soprano; the Helmsman, bass; Pallas Athene, soprano; Leucothea, soprano; Spirit of Tiresias, bass; Spirit of Anticlia, Odysseus' mother, alto; and Hermes, tenor. In performance, however, the parts of Arete and the Spirit of Anticlia, as well as of Nausicaa and Pallas Athene, are usually doubled. The choruses, which are a very important feature of the work, are assigned to Odysseus' companions, Spirits of the Departed, Sirens, Tritons, Nymphs of the sea, Pheaces, Rhapsodes, boatmen and people of Ithaca.

In the first scene Odysseus is discovered on Calypso's enchanted island longing for home. Hermes, the messenger of the gods, appears to him and announces that the Immortals, touched by his sorrow, will rescue him and restore him to Penelope. In the next scene the wanderer has reached the abysses of Erebus, "where, loud thundering, the flood of Cocytus pours its black wave into Acheron's tide." Here he invokes the world of shades. The spirits of children, brides, youths, and old men successively appear to him and narrate their mournful stories. Then Tiresias the bard warns him of the Sirens, and Anticlia his mother bids him hasten to Penelope. In the third scene he passes the isles of the Sirens, and escapes their wiles through the firmness of his companions. The fourth scene describes the storm at sea, the wreck of the vessel, and Odysseus' rescue by Leucothea, who gives him the veil the Immortals have woven, and bids the Oceanides and Tritons guide him safely to land; and the first part closes with our hero peacefully sleeping on the flowery shore of the island of Pheacia.

The second part opens with the lament of Penelope and her prayer to the gods to restore her husband to her. The sixth scene changes to the island again, and discloses Odysseus awakened from his slumbers by the sports and dances of Nausicaa and her joyful maidens. He appeals to her for help and refreshment, and is bidden to partake of their hospitality. In the next scene a sumptuous banquet is spread for him, at which he reveals his identity and asks that he be allowed to return to his home. The fair Nausicaa, though suddenly enamoured of the handsome stranger, conceals her passion and expedites his departure. The eighth scene gives us a sketch of Penelope weaving the garment, the *ruse* by which she kept her suitors aloof.

> "This garment by day I weave in my sorrow,
> And ravel the web in the still hour of night;
> Thus wearying long, yet my tears greet the morrow,
> Hope vanishes as the long years take flight."

The ninth scene opens with the arrival of Odysseus at Ithaca. The sleeping wanderer is borne ashore by his comrades, and upon awaking from his slumbers fails to recognize his own country until Pallas Athene appears to him. The goddess convinces him that he is at home once more, and then discloses the plot of the suitors, who are revelling in his palace, to compel Penelope to select one of them that day in order that they may gain possession of his property, as well as their conspiracy for his destruction, from which she promises to protect him. The final scene describes the glad acclamations of the people as they recognize Odysseus, and the joy of Penelope as she welcomes him home once more.

The orchestral introduction is very free and flowing in character, and its themes are taken from the duet of Odysseus and Penelope, which occurs later on. The opening chorus of Calypso's nymphs ("Here, O Hermes, in midst of the Island") is very graceful in its movement and is set to a most delightful accompaniment. It is followed by Odysseus' lament ("Flow, ye Tears, since Days are hateful"), at first tender in its character, then changing to passionate utterances as the remembrance of Penelope comes to him, and closing with a hopeful strain after the promise of help from Zeus. In the second or Hades scene the music changes from its bright color to a gloomier minor tone. It opens with a male chorus ("The Bounds we have reached of the deep flowing Ocean"), pianissimo, gradually increasing in intensity and accompanied by remarkable effects in tone-color as the orchestra describes "the thundering of the flood Cocytus" and "the surging aloft of the shadows of the departed." It is followed by semi-choruses of the shades, and closes with a very spirited and dramatic male chorus ("Dread on Dread! Lo, surging aloft, the numberless Hosts of Departed"). The third scene opens with a fresh and characteristic male chorus ("Our Sails to the Breezes"), followed by the graceful and alluring chorus of the sirens ("Come, great Odysseus, Hero of Might"). The last scene is almost entirely choral and very dramatic in its effect, especially the opening number for the Oceanides and Tritons ("Hark! the Storm gathers from afar"), with its vigorous instrumental description of the tempest, and the closing number for full chorus ("Yonder beckons the wood-crested Harbor"), which in its tenderness and joyousness forms a striking contrast to the earlier part of the scene.

The second part is introduced with a dignified and sombre recitative ("Thou far-darting Sun"), followed by an aria of the same character ("Oh! Atritone") in which Penelope bewails the absence of Odysseus. In the next scene the music changes to a bright and tripping strain, the chorus of Nausicaa's maidens ("On the flowery Mead, girt by the dimpling Tide"), which closely resembles that of Calypso's nymphs in the first scene. After Odysseus' fervent appeal ("Hark to me! Queen, or heaven-dwelling Goddess") the banquet scene occurs. It begins with an animated chorus of the Pheacians ("Be welcome, Stranger, to Pheacia's Land"), followed by an exquisite unison chorus of the Rhapsodes ("Ten Years now are past since Troy in the Dust was laid"), set to an accompaniment of harps. A simple and tender melody ("Let me then depart in Peace"), sung by Odysseus, in which the chorus singers gradually join, closes the scene. The eighth scene contains the most expressive solo number of the work, Penelope's aria ("This Garment by Day I weave in my Sorrow"), with a characteristic descriptive accompaniment. The gems of the ninth scene are Odysseus' passionate aria ("O my Fatherland! blest Remembrance!") and his furious revenge song ("Miscreant! woe to Thee"). The last scene opens with a joyous chorus of the people ("Say, have ye heard the Tidings of Joy?"), followed by a fervent duet between Odysseus and Penelope ("Omnipotent Zeus! we call on thy Name"). The final chorus begins in chorale style ("In Flames ascending"), and after repeating the melody of Odysseus' song in the seventh scene ("Nowhere abides such Delight"), closes with a fine fugued passage ("Slayer of Darkness").

BUCK.

DUDLEY BUCK, one of the most eminent of American organists and composers, was born March 10, 1839, at Hartford, Conn., where his father was engaged in the mercantile business. He studied both the piano and organ, the latter with such success that at the age of sixteen he was appointed organist at St. John's Church in his native city. In 1858 he went to Europe and entered the Leipsic Conservatory, where he studied the piano with Plaidy and Moscheles, and composition with Hauptmann and Richter. After remaining there a year and a half he went to Dresden and began the study of Bach's music with Johann Schneider. A year and a half later he went to Paris, and there acquainted himself with French music and musicians. He returned to this country in 1862, and accepted the position of organist at the Park Church, Hartford, but after the death of his parents removed to Chicago, where he obtained the position of organist at St. James's Episcopal Church, and also devoted much of his time to teaching and composition. In that city his home became a musical centre. His library, fine organ, and music-room were great attractions, and he had laid the foundation of a brilliant musical career, when the great fire of 1871 swept away his entire property, including many manuscript compositions. Like many other musicians at that time he left the city, seeing no prospect of advantage to him where it would require a long time to recover purely material losses. He went with his family to Boston, where his fame was already established, and obtained the position of organist at St. Paul's Church, as well as the charge of the large organ in the Music Hall. After remaining a short time in that city he removed to New York, where he has since resided. His life has been a very busy one, and he has had an important influence, both personally and in connection with Theodore Thomas, upon the progress of music in this country. It is not extravagant to say that there are few Protestant churches whose music has not been dignified and improved by his contributions, particularly of anthems and Te Deums, as well as of compositions for the organ, of which he is a consummate master. Singing societies are also indebted to him for many elegant four-part songs. Among his larger works are the cantata "Don Munio" (1874); the "Centennial," written for the Centennial at Philadelphia; "The Nun of Nidaros" (1878); "The Golden Legend," which was the prize cantata at the Cincinnati Festival of 1880; an Easter cantata; the Forty-sixth Psalm, written for the Boston Handel and Haydn Society; two volumes of sacred songs and motets;

"Marmion," a symphonic overture, and other works for orchestra; the cantatas "Voyage of Columbus" (1885) and the "Light of Asia" (1886). The last two cantatas were issued in Europe, the one in Germany and the other in England, and thus came to this country bearing a foreign imprint, — a novelty for an American composer.

Don Munio.

"Don Munio," a dramatic cantata for solos, chorus, and orchestra, was written in 1874. The story of it is taken from Washington Irving's Spanish papers, and the scene is laid in the period of the wars with the Moors. While hunting one morning, Don Munio de Hinojosa captures a cavalcade which is escorting the Moorish Prince, Abadil, and his betrothed, Constanza, on the way to their wedding. The Prince, all escape being cut off, seeks to purchase the good-will of Don Munio with his gold and jewels, and implores him not to separate him from his affianced. The Don, touched by their unfortunate condition, invites them to spend a fortnight at his castle, promising that the nuptials shall be celebrated there, and then they shall be released. The lovers accept, and Don Munio is faithful to his promise. Shortly after their departure he is ordered by the king to join in the expedition to Palestine. In one of the encounters of this crusade he is killed by Abadil, who does not recognize his former benefactor with his visor closed. His death is greatly mourned in Spain, but they are consoled when Roderigo, a messenger from Palestine, arrives and tells them that one evening while strolling near the Holy Sepulchre he saw seventy Christian knights riding in ghostly procession, with the late Don Munio at their head. This is regarded as an assurance that all is well with him. *Requiescat in pace.*

These are the incidents which Mr. Buck has chosen for musical treatment, and he has done the work excellently well. After the orchestral introduction follows a spirited hunting-song for male chorus. The next scene opens in the chamber of Donna Maria, wife of Don Munio, who laments his absence in a minor strain, to which succeeds a rondo movement. The third is religious in character, marked " Evening. Close of vesper service in the chapel of the castle. Escobedo, the chaplain, with the women, and such retainers as have not followed Don Munio on his expedition." It begins with a prelude closing with full orchestra and organ, and leading to barytone solo and chorus, and a short exhortation to prayer by Escobedo. The next number is an Ave Maria for full chorus, which is very beautifully harmonized. In the next scene we encounter Don Munio in the forest, and are treated to the conventional hunting-song. The next number hints at the approach of the Moors, which is soon disclosed by a pretty three-part chorus of "the females of the Moorish cavalcade as they journey." The eighth scene contains some powerful chorus work, divided between the furious Spaniards and the frightened women, and set to a very vigorous accompaniment. After the tumult ends, Abadil very melodiously appeals to Don Munio, followed by a brief arioso in which the latter makes his terms, and a spirited chorus of gratitude to the Don, which close the first part.

After a short prelude, the second part opens with a tenor aria for Abadil ("O, thou my Star") which is very refined in sentiment. It is followed by the chorale "Jesu, dulcis Memoria," sung by the chapel choir. A duet ensues between the two lovers on the castle terrace, which is very Italian in its flavor, and one of the most effective numbers in the cantata. The next two numbers furnish the wedding music, — a happy bridal chorus, and a charming bolero for orchestra. These lead to an unaccompanied quartet between Don Munio, Donna Maria, Abadil, and Constanza ("It is the Lot of Friends to part"). In the next scene occurs a vigorous duet between Don Munio and his wife, in which he informs her of his speedy departure for Palestine, followed by a stirring battle-hymn for male chorus. The next scene, "The chapel of the castle, choir chanting the dirge for the dead," is in strong contrast with the preceding. Mr. Buck has rarely written anything better in his sacred music than this beautiful requiem. In the next two numbers the messenger describes the manner of Don Munio's death, and the ghostly vision at the sepulchre, and at the end of his message the requiem changes to a jubilant chorus of gratitude ("In thankful Hymns ascending"). "Don Munio" is one of the most powerful and spontaneous of American compositions, and needs but little more amplification to deserve the name of opera.

The Centennial Meditation of Columbia.

The National Centennial celebration at Philadelphia was inaugurated May 10, 1876, with a special musical programme, in which the cantata with the above formidable title occupied a prominent place. The ode was written by Sydney Lanier, of Georgia, a poet who prior to that time had made considerable reputation by two poems printed in "Lippincott's Magazine." The national idea was satisfied by assigning the music to Dudley Buck, at that time living in Connecticut. It must be acknowledged that the work did not make a deep impression, although it contains some excellent musical writing, and for two sufficient reasons. First, it is not a work of musical genius or inspiration, as it was ordered by a commission for a popular show. It was not singular in this respect. The "Centennial March," written by Richard Wagner, for the same occasion, is page after page of sound and fury, executed for a most exorbitant remuneration. To ascertain its real want of inspiration one has but to place it by the side of the "Kaiser March," with its massive chords, its grand thematic treatment, and its stately movement, the outcome of patriotic fervor and national triumph. Second, the stilted and unmusical lines furnished by Mr. Lanier must have hampered the composer in every verse. This is all the more remarkable because Mr. Lanier himself was a practical musician. He had been for some time a violinist in the Peabody orchestra at Baltimore, under that accomplished leader, Asgar Hamerik. It is remarkable, therefore, that he should not have recognized the difficulties he was placing in the way both of the composer and the performers.

The ode has sixty-one lines, divided into eight stanzas of unequal lengths. It sketches the past and present of the nation, the powers which opposed its progress and hindered the development of its freedom, and the elements which at last produced success, closing with cheering auguries for the future, and a welcome to the world. All this might have been set to smooth and fluent verse, which would readily have adapted itself to music; but what composer could have treated successfully such verses as these? —

> "Mayflower, Mayflower, slowly hither flying,
> Trembling westward o'er yon balking sea,
> Hearts within, 'Farewell, dear England,' sighing,
> Winds without, 'But dear in vain,' replying,
> Gray-lipp'd waves about thee shouted, crying,
>   'No! it shall not be!'

"Jamestown, out of thee —
Plymouth, thee — thee, Albany —
Winter cries, 'Ye freeze; away!'
Fever cries, 'Ye burn; away!'
Hunger cries, 'Ye starve; away!'
Vengeance cries, 'Your graves shall stay!'

"Hark!
Huguenots whispering 'Yea' in the dark,
Puritans answering 'Yea' in the dark!
'Yea,' like an arrow shot true to his mark,
Darts through the tyrannous heart of Denial.
Patience and Labor and solemn-souled Trial,
   Foiled, still beginning,
   Soiled, but not sinning,
Toil through the stertorous death of the Night,
Toil, when wild brother-wars new-dark the light,
Toil, and forgive, and kiss o'er, and re-plight."

Even in the last verse, where the composer must make his climax, and the singers must be most effective, they are confronted with this unsingable line: —

"And wave the world's best lover's welcome to the world."

The only musical verse is the reply of the angel to Columbia in the midst of her ragged and cacophonous meditation, which the composer selected as a solo for bass voice:[1] —

"Long as thine Art shall love true love,
  Long as thy Science truth shall know,
  Long as thine Eagle harms no Dove,
  Long as thy Law by law shall grow,
  Long as thy God is God above,
  Thy brother every man below,
So long, dear Land of all my love,
  Thy name shall shine, thy fame shall grow."

[1] Sung upon that occasion by Mr. Myron D. Whitney.

The prelude for orchestra determines the motive of the whole cantata, and is very spirited; for here, at least, the composer was not hampered by words. The opening verse, —

"From this hundred-terraced height,"

is set very effectively in chorale form; but the next two verses, already quoted, are arranged for semi-chorus and full chorus, and close in a vocal stretto quite as hysterical as the words. Then follows the whispering of the Huguenots and Puritans, commencing *sotto voce*, and gradually increasing to a *forte* at the close. A few bars for the horn lead to the bass solo, "Long as thine Art," with horn obligato, — a very impressive and dignified aria, and one which would speedily become a favorite in the concert-room if adapted to the words. The final number ("Music from this Height of Time") begins in full choral harmony and closes with a vigorous and well-written fugue.

The Golden Legend.

"The Golden Legend" was written in competition for the prize of one thousand dollars, which the Cincinnati May Festival Association offered in 1879 for the best work of a native composer. The judges were Theodore Thomas, Otto Singer, Asgar Hamerik, Carl Zerrahn, and the late Dr. Leopold Damrosch. Their award was made to "The Golden Legend," and it was first performed at the Festival of 1880, with Miss Annie B. Norton as Elsie, Mr. Frederick Harvey as Prince Henry, Mr. J. F. Rudolphsen as Lucifer, and Mr. M. D. Whitney as Friar Paul.

The text of the cantata is composed of a prologue, epilogue, and twelve scenes taken from Longfellow's Episode in "Christus" by the same name. The mediæval story is a very simple one. Prince Henry of Hoheneck, stricken down with an incurable ailment, after vainly seeking a remedy, is visited by Lucifer disguised as a physician, who tempts him to adopt a remedy prescribed by a doctor of Salerno; namely, the blood of a maiden who will voluntarily offer herself as a sacrifice. Elsie devotes her life to the Prince, and they journey together to Salerno, where her death must take place. Arrived at the spot, the Prince, touched by her magnanimity, entreats her to forego her purpose; but she insists upon it, bids him farewell in the school, and enters an inner apartment with Lucifer disguised as a friar. Before the tragedy can be consummated, the Prince bursts open the door, with the aid of his followers, and rescues her. The pair return to the castle on the Rhine, where of course the rapidly convalescing Prince marries Elsie, and the story closes with an epilogue reciting the discomfiture of Lucifer and the triumph of good over evil.

Out of this material the composer has constructed his work, eliminating from and adding to the original matter to suit his musical scheme, but at the same time preserving the general spirit of the story. After a very spirited and energetic prelude, the prologue begins with the fruitless attempt of Lucifer to pull down the cross on the spire of Strasburg cathedral, the protests of the spirits of the air (first and second sopranos), the defiance of the bells (male chorus) as each attempt fails, and the final disappearance of the spirits amid the chanting of the majestic Latin Hymn, " Nocte surgentes," by full chorus in the church, accompanied by the organ. The second scene opens in Prince Henry's chamber in the tower of the Vautsberg castle, and reminds one of the opening scene of " Faust," as set by Gounod. After an expressive declamation of his melancholy and his longing for rest and health (" I cannot sleep, my fervid Brain calls up the vanished Past again "), Lucifer appears in a flash of light, dressed as a travelling physician, and a dialogue ensues, the purport of which has already been told, which closes with an ingenious and beautifully-written number for the two voices, accompanied by a four-part chorus of mixed voices and a small semi-chorus of sopranos and altos (" Golden Visions wave and hover "). The fourth scene is an unaccompanied quartet, " The Evening Song," sung by Elsie, Bertha, Max, and Gottlieb in their peasant home in the Odenwald, as they light the lamps (" O gladsome Light of the Father "). It is a simple, tranquil hymn, but full of that sacred sentiment which this composer expresses so admirably in music. The fifth scene, Elsie's prayer in her chamber (" My Redeemer and my Lord "), in its calm beauty and religious feeling makes a fitting pendant to the quartet. In the next number, the orchestra is utilized to carry on the action, and in march tempo describes the pilgrimage to Salerno with stately intervals, in which is heard the sacred song, "Urbs cœlestis, urbs beata," supposed to be sung by the pilgrims "moving slowly on their long journey with uncovered feet." The seventh scene is laid in the refectory of the convent of Hirschau, in the Black Forest, where Lucifer enters the gaudiolum of monks, disguised as a friar, and sings the rollicking Latin drinking-song, "Ave color vini clari," which Mr. Edmund C. Stedman versified for this work as follows:—

"Hail! thou vintage clear and ruddy!
Sweet of taste and fine of body,
Through thine aid we soon shall study
How to make us glorious!

"Oh! thy color erubescent!
Oh! thy fragrance evanescent!
Oh! within the mouth how pleasant!
Thou the tongue's prætorius!

"Blest the stomach where thou wendest!
Blest the throat which thou distendest!
Blest the mouth which thou befriendest,
And the lips victorious!

CHORUS OF MONKS.

"Pour the wine, then, pour it!
Let the wave bear all before it!
There's none to score it,
So pour it in plenty, pour it!"

The next number is for orchestra only, and once more the instruments are used for a continuance of the action by a description of the carousal of the monks in a characteristic allegro bacchanale, the abbot testifying his indignation through the medium of the trombone and the use of the Gregorian melody. The sentiment of the latter is expressed by the following verse : —

> "What mean this revel and carouse?
> Is this a tavern and drinking-house?
> Are you Christian monks or heathen devils,
> To pollute this convent with your revels?"

The ninth scene changes to Genoa. Elsie, on a terrace overlooking the sea, sings a charming aria ("The Night is calm and cloudless"), with a choral refrain of "Kyrie Eleison." The tenth is a graceful barcarolle for orchestra, but it is somewhat in the nature of an interpolation, and is only connected with the movement of the story by a thin thread, as will be seen from the verse which gives its motive : —

> "The fisherman who lies afloat,
> With shadowy sail in yonder boat,
> Is singing softly to the night.
> A single step and all is o'er ;
> And thou, dear Elsie, wilt be free
> From martyrdom and agony."

The eleventh scene is a spirited and beautifully-written male chorus of sailors ("The Wind upon our Quarter lies"). The twelfth reaches the climax in the scene at the college of Salerno between Lucifer, Elsie, and the Prince, with accompaniment of attendants, and is very dramatic throughout. It is followed by a tender love-duet for Elsie and the Prince on the terrace of the castle of Vautsberg, which leads to the epilogue, "O Beauty of Holiness," for full chorus and orchestra, in which the composer is at his very best both in the construction of the vocal parts and the elaborately worked-up accompaniments.

The Voyage of Columbus.

"The Voyage of Columbus" was written in 1885, and first published in Germany. The text of the libretto was prepared by the composer himself, extracts from Washington Irving's "Columbus" forming the theme of each of the six scenes, all of which are supposed to transpire at evening, and are therefore styled by the composer "night-scenes." Their arrangement, which is very skilfully accomplished, is as follows: —

SCENE I. In the chapel of St. George at Palos, Aug. 2, 1492. "The squadron being ready to put to sea, Columbus, with his officers and crew, confessed themselves to the friar, Juan Perez. They entered upon the enterprise full of awe, committing themselves to the especial guidance and protection of Heaven."

SCENE II. On the deck of the Santa Maria. "Eighteen years elapsed after Columbus conceived his enterprise before he was enabled to carry it into effect. The greater part of that time was passed in almost hopeless solicitation, poverty, and ridicule."

SCENE III. The Vesper Hymn. "In the evening, according to the invariable custom on board the admiral's ship, the mariners sang the Vesper Hymn to the Virgin."

SCENE IV. Discontent and Mutiny. "In this way they fed each other's discontent, gathering into little knots, and fomenting a spirit of mutinous opposition . . . finally breaking forth into turbulent clamor."

SCENE V. In distant Andalusia. "He compares the pure and balmy mornings to those of April in Andalusia, and observes that they wanted but the song of the nightingale to complete the illusion."

SCENE VI. Land and Thanksgiving. "As the evening darkened, Columbus took his station on the top of the castle or cabin, on the high poop of his vessel, ranging his eye along the horizon, and maintaining an intense and unremitting watch."

The cantata opens with a brief orchestral prelude of a sombre character begun by the trombone sounding the Gregorian intonation, and leading to the barytone solo of the priest ("Ye men of Spain, the Time is nigh"), appealing to the crew to commit themselves to Heaven, to which the full male chorus responds with ever-increasing power, reaching the climax in the "Ora pro nobis." Twice the priest repeats his adjuration, followed by the choral response, the last time with joy and animation as the flag of Castile is raised and they bid farewell to the shores of Spain. A short allegro brings the scene to a close.

The second scene is a bass aria for Columbus ("Eighteen long Years of Labor, Doubt, and Scorn"), of a vigorous and spirited character, changing to a solemn adagio in the prayer, "Lord of all Power and Might," and closing with a few spirited phrases in the opening tempo. It is followed by the Vesper Hymn, "Ave Maris Stella," a number in which the composer's eminent ability in sacred music is clearly shown. Its tranquil harmony dies away in the softest of pianissimos, and is followed by an agitated prelude introducing the furious chorus of the mutinous crew "Come, Comrades, come," which gathers intensity as it progresses, voices and instruments uniting in broken but powerful phrases, sometimes in full chorus and again in solo parts, until the climax is reached, when Columbus intervenes in brief solos of great dignity, to which the chorus responds, the scene closing with the renewal of allegiance, — a stirring bass solo with choral accompaniment.

The fifth scene is a tenor recitative and love-song of a most graceful character, and one which will become a favorite when it is well known: —

> "In Andalusia the nightingale
> Sings, — sings through the live-long night;
> Sings to its mate in pure delight:
> But, ah me! ah, my love!
> Vanished and lost to my sight
> In distant Andalusia."

The final scene is very elaborate in its construction, and brings the work to a sonorous and stately close. It opens with a very dramatic recitative by Columbus ("The Night is dark, but many a Sign seen through this Day proclaims the Goal at Hand"), at the close of which there is a short orchestral prelude, which serves to introduce a trio ("Here at your Bidding") for Columbus and two officers (first tenor and first bass). At the cry of a seaman, "Land ho!" the chorus responds with animation. Columbus bids his crew join him "in prayer and grateful praise." The answer comes in a splendidly-written "Hallelujah," which is fairly majestic in its progression, reaching its close in full broad harmony, with the accompanying strains of trumpets.

The Light of Asia.

Mr. Buck's latest cantata, "The Light of Asia," well-nigh reaches the dimensions of an opera or oratorio. It was written in 1886 and first published in England. Its name reveals its source, and the composer has made compensation for the privilege of using Mr. Edwin Arnold's beautiful poem, by a graceful dedication of the work to him. The libretto was prepared by the composer himself, who has shown great skill in making his selections in such manner as not to disturb the continuity of the story. The purely philosophical portions are omitted, and only those are retained which have a human interest. In this manner he has avoided the obstacle which the lack of human sympathy in the poem, beautiful as it is, would otherwise have placed in his way. The text, as will be remembered, has no definite metre, much of it being in blank verse, and does not readily lend itself to musical expression; but it will be conceded that the composer has also overcome this difficulty in a very remarkable manner. The cantata is divided into four parts, — Prologue, the Renunciation and Temptation, the Return, and Epilogue and Finale.

The first part has nine numbers. A brief prelude leads to the opening chorus: —

> "Below the highest sphere four regents sit,
> Who rule the world; and under them are zones
> Nearer, but high, where saintliest spirits dead,
> Wait thrice ten thousand years, then live again."

It begins with a fugue, opened by the basses, simple in its construction but stately in theme and very dignified throughout. It is followed by a bass solo of descriptive character ("The King gave Order that his Town should keep high Festival"), closing with a few choral measures, *sotto voce*, relating that the King had ordered a festival in honor of the advent of Buddha, and how a venerable saint, Asita, recognized the divinity of the child and "the sacred primal signs," and foretold his mission. The third number is the description of the young Siddârtha, set in graceful recitative and semi-chorus for female voices, with a charming accompaniment. The fourth is a spring song ("O come and see the Pleasance of the Spring"), begun by tenors and basses and then developing into full chorus with animated descriptive effects for the orchestra, picturing "the thickets rustling with small life," the rippling waters among the palms, the blue doves' cooings, the jungles laughing with the nesting-songs, and the far-off village drums beating for marriage feasts. A recitative for bass ("Bethink ye, O my Ministers"), in which the King counsels with his advisers as to the training of the child, leads to a four-part song for tenors and basses ("Love will cure these thin Distempers"), in which they urge him to summon a court of pleasure in which the young prince may award prizes to the fair. Then

> "If one or two
> Change the fixed sadness of his tender cheek,
> So may we choose for love with love's own eye."

The King orders the festival, and in the next number — a march and animated three-part chorus for female voices — Kapilavastu's maidens flock to the gate, "each with her dark hair newly smoothed and bound." Then comes the recògnition, briefly told in soprano recitative. Yasôdhara passes, and "at sudden sight of her he changed." A beautiful love-duet for soprano and tenor ("And their Eyes mixed, and from the Look sprang Love") closes the scene. The next number is a bass solo narrating the triumph of Siddârtha over all other suitors, leading to a jubilant and graceful wedding chorus ("Enter, thrice-happy! enter, thrice-desired!"), the words of which are taken from the "Indian Song of Songs."

The second part opens with a soprano solo describing his pleasure with Yasôdhara, in the midst of which comes the warning of the Devas: —

"We are the voices of the wandering wind,
That moan for rest and rest can never find.
Lo ! as the wind is, so is mortal life, —
A moan, a sigh, a sob, a storm, a strife."

This number is a semi-chorus, set for female voices, interspersed with brief phrases for tenor, and after a bass solo, relating the King's dream and the hermit's interpretation, which induces him to doubly guard Siddârtha's pleasure-house, leads up to a beautiful chorus, divided between two sopranos, alto, two tenors, and two basses: —

"Softly the Indian night sunk o'er the plain,
Fragrant with blooms and jewelled thick with stars,
And cool with mountain airs sighing adown
From snow-flats on Himâla high outspread.
The moon above the eastern peaks
Silvered the roof-tops of the pleasure-house,
And all the sleeping land."

The next scene opens with a soprano solo ("Within the Bower of inmost Splendor"), in which Yasôdhara relates her dream of the voice crying "The Time is nigh," to Siddârtha, and closes with a tender duet for soprano and tenor. The next number is a brief chorus ("Then in her Tears she slept"), followed by the tenor solo, "I will depart," in which Siddârtha proclaims his resolve "to seek deliverance and the unknown light," and leading to a richly-colored and majestic chorus:

"There came a wind which lulled each sense aswoon
Of captains and of soldiers:
The gates of triple brass rolled back all silently
On their grim hinges;
Then, lightly treading, where those sleepers lay,

> Into the night Siddârtha passed,
> While o'er the land a tremor spread,
> As if earth's soul beneath stirred with an unknown hope,
> And rich celestial music thrilled the air
> From hosts on hosts of shining ones."

A tenor solo describes the six long years of wandering, followed by a characteristic chorus of voices of earth and air bidding him pass to the tree under whose leaves it was foretold that truth should come to him for the saving of the world. A short bass recitative leads to a vigorous descriptive chorus relating the temptations of Siddârtha, in which the orchestra is used with masterly effect. A brief soprano solo, the apparition of Yasôdhara among the wanton shapes floating about the tree, imploring him to return, and the tenor response, bidding the shadow depart, intervene; and then the chorus resumes with increased vigor, reaching a furious climax as the legions of hell tempt him, but dying away in the close to phrases of tender beauty :—

> " Radiant, rejoicing, strong, Buddha arose,
> And far and near there spread an unknown peace.
> As that divinest daybreak lightened earth,
> The world was glad."

The third part (the Return) opens with a soprano solo of a slow and mournful character, relating the sorrow of Yasôdhara and the visit of her damsels, who announce the arrival of merchants with tidings of Siddârtha. They are summoned, and tell their story in a short chorus, which is followed by a brief soprano solo ("Uprose Yasôdhara with Joy"), an exultant chorus ("While the Town rang with Music"), and another brief phrase for soprano, leading to a fine choral outburst (" 'T is he ! Siddârtha, who was lost"). The next number, a bass solo describing the King's wrath when he learns that Siddârtha has returned as a yellow-robed hermit instead of with "shining spears and tramp of horse and foot," is very sonorous as well as dramatic, and is followed by a tenor and bass dialogue developing into a trio of great beauty (" Thus passed the Three into the Way of Peace"). The final number is a masterpiece of choral work both in the elaborateness of its construction and the majesty of its effect, and brings the cantata to a close with the mystic words : —

> "The Dew is on the Lotus! Rise, great Sun !
> And lift my leaf and mix it with the wave.
> The Sunrise comes! the Sunrise comes!
> The Dewdrop slips into the shining sea.
> Hail, High Deliverer, Hail!"

CORDER.

FREDERICK CORDER, the English composer and conductor, was born at Hackney, London, Jan. 26, 1852. He was a student at the Royal Academy of Music in 1874, and in the following year gained the Mendelssohn scholarship. From 1875 to 1878 he studied at Cologne with Hiller, and in 1879 returned to London, where he engaged for a time in literary pursuits. His abilities as a writer are very clearly shown in the librettos to his works. In 1880 he was appointed conductor of the orchestra at the Brighton Aquarium, and since that time he has devoted himself to teaching and composition. His principal works are "In the Black Forest," an orchestral suite, and "Evening on the Seashore," idyl for orchestra (1876); the opera "Morte d' Arthur" (1877); the one-act opera "Philomel" (1879); cantata, "The Cyclops" (1880); "Ossian," a concert overture for orchestra, produced by the London Philharmonic Society (1882); the cantata "Bridal of Triermain" (1886); and the opera "Nordisa," founded upon a Norwegian subject and brought out with great success in January, 1887 by the Carl Rosa opera troupe. Mr. Corder is one of the most ambitious and promising of all the younger English composers, and his music shows in a special degree the influence of Wagner. That he has also literary talent of a high order is evinced by his contributions to periodical literature and the librettos of his last two works, — "The Bridal of Triermain" and "Nordisa."

The Bridal of Triermain.

"The Bridal of Triermain" was written for the Wolverhampton (England) Festival of 1886, and was one of the most notable successes in the festival performances of that year. The subject is taken from Walter Scott's poem of the same name. The adaptation has been made in a very free manner, but the main incidents of the poem have been carefully preserved. Sir Roland's vision of the "Maid of Middle Earth;" the bard Lyulph's recital of the Arthurian legend, which tells of Gyneth's enchantment in the valley of St. John by Merlin, where she must sleep

> "Until a knight shall wake thee
> For feats of arms as far renowned
> As warrior of the Table Round;"

the magic wrought by Merlin in the valley to delude Roland and thwart his effort to rescue Gyneth; his daring entrance into the palace grounds; the discovery of the Princess in the enchanted hall, and her final rescue are the themes which the composer has treated. In arranging his libretto he has, as has been said, made a free adaptation of the poem, sometimes using verses entire, at other times changing the text and rearranging it to suit the composer's musical demands, even at the expense of the original beauty and symmetry of the work.

The cantata has no overture, but opens with a choral introduction ("Where is the Maiden of Mortal Strain?"). An orchestral interlude in the form of a tender graceful nocturne follows, leading up to the tenor solo, "The Dawn of an autumn Day did creep," in which the Baron relates the apparition he has seen in his dream. A short bass recitative by Lyulph the bard introduces the Legend, which is told in an effective number for soprano solo, bass solo, and chorus ("In Days e'en Minstrels now forget"). The next number, a very dramatic dialogue for soprano and tenor, gives us the conversation between Arthur and Gyneth, and leads to an energetic full chorus with very descriptive accompaniment, picturing the bloody tourney and its sudden interruption by the appearance of Merlin the enchanter. The first part closes with a charming number ("'Madmen,' he cried, 'your Strife forbear'") arranged for bass solo, quartet, and chorus, in which is described the spell which Merlin casts upon Gyneth.

The second part, after a short allegro movement for orchestra, opens with a contralto solo ("Of wasted Fields and plundered Flocks ") which prepares the way for a concerted number for solos and chorus ("And now the Moon her Orb has hid"), describing the magical arts which Merlin employed to thwart the Baron. This number alone is sufficient to stamp Mr. Corder as a composer of extraordinary ability. A succession of bass, tenor, and contralto recitatives ("Wroth waxed the Warrior") leads to another powerful chorus ("Rash Adventurer, bear thee back"), the song of the "four maids whom Afric bore," in which the composer has caught the weird, strange color of the scene and given it vivid expression. A tenor recitative ("While yet the distant Echoes roll") leads up to a graceful, sensuous soprano solo and female chorus ("Gentle Knight, awhile delay"). Its counterpart is found in the tenor recitative and spirited, dignified male chorus ("Son of Honor, Theme of Story"). The *dénouement* now begins. A contralto solo, declamatory in style ("In lofty Hall, with Trophies graced"), and a short soprano solo of a joyous character ("Thus while she sang") lead to the final number ("Gently, lo! the Warrior kneels"), beginning with full chorus, which after short solos for tenor and soprano takes a spirited martial form ("And on the Champion's Brow was found") and closes with a quartet and chorus worked up to an imposing climax.

The work is largely in narrative form; but this, instead of being a hindrance, seems to have been an advantage to the composer, who has not failed to invest his music with dramatic force that is remarkable. Mr. Corder is credited with being an ardent disciple of Wagner, and his cantata certainly shows the influences of that school. It is throughout a vigorous, effective work, and gives promise that its composer will yet be heard from outside the English musical world.

COWEN.

FREDERIC H. COWEN, the favorite English song-writer, was born at Kingston, Jamaica, Jan. 29, 1852, and went to England at a very early age. His first teachers were Benedict and Sir J. Goss, with whom he studied until 1865. During the next three years he continued his musical education at the conservatories of Leipsic and Berlin, returning to England in 1868. His earlier works were an operetta called "Garibaldi," a fantasie-sonata and piano concerto, a few pieces of chamber music, and a symphony in C minor. These served to introduce him to public notice, and since that time nearly all of his works have met with remarkable success, among them "The Rose Maiden" (1870); music to Schiller's "Joan of Arc" (1871); festival overture (1872); "The Corsair," composed for the Birmingham Festival of 1876; a symphony in F major and the Norwegian symphony, which have been favorably received in this country. His most important opera is "Pauline," which was produced in London with great success by the Carl Rosa company, Nov. 22,

1876. As a song-writer, Mr. Cowen is also well known; many of his lyrics, especially those written for Antoinette Sterling and Mrs. E. Aline Osgood, the American singers, having obtained a wide-spread popularity.

The Sleeping Beauty.

"The Sleeping Beauty," written for the Birmingham Festival of 1885, the poem by Francis Hueffer, has for its theme the well-known fairy tale which has been so often illustrated in music and upon canvas. It is a great favorite in England, and has also met with a successful reception in Paris, where it was brought out not long since by the Concordia Society of that city, under the title of "La Belle au Bois Dormant," the translation having been made by Miss Augusta Holmes, herself a musician of considerable repute.

After a brief orchestral introduction, a three-part chorus (altos, tenors, and basses) tells the story of the ancient King to whom an heiress was born when all hope of offspring had been abandoned, the gay carousal which he ordered, and the sudden appearance of the twelve fays, guardians of his house, with their spinning-wheels and golden flax, who sing as they weave: —

> "Draw the thread and weave the woof
> For the little child's behoof:
> Future, dark to human eyes,
> Openly before us lies;

> As we will and as we give,
> Haply shall the maiden live;
> Draw the thread and weave the woof
> For the little child's behoof."

In beauty of melody and gracefulness of orchestration this chorus of the fays is specially noticeable. Its charming movement, however, is interrupted by a fresh passage for male chorus, of an agitated character, describing the entrance of the Wicked Fay, who bends over the cradle of the child and sings a characteristic contralto aria: —

> "From the gold of the flaxen reel
> Threads of bliss have been spun to thee;
> By the whirl of the spinning wheel
> Cruel grief shall be done to thee.
> Thy fate I descry:
> Ere the buds of thy youth are blown,
> Ere a score of thy years have flown,
> Thou shalt prick thy hand, thou shalt die."

Following this aria, the male chorus has a few measures, invoking a curse upon the Fay, which leads to a full chorus of an animated character, foretelling that there shall dawn a day when a young voice, more powerful than witchcraft, will save her; at the close of which the guardian fays are again heard drawing the thread and weaving the woof in low, murmuring tones, with a spinning accompaniment. It is followed by a trio (soprano, tenor, and bass), with chorus accompaniment, announcing the departure of the fays, and leading to a very melodious tenor solo, with two graceful orchestral interludes, which moralizes on what has occurred and closes the prologue.

The first scene opens in a hall in the King's palace, and is full of animation. A brilliant orchestral prelude leads to the full chorus in waltz time ("At Dawn of Day on the first of May"), which moves along with a fascinating swing, and closes in a very vigorous climax. At this point the King makes his appearance and expresses his joy that the time has passed when the prophecy of the Wicked Fay could take effect, for this is the Princess's twentieth birthday. A dialogue follows between the King and his daughter, closing with a beautiful chorus ("Pure as thy Heart"), after which the dance-music resumes. Unobserved the Princess leaves the banqueting-hall, glides along a gallery, and ascends the staircase to a turret chamber. Before she enters she sings an aria, of a tranquil, dreamy nature ("Whither away, my Heart?"), and interwoven with it are heard the gradually lessening strains of the dance-music, which ceases altogether as her song comes to an almost inaudible close.

The second scene opens in the turret chamber, where the Wicked Fay, disguised as an old crone, is spinning. After a short dialogue, in which the Fay explains to the Princess the use of the wheel, she bids her listen, and sings a weird ballad ("As I sit at my Spinning-wheel, strange Dreams come to me"), closing with the refrain of the old prophecy, "Ere the Buds of her Youth are blown." The Princess dreamily repeats the burden of the song, and then, fearing the presence of some ill-omen, opens the door to escape. She hears the dance-music again, but the Fay gently draws her back and induces her to touch the flax. As she does so, the Fay covertly pricks her finger with the spindle. She swoons away, the dance-music suddenly stops, and there is a long silence, broken at last by the Fay's triumphant declaration: "Thus have I wrought my Vengeance." The next number is the Incantation Music ("Spring from the Earth, red Roses"), a very dramatic declamation, sung by the Fay and interwoven with snatches of chorus and the refrain of the prophecy. A choral interlude ("Sleep in Bower and Hall") follows, describing in a vivid manner, both with voices and instruments, the magic sleep that fell upon the castle and all its inmates, and the absence of all apparent life save the spiders weaving their webs on the walls as the years go by: —

"The spells of witchcraft which enthrall
Each sleeper in that desolate hall,
Who can break them?
Say, who can lift the deathly blight
That covers king and lord and knight,
To give them back to life and light,
And awake them?"

The answer comes in an animated prelude, through which is heard the strain of a horn signal, constantly growing louder, and heralding the Prince, who enters the silent palace, sword in hand, among the sleeping courtiers, knights, and ladies. After a vigorous declamation ("Light, Light at last") he passes on his way to the turret chamber, where he beholds the sleeping Princess. The love-song which follows

("Kneeling before Thee, worshipping wholly") is one of the most effective portions of the work. His kiss awakes her, and as she springs up, the dance-music at once resumes from the bar where it had stopped in the scene with the Wicked Fay. An impassioned duet follows, and the work closes with the animated waltz-chorus which opened the first scene.

DVOŘÁK.

ANTON DVOŘÁK, the Bohemian composer who has risen so suddenly into prominence, was born at Mülhausen, near Prague, Sept. 8, 1841. His father combined the business of tavern-keeper and butcher, and young Dvořák assisted him in waiting upon customers, as well as in the slaughtering business. As the laws of Bohemia stipulate that music shall be a part of common-school education, Dvořák learned the rudiments in the village school, and also received violin instruction. At the age of thirteen he went to work for an uncle, who resided in the village where the schoolmaster was a proficient musician. The latter, recognizing his ability, gave him lessons on the organ, and allowed him to copy music. Piano lessons followed, and he had soon grounded himself quite thoroughly in counterpoint. At the age of sixteen he was admitted to the organ-school of Prague, of which Joseph Pitsch was the principal. Pitsch died soon after, and was succeeded by Kreyci, who made Dvořák acquainted with the music of Mozart, Beethoven, and Mendelssohn.

The first orchestral work he heard was Beethoven's "Ninth Symphony," during its rehearsal under Spohr's direction. In 1860, being then in his nineteenth year, he obtained an engagement, with the meagre salary of one hundred and twenty-five dollars a year, as violinist in a band that played at cafés and dances. Two years later he secured a position in the Bohemian Opera House at Prague, then under the direction of Mayer, where he remained until 1871, in which year he left the theatre and devoted himself to teaching, with the prospect of earning two hundred and fifty dollars a year. These were hard days for the young musician; but while he was there struggling for a bare subsistence, he continued writing compositions, though he had no prospect of selling them or of having them played. About this time he wrote his "Patriotic Hymn" and the opera "König und Köhler." The latter was rejected after an orchestral trial; but he continued his work, undaunted by failure. Shortly after this he received the appointment of organist at the Adelbert Church, Prague, and fortune began to smile upon him. His Symphony in F was laid before the Minister of Instruction in Vienna, and upon the recommendation of Herbeck secured him a grant of two hundred dollars. When Brahms replaced Herbeck on the committee which reported upon artists' stipends, he fully recognized Dvořák's ability, and not only encouraged him, but also brought him before the world by securing him a publisher and commending him to Joachim, who still further advanced his interests by securing performances of his works in Germany and England. Since that time he has risen rapidly, and is now recognized as one of the most promising of living composers. Among his works which have been produced during the past few years are the "Stabat Mater," the cantata "The Spectre's Bride," three operas in the Czechist dialect, three orchestral symphonies, several Slavonic rhapsodies, overtures, violin and piano concertos, an exceedingly beautiful sextet, and numerous songs.

The Spectre's Bride.

The legend of the Spectre's Bride is current in various forms among all the Slavonic nations. The Russians, Servians, Slovaks, Lithuanians, and Poles all have poems in which the ghostly ride of the spectre and the maiden forms the theme. The German version, told by Bürger in his famous ballad "Lenore," is best known; and Raff has given it a musical setting in his Lenore Symphony. In general, the story is the same. The Spectre comes for his Bride and she rides away with him through the night, amid all manner of supernatural horrors, only to find at the end that she has ridden to the grave with a skeleton. The Bohemian poem used by Dvořák is that of Karel Jaromir Erben, a poet who obtained a national fame by making collections of the songs and legends of his country during his service as Secretary of the Royal Bohemian Museum and Keeper of the Archives at Prague. In his version, unlike the German, the Spectre and his Bride make their grewsome journey on foot. The *dénouement* in the churchyard differs also, as the maiden is saved by an appeal to the Virgin. In the opening scene she is represented gazing at a picture of the Virgin, mourning the death of her parents and the absence of her lover, who has failed to keep his promise to return. His parting words were: —

> "Sow flax, my love, I counsel thee,
> And every day remember me.
> Spin in the first year, spin with care,
> Bleach in the next the fabric fair;
> Then garments make, when the years are three,
> And every day remember me.
> Twine I that year a wreath for thee;
> We two that year shall wedded be."

She has faithfully followed the counsel. The three years have expired, but still no tidings have come. As she appeals to the Virgin to bring him back, the picture moves, the flame of the lamp upleaps, there is an ominous knock at the door, and the voice of the apparition is heard urging her to cease praying and follow him to his home. She implores him to wait until the night is past, but the importunate Spectre bids her go with him, and she consents. On they speed over rough bowlders, through thorny brakes and swamps, attended by the baying of wolves, the screeching of owls, the croaking of frogs, and the fitful glow of corpse-candles. One by one he compels her to throw away her prayer-book, chaplet, and cross, and resisting all her appeals to stop and rest, at last they reach the churchyard wall. He calms her fears with the assurance that the church is his castle and the yard his garden, and bids her leap the wall with him. She promises to follow him, but after he has cleared it, sudden fear seizes her; she flies to a tiny house near by and enters. A ghastly scene takes place; spectres are dancing before the door, and the moonlight reveals to her a corpse lying upon a plank. As she gazes, horror-stricken, a knock is heard, and a voice bids the dead arise and thrust the living one out. Thrice the summons is repeated, and then as the corpse opens its eyes and glares upon her, she prays once more to the Virgin. At this instant the crowing of a cock is heard. The dead man falls back, the ghastly, spectral crew disappear, and night gives way to a peaceful morning.

> "All who to Mass at morning went
> Stood still in great astonishment;
> One tomb there was to ruin gone,
> And in the dead-house a maiden wan;
> On looking round, amazed were they,
> On every grave a garment lay.

> "Well was it, maiden, that thy mind
> Turned unto God, defence to find,
> For He thy foes did harmless bind;
> Had'st thou thyself, too, nothing done,
> Ill with thy soul it then had gone;
> Thy body, as the garments were,
> Mangled had been, and scattered there."

Such is the horrible story which forms the theme of Dvořák's cantata. It was written for the Birmingham Festival of 1884, and the text was translated by the Rev. Dr. Troutbeck, from a German translation of the original poem made by K. J. Müller. It contains eighteen numbers, each of considerable length, of which eleven are descriptive, the barytone, with chorus response, acting the part of the narrator, and accompanied by instrumentation which vividly paints the horrors of the nocturnal tramp, even to the realistic extent of imitating the various sounds described. It is unnecessary to specify each of these numbers in detail, as they are all closely allied in color and general effect. The music which accompanies them is picturesque and weird, increasing in its power and actual supernaturalism until it reaches its climax in the dead-house where the maiden takes refuge ; and in these numbers the orchestra bears the burden of the work. The remaining numbers are almost magical in their beauty and fascination, particularly the first song of the maiden, lamenting her lover, and closing with the prayer to the Virgin, which is thoroughly devotional music, and the second prayer, which saves her from her peril. There are four duets, soprano and tenor, between the Bride and Spectre, and one with chorus, in which are recounted the episodes of the chaplet, prayer-book, and cross, besides the hurried dialogue between them as he urges her on. These, too, abound in quaint rhythms and strange harmonies set against a highly-colored instrumental background. The story is not a pleasant one for musical treatment, — at least for voices, — and the prevailing tone of the composition is sombre ; but of the wonderful power of the music and its strange fascination there can be no doubt.

FOOTE.

ARTHUR FOOTE, a rising young composer of Boston, whose works have already made more than a local reputation, was born at Salem, Mass., March 5, 1853. While at Harvard College he studied composition with Prof. J. K. Paine, and after graduation determined to devote himself to the musical profession. He studied the piano-forte and organ with Mr. B. J. Lang of Boston, and soon made his mark as a musician of more than ordinary promise. Among his published works which have attracted favorable attention are various songs and piano compositions; pieces for violin and piano, violoncello and piano; a string quartet; trio for piano, violin, and violoncello; and "Hiawatha," a ballad for male voices and orchestra. A suite for strings, in manuscript, has obtained the honor of performance at the London symphony concerts (January, 1887), and an overture, "In the Mountains," also in manuscript, was played by the Boston Symphony Orchestra in February, 1887. He is now living in Boston, where he is engaged in teaching the piano and organ.

Hiawatha.

"The Farewell of Hiawatha," for barytone solo, male voices, and orchestra, modestly styled by its composer a ballad, is a cantata in its lighter form. Its subject is taken from Longfellow's familiar poem, and includes the beautiful close of the legend beginning with the stanza: —

> " From his place rose Hiawatha,
> Bade farewell to old Nokomis,
> Spake in whispers, spake in this wise,
> Did not wake the guests, that slumbered."

The composer has made use of the remainder of the poem without change, except in repetitions demanded by musical necessity and in the omission of the seven lines immediately preceding the final words of farewell, which does not mar the context. A short orchestral introduction, *andante con moto*, followed by a chorus of tenors and basses in a few bars, recitative in form and sung pianissimo, lead to a barytone solo for Hiawatha ("I am going, O Nokomis") of a quiet and tender character. A graceful phrase for the violoncello introduces another choral morceau relating Hiawatha's farewell to the warriors (" I am going, O my People ") a melodious combination of sweetness and strength, though it only rises to a display of energy in the single phrase, " The Master of Life has sent them," after which it closes quietly, and tenderly, in keeping with the sentiment of the text. The remainder of the work is choral. The westward sail of Hiawatha into the "fiery sunset," "the purple vapors," and "the dusk of evening" is set to a very picturesque accompaniment, which dies away in soft strains as he disappears in the distance. An allegro movement with a crescendo of great energy introduces the farewell of "the forests dark and lonely," moving "through all their depths of darkness," of the waves "rippling on the pebbles," and of "the heron, the Shuh-shuh-gah, from her haunts among the fen-lands." The last division of the chorus is an allegro, beginning pianissimo and closing with an exultant outburst: —

"Thus departed Hiawatha,
Hiawatha the Beloved,
In the glory of the sunset,
In the purple mists of evening,
To the regions of the home-wind,
Of the Northwest wind Keewaydin,
To the Islands of the Blessed,
To the kingdom of Ponemah,
To the land of the Hereafter!"

The work, which was written for the Apollo Club of Boston, is not a long one, nor is it at all ambitious in style. The composer has evidently tried to reflect the quiet and tender sentiment of the farewell in his music, and has admirably succeeded. Poetic beauty is its most striking feature, both in the instrumental parts, which are well sustained, and in the vocal, which are earnest, expressive, and at times very pathetic, of this pretty tone-picture.

GADE.

NIELS W. GADE was born at Copenhagen, Oct. 22, 1817. His father was a musical-instrument maker and intrusted his early education to the Danish masters Wershall, Berggren, and Weyse. He made such good progress that he soon entered the royal orchestra of that city as a violinist and began to be known as a composer. His first important work, the overture "Nachklänge von Ossian," obtained a prize from the Copenhagen Musical Union and also secured for him the favor of the King, who provided him with the means for making a foreign journey. Prior to starting he sent a copy of a symphony to Mendelssohn, which met with the latter's enthusiastic approval. He arrived at Leipsic in 1843, and after producing his first symphony with success, travelled through Italy, returning to Leipsic in 1844, where during the winter of that year he conducted the Gewandhaus concerts in the place of Mendelssohn, who was absent in Berlin. In the season of 1845-46 he assisted Mendelssohn in the same concerts, and after the latter's death became the principal director, a post which he held until 1848, when he returned to Copenhagen and took a position as organist, and also conducted the concerts of the Musical Union. In 1861 he was appointed Hofcapellmeister, and was honored with the title of Professor of Music. Since that time he has devoted himself to composition, and has produced many excellent works, especially for festivals in England and elsewhere. Among them are the cantatas "Comala," "Spring Fantasie," "The Erl King's Daughter," "The Holy Night," "Spring's Message," "The Crusaders," and "Zion;" the overtures "In the Highlands," "Hamlet," and "Michael Angelo;" seven symphonies, and a large number of songs and piano pieces, as well as chamber-music compositions.

Comala.

"Comala," one of the earliest of Gade's larger vocal works, was first produced at Leipsic in March, 1843. Its subject is taken from Ossian, and relates the tragedy of "Comala," daughter of Sarno, King of Innistore, who had conceived a violent passion for Fingal, King of Morven. Her love is returned by the warrior, and disguised as a youth the princess follows him on his expedition against Caracul, King of Lochlin. On the day of the battle Fingal places her on a height, near the shore of the Carun, whence she can overlook the fight, and promises her if victorious that he will return at evening. Comala, though filled with strange forebodings, hopefully waits her royal lover's coming. As the tedious hours pass on a fearful storm arises, and amid the howling of the blast the spirits of the fathers sweep by her on their way to the battlefield to conduct to their home the souls of the fallen, — the same majestic idea which Wagner uses with such consummate power in his weird ride of the Valkyries. Comala imagines that the battle has been lost, and evercome with grief falls to the ground and dies. The victorious Fingal returns as evening approaches, accompanied by the songs of his triumphant warriors, only to hear the tidings of Comala's death from her weeping maidens. Sorrowing he orders the bards to chant her praises, and joining with her attendants to waft her departing soul "to the fathers' dwelling" with farewell hymns.

The cantata is almost equally divided between male and female choruses, and these are the charm of the work. Many of the songs of Comala and her maids are in graceful ballad form, fresh in their melody, and marked by that peculiar refinement which characterizes all of Gade's music. The parting duet between Fingal and Comala is very beautiful, but the principal interest centres in the choruses. Those of the bards and warriors are very stately in their style and abound in dramatic power, particularly the one accompanying the triumphal return of Fingal. The chorus of spirits is very impressive, and in some passages almost supernatural. The female choruses, on the other hand, are graceful, tender, and pathetic; the final full chorus, in which the bards and maidens commend the soul of Comala to "the fathers' dwelling," has rarely been surpassed in beauty or pathos. The music of the cantata is in keeping with the stately grandeur and richly-hued tones of the Ossianic poem. The poetry and music of the North are happily wedded.

Spring Fantasie.

Though the "Spring Fantasie" is in undoubted cantata form, Gade designates it as a "Concertstück;" that is, a musical composition in which the instrumental parts are essential to its complete unity. Its origin is unquestionably to be found in the idea of Beethoven's "Choral Fantasie," which was subsequently developed in the choral symphony on a still larger and grander scale. The instrumental elements of the "Spring Fantasie" are unquestionably the most prominent. They do not play the subordinate part of accompaniment, but really enunciate the ideas of the poem, which are still further illustrated by the voices, acting as the interpreters of the meaning of the instrumentation.

The "Fantasie" was written in 1850, its subject being a poem by Edmund Lobedanz, which of itself might appropriately be called a fantasy. The work consists of four movements, for four solo voices, orchestra, and piano-forte. The prominence which Gade has given to the instrumental parts is shown by his characterizing the movements, — I. *Allegro moderato e sostenuto;* II. *Allegro molto e con fuoco;* III. *Allegro vivace.* The poem in the original is one of more than ordinary excellence. The translation in most common use is one made by Mrs. Vander Weyde for a performance of the work in London in 1878 at the Royal Normal College and Academy of Music for the Blind, under the direction of Herr von Bülow.

The first movement is in the nature of an invocation to spring, in which the longing for May and its flowers is very tenderly expressed. The second movement depicts with great vigor the return of the wintry storms, the raging of the torrents, the gradual rolling away of the clouds, the approach of more genial breezes, and the rising of the star, typifying "the joy of a fair maiden's love." The closing movement is full of rejoicing that the spring has come. Voices and instruments share alike in the jubilation: —

> "For the spring-time has come, the May is here,
> On hill and in vale all is full of delight.
> How sweet is the spring-time, how lovely and bright, —
> Its kingdom is over us all."

The Erl King's Daughter.

"The Erl King's Daughter" was written in 1852. Its story differs from that told in Goethe's famous poem, and set to music equally famous by Schubert in his familiar song. In Goethe's poem the father rides through the night clasping his boy and followed by the Erl King and his daughters, who entice the child unseen by the parent. In vain he assures him that the Erl King's voice is but the "sad wind sighing through the withered leaves," that his train is but the mist, and that his daughters are the aged gray willows deceiving his sight. The boy at first is charmed with the apparition, but cries in mortal terror as the Erl King seizes him, while the father gallops at last into the courtyard, only to find his child dead in his arms.

In the poem used by Gade it is the Erl King's daughter who tempts a knight to his death. The prologue relates that Sir Oluf at eve stayed his steed and rested beneath the alders by the brook, where he was visited by two of the daughters, one of whom caressed him while the other invited him to join their revels. At sound of the cock-crow, however, they disappeared. It was the eve of Sir Oluf's wedding day. He arrives home in a distraught condition, and in spite of his mother's appeals decides to return to the alder grove in quest of the beauties who had bewitched him. He finds the alder-maids dancing in the moonlight, singing and beckoning him to join them. One of the fairest tempts him with a silken gown for the bride and silver armor for himself. When he refuses to dance with her, she seizes him by the arm and predicts his death on the morrow morning. " Ride home to your bride in robe of red," she cries as he hastens away. In the morning the mother anxiously waits his coming, and at last beholds him riding desperately through "the waving corn." He has lost his shield and helmet, and blood drips from his stirrups. As he draws rein at the door of the castle he drops dead from his saddle. A brief epilogue points the moral of the story in quaint fashion. It is to the effect that knights who will on horseback ride should not like Oluf stay in elfin groves with elfin maidens till morning. It is unnecessary to specify the numbers in detail; as with the exception of the melodramatic finale, where the music becomes quite vigorous, it is all of the same graceful, flowing, melodic character, and needs no key to explain it to the hearer.

The Crusaders.

"The Crusaders" is one of the most powerful as well as beautiful of modern cantatas. It was written for performance in Copenhagen in 1866, and ten years later was produced at the Birmingham Festival, under the composer's direction. It is divided into three parts, and its story may be told in a word. Its theme is the same as that which Wagner has treated in "Lohengrin" and "Tännhauser," — the conflict of the human soul with the powers of darkness, sensual beauty and sorcery, and its final triumph. It is the story of the temptation of Rinaldo d'Este, the bravest of the Crusaders, by

Armida and her sirens, who at last calls upon the Queen of Spirits to aid them in their hopeless task, the thwarting of the powers of evil, and the final triumph before Jerusalem.

The first part opens with a chorus of pilgrims and women in the band of the Crusaders, expressive of the weariness and sufferings they have endured in their long wanderings, the end of which still appears so far away. As the beautiful music dies away, the inspiring summons of Peter the Hermit is heard, leading up to the Crusaders' song, — a vigorous, warlike melody, full of manly hope and religious fervor. An evening prayer of pious longing and exalted devotion closes this part.

The second part is entitled "Armida," and introduces the evil genius of the scene. A strange, mysterious orchestral prelude indicates the baneful magic of the sorcerer's wiles. In a remarkably expressive aria, Armida deplores her weakness in trying to overcome the power of the cross. As she sees Rinaldo, who has left his tent to wander for a time in the night air, she calls to the spirits to obey her incantation : —

> "Cause a palace grand to rise,
> Let a sea before it glimmer.
> In the walls of richest gold
> Let the purest diamonds shimmer;
> Round the fountains' pearly rim,
> Where bright the sunbeams are glancing,
> Plashing low and murmuring sweet,
> Set the merry wavelets dancing.
> In yon hedge of roses where fairies rock in softest dreaming,
> Fays and elfins bid appear, and sirens float in waters dreaming.

> All around let music ring,
> Fill the air with sweetest singing;
> Lure them on with magic power,
> To our midst all captive bringing.
> Sing remembrance from their hearts,
> Till they bow, my will fulfilling;
> Make them every thought forego,
> Every wish, save mine own, stilling."

After another invocation of the spirits, the sirens appear, singing a sensuous melody ("I dip my white Breast in the soft-flowing Tide"). Then begins the temptation of the wandering Knight. He starts in surprise as he hears the voices rising from the waves, and again they chant their alluring song. They are followed by Armida, who appeals to him in a seductive strain ("O Rinaldo, come to never-ending Bliss"). The Knight joins with her in a duet of melodious beauty. He is about to yield to the temptation, when he hears in the distance the tones of the Crusaders' song. He wavers in his resolution, Armida and the sirens appeal to him again, and again he turns as if he would follow them. The Crusaders' song grows louder, and rouses the Knight from the spell which has been cast about him, and the scene closes with a beautifully concerted number, in which Rinaldo, Armida, the chorus of Crusaders and of sirens contend for the mastery. The fascination of the Crusaders' song is the strongest. The cross triumphs over the sorceress, and in despair she sings, —

> "Sink, scenes illusive, deep in dark abyss of doom!
> The light of day is turned to blackest night of gloom."

The third part, entitled "Jerusalem," is religious in character, and mostly choral. In rapid succession follow the morning hymn with beautiful horn accompaniment, the march of the Pilgrims full of the highest exaltation, the hermit's revelation of the Holy City to them, their joyous greeting to it, Rinaldo's resolution to expiate his offence by his valor, the hermit's last call to strife, their jubilant reply, and the final victory: —

> "As our God wills it. Up, arouse thee!
> Up! yon flag with hope endows thee.
> Jerusalem! the goal is there.
> We cry aloud, 'Hosanna!'"

GILCHRIST.

WILLIAM W. GILCHRIST, the American composer, was born at Jersey City, N. J., in 1846. He began his studies with H. A. Clarke, professor of music in the University of Pennsylvania. In 1872 he accepted the position of organist at the New Jerusalem Church in Cincinnati, Ohio, and was also appointed teacher in the Conservatory of Miss Bauer. A year later he returned to Philadelphia, where he has since resided. During this time he has done a great work for music in that city, having been conductor of several societies. He has been the recipient of honors on many occasions, having obtained several prizes from the Philadelphia Abt Society and others for his compositions. In 1880 he contended for the prize offered by the Cincinnati Musical Festival Association, but stood third on the list, Dudley Buck being first and George E. Whiting second. In 1882 he made another trial for the Association's prize, and was successful; the committee, consisting of Carl Reinecke of Leipsic, M. Saint-Saens of Paris, and Theodore Thomas of New York, making him the award.

The Forty-sixth Psalm.

The composition referred to in the sketch of Mr. Gilchrist's life which secured for him the Cincinnati prize in 1882 was "The Forty-sixth Psalm." The composer's own analysis of the work, furnished at the time, is appended: —

"The composition is a setting of the Forty-sixth Psalm for soprano solo, chorus, orchestra, and organ, and has four principal divisions exclusive of an introduction, each following the other without pause, and connected by a gradual decrescendo in the orchestra. The opening of the Psalm seemed to me to indicate a strong outburst of praise or of thanksgiving for a deliverance from trials, which the introduction is intended to convey. But instead of beginning with a strong outburst, I lead up to it from a very subdued beginning, working gradually to a climax at the entrance of the chorus on the words, 'God is our refuge and our strength.' The opening movement of the chorus becomes a little subdued very shortly as it takes up the words, 'A very present help in trouble,' which is followed again by an *allegro con fuoco* movement on the words, ' Therefore we will not fear though the earth be removed, though the mountains be carried into the midst of the sea.' This movement leads into still another, a furioso movement on the words, 'Though the waters thereof roar, though the mountains shake with the swelling thereof.' This is followed by an elaborate coda, in which all the themes of the preceding movement are worked together, and which brings the chorus to a close.

The second division, in E major, is marked by an *andante contemplativo* on the words, 'There is a river the streams whereof shall make glad the city of God.' This movement is intended to be one of tranquillity, varied with occasional passionate outbursts on the words, 'God is in the midst of her; she shall not be moved.' A peculiar rhythmical effect is sought by the alternation of $\frac{4}{4}$ and $\frac{3}{4}$ time, three bars of the first being answered by two bars of the second. This movement ends very tranquilly on the words, 'God shall help her, and that right early,' and is immediately followed by an *allegro molto*, in B minor, on the words, 'The heathen raged, the kingdoms were moved; he uttered his voice, the earth melted.' In the middle of this chorus the soprano solo enters for the first time on the words, 'He maketh wars to cease unto the end of the earth; He breaketh the bow and cutteth the spear in sunder.' The chorus works up to a strong climax on the words, 'He burneth the chariot with fire,' which is suddenly interrupted by a decrescendo on the words, 'Be still, and know that I am God.'

This leads to the third division, which is a return of the second division in E major, and which is played through almost entirely by the orchestra, the chorus merely meditating on the words last quoted. This leads to the final chorus, which is a fugue, in E major, with *alla breve* time, on the words, 'And the Lord of Hosts is with us; the God of Jacob is our refuge,' towards the close of which a *Gloria Patri* is introduced, being woven in with fragments of the fugue to a strong climax. The whole composition finishes with an impetuous accelerando. My central idea was to make a choral and orchestral work, the solo, while requiring a good singer, being only secondary. The Psalm seemed to me particularly adapted for musical composition, as being capable of a varied, even dramatic effect."

GLEASON.

FREDERICK GRANT GLEASON was born at Middletown, Conn., Dec. 17, 1848. He inherited the love of music from his parents, — his father having been a flutist and his mother an alto singer and pianist. In his sixteenth year he showed a decided talent for composition; and two of his works, an oratorio, "The Captivity," and a Christmas oratorio, though crudely written, gave such promise that he was placed under the tuition of Dudley Buck, with whom he studied the piano and composition. He made such rapid progress that his parents were induced to send him to Germany, where he at once entered the Leipsic Conservatory. Moscheles taught him the piano, and Richter harmony, and he also took private lessons from Plaidy and Lobe. In 1870 he went to Berlin, where he continued his piano studies with Raif, a pupil of Tausig, and his tuition in harmony with Weitzmann. After a visit home he went to England and resumed lessons on the piano with Berringer, another pupil of Tausig, and also studied English music. He subsequently made a second visit to Berlin, and improved his time by studying theory with Weitzmann, the piano with Loeschorn, and the organ with Haupt. During this visit he also issued a valuable work entitled "Gleason's Motet Collection." After the completion of his studies he returned home and accepted the position of organist at one of the Hartford churches. In 1876 he removed to Chicago and engaged as teacher in the Hershey School of Musical Art. At present he is still occupied in teaching and also fills the position of musical critic for the "Tribune" of that city. During these years his pen has been very busy, as the list of his compositions shows. Among his principal works are two operas, still in manuscript, — "Otho Visconti" and "Montezuma;" the cantatas "God our Deliverer," "The Culprit Fay," and "Praise of Harmony;" and several trios, sonatas, and other works for the chamber, as well as many songs. The selections from his operas which have been played by the Thomas orchestra show that they are compositions of unusual excellence and scholarship.

The Culprit Fay.

"The Culprit Fay," a musical setting of Joseph Rodman Drake's well-known fairy poem, was written in 1879. It is divided into three parts, — the first containing five, the second five, and the third eight numbers; the solos being divided among soprano, alto, tenor, and barytone, the last named taking the part of the Fairy King. The exquisitely graceful fairy story told in the poem is too well known to need description. It is admirably adapted to music by its rhythmic fluency as well as by the delicacy of its poetical sentiment; and while it does not call for earnestness or strength in any of its movements, there is ample opportunity for melodious and attractive pictures in tone of the dainty descriptions of the poet. The composer has improved these opportunities with much skill, and, notwithstanding the intrinsic lightness of the score, has secured musical unity and poetical coherence by the artistic use of the *leit-motif.* Nine of these motives are employed, characterizing the summer night, the elfin mystery, the life of the fairies, the fay's love for the mortal maid, the penalty for this violation of fairy law, night on the river, the spells of the water imps, the penalties imposed upon the culprit, and the Sylphide Queen's passion for the Fay. The skilfulness with which these motives are adapted to characters and situations, and interwoven with the general movement in their proper recurrence, shows that the composer has not studied Wagner, the master of the *leit-motif,* in vain.

After a short introduction for the horns and strings, the cantata opens with a full chorus of graceful, flowing character ("'T is the Middle Watch of a Summer's Night") describing the moonlight scene about "Old Cro' Nest." It is followed by the mystery motive announcing a weird alto solo, "'T is the Hour of Fairy Ban and Spell." It is the summons of the sentry elf, ringing the hour of twelve, indicated in the score by the triangle, and calling the fairies to confront the culprit. A stirring and blithe instrumental introduction, followed by a short chorus ("They come from Beds of Lichen green"), describes the gathering of the fays, retarded at the close, and growing sombre as it is announced that "an ouphe has broken his vestal vow." A tenor solo ("He has loved an earthly Maid") tells the sad story of the guilty one who "has lain upon her lip of dew" and "nestled on her snowy breast." They gather about to hear his doom, and do not have to wait long; for the tenor song leads without break to a barytone solo, in recitative form, by the Fairy King ("Fairy, Fairy, list and mark"), pronouncing the penalties he must pay for his transgression, — the catching of a drop from the sturgeon's silver bow to wash away the stain on his wings, and the relighting of his flamewood lamp by the last faint spark in the train of a shooting star.

A graceful chorus ("Soft and pale is the moony Beam") opens the second part, picturing the scene upon the strand bordering the elfin land, and the leaps of the sturgeon, followed by a tenor solo and recitative describing the sorrow of the lonely sprite and his desperate effort to push his musselshell boat down to the verge of the haunted land. The alto, which does all the mystery work, goes on with the description of the vain attempt of the river imps to wreck his frail craft, and his discovery and pursuit of the sturgeon; then there is a pause. The full chorus, in a quick movement, pictures the pretty scene of the sturgeon's leap, the arch of silver sheen, and the puny goblin waiting to catch the drop. The tenor recitative announces his success, and a full jubilant chorus of the sprites ("Joy to thee, Fay! thy Task is done") bids him hasten back to the elfin shore.

The third part opens with a full chorus, very animated in its progression ("Up to the Cope, careering swift"), describing the ride of the Fay past the sphered moon and up to the bank of the Milky Way, where he checks his courser to wait for the shooting star. In the next number, a short recitative, the alto has a more grateful task; this time it is the graceful sylphs of heaven who appear, weaving their dance about the Fay, and leading him on to the palace of the Sylphide Queen. It is followed by two charming soprano solos, — the one descriptive of her beauty as she listens to the story of the Fay, and the other ("O Sweet Spirit of Earth") of her sudden passion and the tempting inducements by which she seeks to make him forget the joys of fairyland. Once more the tenor, who plays the part of narrator, enters, and in solo and recitative assures us how like a brave homunculus the Fay resisted her blandishments. A very vigorous and descriptive chorus, as fast as can be sung, pictures the Fay careering along on the wings of the blast up to the northern plain, where at length a star "bursts in flash and flame." The tenor announces his second success, and the final chorus ("Ouphe and Goblin!

Imp and Sprite ") sings his welcome back in an animated manner, beginning with a moderate movement which constantly accelerates and works up to a fine climax; after which —

> "The hill-tops glow in morning's spring,
> The skylark shakes his dappled wing,
> The day glimpse glimmers on the lawn,
> The cock has crowed and the fays are gone."

The Praise Song to Harmony.

"The Praise Song to Harmony," written in 1886, is a musical setting of a poem of the same name by David Ebeling, a German poet who lived in the latter part of the eighteenth century. The composition is in a strict sense a symphonic cantata, somewhat in the manner of Mendelssohn's "Hymn of Praise," being prefaced with a symphonic allegro in the classical form which is written in a very scholarly manner and displays great skill in thematic treatment.

The cantata proper opens with a short introduction, consisting of massive chord foundations for the full orchestra, connected by a figure for the strings, ushering in a chorus for male voices ("Hail thee, O Harmony, offspring of Heaven"). The words contain a description of the creation of worlds and of music, as the song of stars unites with the angel chorus in praise of the Almighty. At the close of this number begins a choral theme for trumpets, horns, and trombones, followed by strings and woodwinds, and introducing a soprano recitative ("With Grace, thy Gaze, O Harmony") descriptive of the blessing brought into the world by music, followed by a picture of the misery of the race without its consolation. At the close the brasses give out a solemn march-like theme. A short chorus ("Joy to us! Again descending, thou Heavenly One") describes the might of song. A brief orchestral interlude follows, preparing the entrance of a barytone solo with chorus ("Blessed Comforter in Grief"). The work closes with a partial repetition of the opening chorus, with a more elaborate and brilliant figural accompaniment, in the course of which the march-like subject is heard again in the brasses. At the end the strings maintain a tremolo while the rest of the orchestra presents a passage with varied harmonies. The opening theme of the cantata, though not a repetition, bears a strong analogy to the introduction of the symphony movement.

HANDEL.

GEORGE FREDERICK HANDEL was born at Halle, in Lower Saxony, Feb. 23, 1685, and like many another composer revealed his musical promise at a very early age, only to encounter parental opposition. His father intended him to be a lawyer; but Nature had her way, and in spite of domestic antagonism triumphed. The Duke of Saxe-Weissenfels recognized his ability and overcame the father's determination. Handel began his studies with Zachau, organist of the Halle cathedral. After the death of his father, in 1697, he went to Hamburg, and for a time played in the orchestra of the German opera. It was during his residence in that city that he wrote his first opera, "Almira" (1705). In the following year he went to Italy, where he remained several months under the patronage of the Grand Duke of Florence. During the next two years he visited Venice, Rome, and Naples, and wrote several operas and minor oratorios. In 1709 he returned to Germany, and the Elector of Hanover, subsequently George I. of England, offered him the position of capellmeister, which he accepted upon the condition that he might visit England, having received many invitations from that country. The next year he arrived in London and brought out his opera of "Rinaldo," which proved a great success. At the end of six months he was obliged to return to his position in Hanover; but the English success made him impatient of the dulness of the court. In 1712 he was in London again, little dreaming that the Elector would soon follow him as king. Incensed with him for leaving Hanover, the King at first refused to receive him; but some music which Handel composed for an aquatic fête in his honor brought about the royal reconciliation. In 1718 he accepted the position of chapel-master to the Duke of Chandos, for whom he wrote the famous Chandos Te Deum and Anthems, the serenata "Acis and Galatea," and "Esther," his first English oratorio. In 1720 he was engaged as director of Italian opera by the society of noblemen known as the Royal Academy of Music, and from that time until 1740 his career was entirely of an operatic character. Opera after opera came from his pen. Some were successful, others failed. At first composer, then director, he finally became *impresario*, only to find himself confronted with bitter rivalry, especially at the hands of Bononcini and Porpora. Cabals were instituted against him. Unable to contend with them alone, he formed a partnership with Heidegger, proprietor of the King's Theatre, in 1729. It was broken in 1734,

and he took the management of Covent Garden.
The Italian conspiracies against him broke out
afresh. He failed in his undertaking and became
a bankrupt. Slanders of all sorts were circulated,
and his works were no longer well received. In
the midst of his adversity sickness overtook him,
ending with a partial stroke of paralysis. When
sufficiently recovered he went to the Continent,
where he remained for a few months. On his return to London he brought out some new works,
but they were not favorably received. A few friends
who had remained faithful to him persuaded him to
give a benefit concert, which was a great success.
It inspired him with fresh courage; but he did not
again return to the operatic world. Thenceforward
he devoted himself to oratorio, in which he made
his name famous for all time. He himself said:
"Sacred music is best suited to a man descending
in the vale of years." "Saul" and the colossal
"Israel in Egypt," written in 1740, head the list of
his wonderful oratorios. In 1741 he was invited to
visit Ireland. He went there in November, and
many of his works were produced during the winter
and received with great enthusiasm. In April, 1742,
his immortal "Messiah" was brought out at Dublin.
It was followed by "Samson," "Joseph," "Semele,"
"Belshazzar," and "Hercules," which were also
successful; but even in the midst of his oratorio
work his rivals did not cease their conspiracies
against him, and in 1744 he was once more a
bankrupt. For over a year his pen was idle. In

1746 the "Occasional Oratorio" and "Judas Maccabæus" appeared, and these were speedily followed by "Joshua," "Solomon," "Susanna," "Therodora," and "Jephthah." It was during the composition of the last-named work that he was attacked with the illness which finally proved fatal. He died April 14, 1759, and was buried in Westminster Abbey. During the last few days of his life he was heard to express the wish that "he might breathe his last on Good Friday, in hopes of meeting his good God, his sweet Lord and Saviour, on the day of His resurrection." The wish was granted him; for it was on Good Friday that he passed away, leaving behind him a name and fame that will be cherished so long as music retains its power over the human heart.

Acis and Galatea.

The first idea of Handel's famous pastoral, "Acis and Galatea," is to be found in a serenata, "Aci, Galatea, e Polifemo," which he produced at Naples in July, 1708. The plan of the work resembles that of the later pastoral, though its musical setting is entirely different.[1] Little was known of it however until nearly a quarter of a century afterwards,

---

[1] The superior attractions of the English serenata will probably prevent the earlier work from ever becoming a popular favorite; more especially since the rôle of Polifemo needs a bass singer with a voice of the extraordinary compass of two octaves and a half. — *Rockstro's Life of Handel.*

when the composer revived portions of it in one of his London concerts, as will shortly be seen.

In 1718 Handel entered the service of James, Duke of Chandos, as chapel-master, succeeding Dr. Pepusch. His patron had accumulated an immense fortune and spent it in a princely manner. He had built a marble palace, at an enormous expense, at Cannons in Middlesex, where he lived in almost regal state. It was the chapel attached to this mansion over which Handel was called to preside, and there were ready for his use a large choir, a band of instrumental performers, and a fine organ. The anthems and services of his predecessor were laid aside, and that year Handel's busy pen supplied two new settings of the Te Deum and the twelve Chandos Anthems, which are really cantatas in form. His first English opera, "Esther," was also composed at Cannons, and was followed by the beautiful pastoral which forms the subject of this sketch. "Esther" was first performed Aug. 20, 1720, and it is generally agreed that "Acis and Galatea" followed it in the same year, though Schoelcher in his biography assigns 1721 as the date. Nine characters are contained in the original manuscript, — Galatea, Clori, and Eurilla, sopranos; Acis, Filli, Dorinda, and Damon, altos; Silvio, tenor; and Polifemo, bass.

After this private performance the pastoral was not again heard from until 1731–32, when it was given under peculiar circumstances. On the 13th of March, 1731, it was performed for the benefit of one Rochetti, who took the rôle of Acis; but with this representation Handel had nothing to do. The act of piracy was repeated in the following year, when Mr. Arne, father of Dr. Arne the composer, and the lessee of the Little Theatre in the Haymarket, announced its performance as follows:—

"At the new theatre in the Haymarket, on Thursday next, 11th May, will be performed in English a pastoral opera called 'Acis and Galatea,' with all the choruses, scenes, machines, and other decorations, etc. (as before), being the first time it was ever performed in a theatrical way. The part of Acis by Mr. Mourtier, being the first time of his appearance in character on any stage; Galatea, Miss Arne.[1] Pit and boxes, 5s."

Handel had taken no notice of the 1731 performance; but this representation, given at a theatre directly opposite the one of which he was manager, roused his resentment, though piracy of this kind was very common in those days. He determined to outdo the manager "over the way." On the 5th of June he announced in the "Daily Journal":—

"In the King's Theatre in the Haymarket, the present Saturday, being the 10th of June, will be performed a serenata called 'Acis and Galatea,' formerly composed by Mr. Handel, and now revised by him, with several additions, and to be performed by a great

---

[1] Miss Arne, afterwards Mrs. Cibber, enjoyed, under the latter name, a great reputation as a singer. Her husband was Theophilus Cibber, the brother of Colley Cibber, a poet laureate in the reign of George II. — *Schoelcher's Life of Handel.*

number of the best voices and instruments. There will be no action on the stage,[1] but the scene will represent in a picturesque manner a rural prospect, with rocks, groves, fountains, and grottos, among which will be disposed a chorus of nymphs and shepherds; the habits, and every other decoration, suited to the subject. Also on the 13th, 17th, 20th. The libretto printed for J. Watts, in three acts."

The rival establishment had produced the work as it was originally given at Cannons; but as intimated in his advertisement, Handel made additions, interpolating a number of airs and choruses from the serenata which he had composed at Naples, thus requiring the work to be sung both in Italian and English, — a polyglot practice from which our own times are not exempt. The part of Acis was sung by Senesino, a male soprano; Galatea by Signora Strada; and Polyphemus by Montagnana. The other parts — Clori and Eurilla sopranos, Filli and Dorinda contraltos, and Silvio tenor — were also represented. It was performed eight times in

[1] This undoubtedly is the manner in which this charming little piece ought to be performed. It is a dramatic poem, but not an acting play, and the incidents are such as cannot be represented on the stage. A few years ago another attempt was made to perform it as an opera, but without success. Polyphemus is entirely an ideal character, and any attempt to personate him must be ridiculous; and the concluding scene, in which the giant throws a huge rock at the head of his rival, produced shouts of merriment. "Acis and Galatea" is performed in an orchestra in the manner in which oratorios are performed; but its effect would certainly be heightened by the picturesque scenery and decorations employed by Handel himself. — *Hogarth's Musical Drama.*

1732, and was brought out in the same form at Oxford in 1733; but in 1739 Handel restored it to its original shape as it had been given at Cannons. It is now generally performed in two parts with the three characters Galatea, Acis, and Polyphemus, and choruses of nymphs and shepherds.

The pretty pastoral will always possess more than ordinary interest, as four celebrated poets are represented in the construction of the poem. Gay wrote the most of it. It also contains a strophe by Hughes, a verse by Pope,[1] and an extract from Dryden's translation of the Galatea myth in the Metamorphoses of Ovid.[2] The story is based on the seventh fable in the thirteenth book of the Metamorphoses,—the sad story which Galatea, daughter of Nereus, tells to Scylla. The nymph was passionately in love with the shepherd Acis, son of Faunus and of the nymph Symœthis, and pursued him incessantly. She too was pursued by Polyphemus, the one-eyed Cyclops of Ætna, contemner of the gods. One day, reclining upon the breast of Acis, concealed behind a rock, she hears the giant pouring out to the woods and mountains his story of love and despair: "I, who despise Jove and the heavens and the piercing lightnings, dread thee, daughter of Nereus; than the lightnings is thy wrath

[1] "Not showers to larks so pleasing,
Not sunshine to the bee,
Not sleep to toil so easing,
As these dear smiles to me."

[2] "Help! Galatea! Help, ye parent gods!
And take me dying to your deep abodes."

more dreadful to me. But I should be more patient under these slights if thou didst avoid all men. For why, rejecting the Cyclop, dost thou love Acis? And why prefer Acis to my embraces?" As he utters these last complaints, he espies the lovers. Then, raging and roaring so that the mountains shook and the sea trembled, he hurled a huge rock at Acis and crushed him. The shepherd's blood gushing forth from beneath the rock was changed into a river; and Galatea, who had fled to the sea, was consoled.

The overture to the work, consisting of one movement, is thoroughly pastoral in its style and marked by all that grace and delicacy which characterize the composer's treatment of movements of this kind. It introduces a chorus ("O the Pleasures of the Plains!") in which the easy, careless life of the shepherds and their swains is pictured. Galatea enters seeking her lover, and after the recitative, "Ye verdant Plains and woody Mountains," relieves her heart with an outburst of melodious beauty:—

> "Hush, ye pretty warbling choir!
> Your thrilling strains
> Awake my pains
> And kindle fierce desire.
> Cease your song and take your flight;
> Bring back my Acis to my sight."

Acis answers her, after a short recitative, with another aria equally graceful ("Love in her Eyes sits playing and sheds delicious Death"). The melodious and sensuous dialogue is continued by Galatea, who once more sings: —

> " As when the dove
> Laments her love
> All on the naked spray;
> When he returns
> No more she mourns,
> But loves the live-long day.
> Billing, cooing,
> Panting, wooing,
> Melting murmurs fill the grove,
> Melting murmurs, lasting love." —

Then in a duet, sparkling with the happiness of the lovers (" Happy We "), closing with chorus to the same words, this pretty picture of ancient pastoral life among the nymphs and shepherds comes to an end.

In the second part there is another tone both to scene and music. The opening chorus of alarm (" Wretched Lovers ") portends the coming of the love-sick Cyclops; the mountains bow, the forests shake, the waves run frightened to the shore as he approaches roaring and calling for " a hundred reeds of decent growth," that on " such pipe ", his capacious mouth may play the praises of Galatea. The recitative, " I melt, I rage, I burn," is very characteristic, and leads to the giant's love-song, an unctuous, catching melody almost too full of humor and grace for the fierce brute of Ætna: —

> " O ruddier than the cherry!
> O sweeter than the berry!
> O nymph more bright
> Than moonshine night,
> Like kidlings, blithe and merry.

> "Ripe as the melting cluster,
> No lily has such lustre.
> Yet hard to tame
> As raging flame,
> And fierce as storms that bluster."

In marked contrast with this declaration follows the plaintive tender song of Acis ("Love sounds the Alarm"). Galatea appeals to him to trust the gods, and then the three join in a trio ("The Flocks shall leave the Mountain"). Enraged at his discomfiture, the giant puts forth his power. He is no longer the lover piping to Galatea and dissembling his real nature, but a destructive raging force; and the fragment of mountain which he tears away buries poor Acis as effectually as Ætna sometimes does the plains beneath. The catastrophe accomplished, the work closes with the sad lament of Galatea for her lover ("Must I my Acis still bemoan?") and the choral consolations of the shepherds and their swains:—

> "Galatea, dry thy tears,
> Acis now a god appears;
> See how he rears him from his bed!
> See the wreath that binds his head!
> Hail! thou gentle murmuring stream;
> Shepherds' pleasure, Muses' theme;
> Through the plains still joy to rove,
> Murmuring still thy gentle love."

Alexander's Feast.

Handel composed the music for Dryden's immortal ode in 1736. In the original score the close of the first part is dated January 5, and the end of the work January 17, showing rapid composition. Three years before this time he had had a violent quarrel with Senesino, his principal singer at the opera-house in the Haymarket, which led to his abandonment of the theatre and its occupancy by his rival, Porpora. After an unsuccessful attempt to compete with the latter, which nearly bankrupted him in health and purse, he decided to quit opera altogether. He sought relief for his physical ailments at Aix-la-Chapelle, and upon his return to London in October, 1735, publicly announced that "Mr. Handel will perform Oratorios and have Concerts of Musick this Winter at Covent Garden Theatre." One of the first works for these concerts was "Alexander's Feast," completed, as stated above, Jan. 17, 1736. The poem was prepared by Newburgh Hamilton, who says in his preface: —

"I determined not to take any unwarrantable liberty with the poem, which has long done honor to the nation, and which no man can add to or abridge in anything material without injuring it. I therefore confined myself to a plain division of it into airs, recitatives or choruses, looking upon the words in general so sacred as scarcely to violate one in the order of its first place. How I have succeeded the world is to judge, and whether I have preserved that beautiful description of the passions, so exquisitely drawn, at the same time I strove to reduce them to the present taste in sounds. I confess my principal view was, not to lose this favorable opportunity of its being set to music by that great master who has with pleasure undertaken the task, and who only is capable of doing it justice; whose compositions have long shown that they can conquer even the most obstinate partiality, and inspire life into the most senseless words. If this entertainment can in the least degree give satisfaction to the real judges of poetry or music, I shall think myself happy in having promoted it; being persuaded that it is next to an improbability to offer the world anything in those arts more perfect than the united labors and utmost efforts of a Dryden and a Handel."

In addition to the preface Hamilton appended a poem "To Mr. Handel on his setting to Musick Mr. Dryden's Feast of Alexander," in which he enthusiastically sings: —

> "Two glowing sparks of that celestial flame
> Which warms by mystick art this earthly frame,
> United in one blaze of genial heat,
> Produced this piece in sense and sounds complete.
> The Sister Arts, as breathing from one soul,
> With equal spirit animate the whole.
> Had Dryden lived the welcome day to bless,
> Which clothed his numbers in so fit a dress,
> When his majestick poetry was crowned
> With all your bright magnificence of sound,
> How would his wonder and his transport rise,
> Whilst famed Timotheus yields to you the prize!"

The work was first performed at Covent Garden Theatre, February 19, about a month after it was written; the principal singers being Signora Strada, Miss Young,[1] John Beard, and Mr. Erard. It met with

---

[1] Cecilia, a pupil of Geminiani, and afterwards wife of Dr. Arne.

remarkable success. The London "Daily Post," on the morning after its production, said:—

"Never was upon the like Occasion so numerous and splendid an Audience at any Theatre in London, there being at least 1,300 Persons present; and it is judged that the Receipt of the House could not amount to less than £450."

It was repeated four times, and then withdrawn to make room for "Acis and Galatea" and the oratorio of "Esther." In March, 1737, it was revived, with two additional choruses made by Hamilton for the work; and upon the same occasion an Italian cantata in praise of Saint Cecilia was sung.

It is unnecessary to inform the reader of the nature of a poem familiar the world over. The overture is written for strings and two oboes. Throughout the work the orchestration is thin, bassoons and horns being the only instruments added to those named above; but in 1790 Mozart amplified the accompaniments, — an improvement which he also made for the score of "Acis and Galatea." The great solos of the composition are the furious aria, "'Revenge, Revenge!' Timotheus cries," and the descriptive recitative, "Give the Vengeance due to the valiant Crew," in which Handel employs his imitative powers with consummate effect. Clouet, in his "Chants Classiques," says of the passage "And the king seized a flambeau with zeal to destroy:"—

"He paints Alexander issuing forth in the midst of an orgie, arming himself with a torch, and followed by his generals, running to set fire to Persepolis. While the accompaniment sparkles with the confused and unequal glare of the torches, the song expresses truthfully the precipitation and the tumult of the crowd, the rolling of the flames, and the living splendor of a conflagration."

The choruses of the work are equally strong, and some of them are among the best Handel ever wrote, particularly, "He sang Darius great and good," "Break his Bands of Sleep asunder," "Let old Timotheus yield the Prize," and "The many rend the Skies with loud Applause." They are as genuine inspirations as the best choruses of the "Messiah" or of "Israel in Egypt."

In 1739 Handel also set to music Dryden's shorter "Ode for St. Cecilia's Day," beginning,

> "From Harmony, from heavenly Harmony
> This universal frame began,"

the music for which had been originally composed in 1687 by Giovanni Baptista Draghi, an Italian, who was music-master to Queen Anne and Queen Mary, and at that time was organist to Catharine of Braganza, widow of Charles II. Handel's setting was first performed on the anniversary of the saint's festival, Nov. 22, 1739. The programme announced:

"Lincoln's Inn Fields. At the Theatre Royal in Lincoln's Inn Fields, Thursday next, November 22 (being St. Cecilia's Day), will be performed an Ode of Mr. Dryden's, with two new Concertos for several instruments, which will be preceded by Alexander's Feast and a Concerto on the organ."

Though one of the shortest of his vocal works, it contains some magnificent choruses.

L' Allegro.

"L' Allegro, il Penseroso ed il Moderato," the first two movements of which contain a musical setting of Milton's well-known poem, was written in the seventeen days from Jan. 19 to Feb. 6, 1740, and was first performed on the 27th of the latter month at the Royal Theatre, Lincoln's Inn Fields, London. Upon this occasion the first and second parts were preceded, according to the handbook, by "a new concerto for several instruments," and the third by "a new concerto on the organ," which was played by the composer himself. It was performed again Jan. 31, 1741, with the addition of ten new numbers to the music, which in the original manuscript appear at the end, marked by Handel, "l' Additione." At a still later period Handel omitted the third part ("Moderato") entirely, and substituted for it Dryden's "Ode on St. Cecilia's Day," which he composed in 1739.

The text of the first two parts is by Milton, Allegro, as is well known, chanting the praises of pleasure, Penseroso those of melancholy; Allegro represented by tenor and Penseroso by soprano, and each supported by a chorus which joins in the discussion of the two moods. There is a radical difference between the poem as Milton wrote it and as it appears set to Handel's music. Milton presented two distinct poems, though allied by antithesis, and Penseroso does not speak until Allegro has finished. In the poem as adapted for music they alternate in sixteen strophes and antistrophes. The adaptation of these two parts was made by Charles Jennens, who was a frequent collaborator with Handel.[1] He also suggested the addition of a third part, the Moderato, and wrote the words, in which he counsels both Allegro and Penseroso to take the middle course of moderation as the safest. The wisdom of the poet in suggesting the *via media* is more to be commended than his boldness in supplementing Milton's stately verse with commonplaces, however wise they may have been. Chrysander, the German biographer of Handel presents a philosophical view of the case. He says:

"In the two pictures a deeply thoughtful mind has fixed for itself two far-reaching goals. With these the poem has reached its perfect end, and in the sense of its inventor there is nothing further to be added. The only possible, the only natural outlet was that into a *life of action*, according to the direction which the spirit now should take; already it was the first step into this new domain which called forth the divided feeling. The two moods do not run together into any third mood as their point of union, but into active real life, as different characters, forever separate. Therefore 'Moderation' could not bring about the

---

[1] Jennens was an amateur poet of the period, descended from a manufacturing family of Birmingham, from whom he inherited a large fortune. He lived on terms of close intimacy with Handel, and was mentioned in his will. He died Nov. 20, 1773.

reconciliation; only life could do it; not contemplation, but deeds. Gladness and Melancholy are symptoms of a vigorous soul; moderation would be mediocrity. And herein lies the unpoetic nature of the addition by Jennens; read according to Milton, the concluding moral of a rich English land-owner whose inherited abundance points to nothing but a golden mean, and whose only real problem is to keep the balance in the lazy course of an inactive life, makes a disheartening impression."

The work as a whole is one of Handel's finest inspirations. The Allegro is bright and spirited throughout; the Penseroso grave and tender; and the Moderato quiet and respectable, as might be expected of a person who never experiences the enthusiasms of joy or the comforts of melancholy. The most of the composition is assigned to solo voices which carry on the discussion, though in the Moderato it is mainly the chorus which urges the sedate compromise between the two.

The work opens without overture, its place having originally been supplied by an orchestral concerto. In vigorous and very dramatic recitative Allegro bids "loathed Melancholy" hence, followed by Penseroso, who in a few bars of recitative far less vigorously consigns "vain, deluding joys" to "some idle brain;" Allegro replies with the first aria ("Come, come, thou Goddess fair"), a beautifully free and flowing melody, responded to by Penseroso, who in an aria of stately rhythm appeals to his goddess, "Divinest Melancholy." Now Allegro summons his retinue of mirth: —

"Haste thee, nymph, and bring with thee
Jest and youthful jollity,
Quips and cranks and wanton wiles,
Nods and becks and wreathèd smiles,
Such as hang on Hebe's cheek,
And love to live in dimple sleek,
Sport, that wrinkled care derides,
And Laughter, holding both his sides;"

and the chorus takes up the jovial refrain in the same temper. The aria itself is well known as the laughing song. Indeed, both aria and chorus are full of unrestrained mirth, and go laughingly along in genuine musical giggles.[1] The effect is still further enhanced by the next aria for Allegro ("Come and trip it as you go"), a graceful minuet, which is also taken by the chorus. After a recitative

---

[1] I was lucky enough to meet with the approbation of Mr. Bates in the recitative of "Deeper and deeper still;" my next song was the laughing one. Mr. Harrison, my predecessor at those concerts, was a charming singer: his singing "Oft on a plat of rising ground," his "Lord, remember David," and "O come let us worship and fall down," breathed pure religion. No divine from the pulpit, though gifted with the greatest eloquence, could have inspired his auditors with a more perfect sense of duty to their Maker than Harrison did by his melodious tones and chaste style; indeed, it was faultless: but in the animated songs of Handel he was very deficient. I heard him sing the laughing song without moving a muscle, and determined, though it was a great risk, to sing it my own way, and the effect produced justified the experiment; instead of singing it with the serious tameness of Harrison, I laughed all through it, as I conceived it ought to be sung, and as must have been the intention of the composer. The infection ran; and their Majesties, and the whole audience, as well as the orchestra, were in a roar of laughter, and a signal was given from the royal box to repeat it, and I sang it again with increased effect. — *Michael Kelly's Reminiscences*, 1789.

by Penseroso ("Come, pensive Nun"), and the aria, "Come, but keep thy wonted State" the first Penseroso chorus occurs ("Join with thee calm Peace and Quiet"), a short but beautiful passage of tranquil harmony. Once more in recitative Allegro bids "loathed Melancholy" hence, and then in the aria, "Mirth, admit me of thy Crew," leading into chorus, sings of the lark, "startling dull Night" and bidding good-morrow at his window, — a brilliant number accompanied with an imitation of the lark's song. Penseroso replies with an equally brilliant song ("Sweet Bird, that shuns't the Noise of Folly"), in which the nightingale plays the part of accompaniment. Another aria by Allegro ("Mirth, admit me of thy Crew") gives an opportunity for a blithe and jocund hunting-song for the bass, followed by one of the most beautiful numbers in the work ("Oft on a Plat of rising Ground") sung by Penseroso, in which the ringing of the far-off curfew, "swinging slow, with sullen roar," is introduced with telling effect. This is followed by a quiet meditative aria ("Far from all Resorts of Mirth"), when once again Allegro takes up the strain in the two arias, "Let me wander not unseen," and "Straight mine Eye hath caught new Pleasures." The first part closes with the Allegro aria and chorus ("Or let the merry Bells ring round"), full of the very spirit of joy and youth; and ending with an exquisite harmonic effect as the gay crowd creep to bed, "by whispering winds soon lulled to sleep."

The second part begins with a stately recitative and aria by Penseroso ("Sometimes let gorgeous Tragedy"), followed by one of the most characteristic arias in the work ("But O, sad Virgin, that thy Power might raise!") in which the passage,

> " Or bid the soul of Orpheus sing
> Such notes as warbled to the string
> Drew iron tears down Pluto's cheek,"

is accompanied by long persistent trills that admirably suit the words. The next number (" Populous Cities please me then ") is a very descriptive solo for Allegro, with chorus which begins in canon form for the voices and then turns to a lively movement as it pictures the knights celebrating their triumphs and the "store of ladies" awarding prizes to their gallants. Again Allegro in a graceful aria sings, "There let Hymen oft appear." It is followed by a charming canzonet ("Hide me from Day's garish Eye") for Penseroso, which leads to an aria for Allegro ("I'll to the well-trod Stage anon"), opening in genuinely theatrical style, and then changing to a delightfully melodious warble at the words, —

> "Or sweetest Shakspeare, Fancy's child,
> Warble his native wood-notes wild."

This is followed by three characteristic arias, "And ever, against eating Cares," "Orpheus himself may heave his Head," and "These Delights, if thou canst give," — the last with chorus. Penseroso has a short chorus in plain but stately harmony ("There let the pealing Organ blow "), with pauses for the organ *ad libitum*, followed by the aria, "May at last my weary Age," and the majestic devotional fugued chorus, "These Pleasures, Melancholy, give!" which close the second part.

The third part, "Il Moderato," is rarely given, and the work may well close with the fugue that so beautifully and harmoniously ends the second part. It opens with an aria in which Moderato tenders the sage advice: —

> "Come, with native lustre shine,
> Moderation, grace divine,
> Whom the wise God of nature gave,
> Mad mortals from themselves to save.
> Keep as of old the middle way,
> Nor deeply sad nor idly gay;
> But still the same in look and gait,
> Easy, cheerful, and sedate,
> Keep as of old the middle way."

With such didactic commonplaces as the above, Moderato commends temperance, health, contentment, frugality, equanimity, and chaste love, and bids them, —

> "Come, with gentle hand restrain
> Those who fondly court their bane;
> One extreme with caution shunning,
> To another blindly running.
> Kindly teach how blest are they
> Who nature's equal rules obey,
> Who safely steer two rocks between,
> And prudent keep the golden mean."

Thus Mr. Jennens's mild philosophy goes on, one of his verses, "As steals the Morn upon the Night," set to a brilliant tenor and soprano duet, followed by the closing chorus, "Thy Pleasures, Moderation, give," in full, broad, rich harmony. There needs no other proof of Handel's genius, than that he could link such Tupperisms to his grand measures.

HATTON.

JOHN LIPHOT HATTON, a composer well known in America, not only by his songs and other works, but also by his visits here, was born in Liverpool in 1809. Though his early musical education was very scanty, he soon became known as a composer after his removal to London in 1832, and his works met with a very cordial reception. In 1842 he became conductor at Drury Lane Theatre, and while acting in that capacity brought out one of his operettas, called "The Queen of the Thames." In 1844 he went to Vienna and produced his opera "Pascal Bruno." Shortly afterwards he issued several songs under the *nom de plume* of "Czapek," which secured for themselves widespread popularity. In 1848 he came to this country, and some years later made a concert-tour here. Upon his return to England he assumed direction of the music at the Princess' Theatre, and while engaged there wrote incidental music for "Macbeth," "Sardanapalus," "Faust and Marguerite," "King Henry VIII.," "Pizarro," "King Richard II.," "King Lear," "The Merchant of

Venice," and "Much Ado About Nothing." In 1856 he wrote "Robin Hood," a cantata; in 1864 the opera "Rose, or Love's Ransom," for Covent Garden; and in 1877 "Hezekiah," a sacred drama, which was performed at the Crystal Palace. He has also written a large number of part songs, which are great favorites with quartet clubs, and nearly two hundred songs which are very popular; among them, "Good-by, Sweetheart, good-by," which has been a stock piece with concert tenors for years, and which the late Signor Brignoli used to sing with excellent effect. His music is specially characterized by grace and melodiousness. Hatton died in 1886.

Robin Hood.

The pastoral cantata of "Robin Hood" was written for the Bradford (England) Triennial Festival of 1856, Sims Reeves creating the part of the hero. Its name suggests the well-known story of the greenwood outlaw which has been charmingly versified by George Linley in the libretto. The personages are Maid Marian, Robin Hood, Little John, and "The Bishop." Maid Marian, it will be remembered, was the mistress who followed Robin into the Sherwood Forest and shared his wild life; and Little John was his stalwart lieutenant, whose name was transposed after he joined the band, thus heightening the incongruity between his name and his great size. The incident contained in Linley's poem appears to have been suggested by Robin Hood's penchant for capturing bishops and other ecclesiastics, notwithstanding his religious professions, which were exemplified by the retention of Friar Tuck as chaplain in the bold archer's household; or it may be based upon the historical story of the expedition which Edward II. and some of his retainers, disguised as monks, made into the forest for the purpose of exterminating the outlaws and thus stopping their slaughter of the royal deer. As the old story goes, they were led into an ambuscade by a forester who had agreed to conduct them to the haunts of Robin, and were captured. When Robin recognized the King in the disguise of the abbot, he craved forgiveness for himself and his band, which was granted upon condition that he should accompany his sovereign to Court and take a place in the royal household. The old collection of ballads, "The Lytell Geste of Robyn Hood," tells the same story and continues it, relating how after "dwelling in the Kynge's courte" a year, he tired of it and obtained permission to make a visit to the woods again, but forfeited his word and never returned, dying at last in Kirklees priory, through the treachery of the abbess, and how in his last moments he blew a loud blast on his horn, summoning Little John from the forest, to whom, after he had forced his way into his chamber, the dying Robin said:

> "Give me my bent bow in my hand,
> And an arrow I 'll let free,
> And where that arrow is taken up,
> There let my grave digged be."

The cantata opens with a chorus of the outlaws, who vigorously assert their independence of tribute, laws, and monarchs, followed by a bombastic bass aria by the Bishop, who threatens them for destroying the King's deer. His grandiloquence is speedily interrupted by the outlaws, with Robin at their head, who surround him without further ado and make him the butt of their sport. Robin Hood sings a charmingly melodious ballad, "Under the Greenwood Tree," in which the Bishop is invited to become one of their number and share their sylvan enjoyments. A trio and chorus follow, in the course of which the Bishop parts with his personal possessions in favor of the gentlemen around him in Lincoln green with "bent bows." A chorus ("Strike the Harp") also informs us that the ecclesiastic is forced to dance for the genial band much against his will as well as his dignity. Robin's sentimentalizing about the pleasures under the greenwood tree is still further emphasized by a madrigal for female voices, supposed to be sung by the forest maidens, though their identity is not very clear, as Marian was the only maid that accompanied the band. After the plundering scene, the cantata grows more passionate in character, describing a pretty and tender love-scene between Robin and Marian, which is somewhat incongruous, whether Marian be considered as the outlaw's mistress, or, as some of the old chroniclers have it, his wife Matilda, who changed her name when she followed him into the forest. From the musical standpoint, however, it affords an opportunity for another graceful ballad of sentiment, in which Marian describes her heart as "a frail bark upon the waters of love;" a duet in which the lovers passionately declare their love for each other as well as their delight with the forest; and a final chorus of the band, jubilantly proclaiming their hatred of kings and courtiers, and their loyalty to Robin Hood and Maid Marian. It may be worthy of note in this connection that Bishop, the English composer, wrote a legendary opera called "Maid Marian, or the Huntress of Arlingford," in which the heroine is Matilda.

HAYDN.

JOSEPH HAYDN, the creator of the symphony and the string quartet, was born at Rohrau, a little Austrian village on the river Leitha, March 31, 1732. His father was a wheelwright and his mother a cook, in service with Count Harrach. Both the parents were fond of music, and both sang, the father accompanying himself upon the harp, which he played by ear. The child displayed a voice so beautiful that in his sixth year he was allowed to study music, and was also given a place in the village church-choir. Reutter, the capellmeister of St. Stephen's, Vienna, having heard him, was so impressed with the beauty of his voice that he offered him a position as chorister. Haydn eagerly accepted it, as it gave him an opportunity for study. While in the service of St. Stephen's he had lessons on the violin and piano, as well as in composition. When his voice broke, and his singing was of no further value, he was thrown upon the tender mercies of the world. Fortune favored him, however. He obtained a few pupils, and gave himself to composition. He made the acquaintance of Metastasio, Porpora, and Gluck. His trios began to attract attention, and he soon found himself rising into prominence. In 1759, through the influence of a wealthy friend and amateur, he was appointed to the post of musical director and composer in the service of Count Morzin, and about this time wrote his first symphony. When the Count dismissed his band, Prince Paul Anton Esterhazy received him as his second capellmeister, under Werner. When the latter died, in 1766, Haydn took his place as sole director. His patron meanwhile had died, and was succeeded by his son Nicolaus, between whom and Haydn there was the utmost good feeling. Up to this time Haydn had written thirty symphonies, a large number of trios, quartets, and several vocal pieces. His connection with the Prince lasted until 1790, and was only terminated by the latter's death. During this period of twenty-eight years his musical activity was unceasing; and as he had an orchestra of his own, and his patron was ardently devoted to music, the incentive to composition was never lacking. Anton succeeded Nicolaus, and was generous enough to increase Haydn's pension; but he dismissed the entire chapel, and the composer took up his abode in Vienna. He was hardly established before he received a flattering proposition from Salomon, the manager, to go to England. He had already had many pressing invitations from others, but could not accept them, owing to his engagement to Esterhazy. Now that he was free, he decided to make the journey. On New Year's Day, 1791, he arrived in London. Success greeted him at once. He became universally popular. Musicians and musical societies paid him devoted attention. He gave a series of symphony concerts which aroused the greatest enthusiasm. He was treated with distinguished courtesy by the royal family. Oxford gave him the honorary degree of Doctor of Music. The nobility entertained him sumptuously. After a year of continuous fêtes he returned to Germany, where he remained two years, during a portion of which time Beethoven was his pupil. In 1794 he made his second journey to England, where his former successes were repeated, and fresh honors were showered upon him. In 1804 he was notified by Prince Esterhazy that he was about to reorganize his chapel, and wished him for its conductor again. Haydn accordingly returned to his old position, where he remained during the rest of his life. He was already an old man, but it was during this period that his most remarkable works were produced, among them the Austrian National Hymn ("Gott erhalte Franz den Kaiser"), the "Seven Words," the "Creation," the "Seasons," and many of his best trios and quartets. He died May 31, 1809, a few days after the occupation of Vienna by the French, and among the mourners at his funeral were many French officers. Funeral services were held in all the principal European cities. Honored and respected all over Europe, he was most deeply loved by his own countrymen, who still affectionately speak of him as "Papa" Haydn.

The Seven Words.

"The Seven Words of Jesus on the Cross," sometimes called "The Passion," was written by Haydn in 1785, for the cathedral of Cadiz, upon a commission from the chapter for appropriate music for Good Friday. It was at first composed as an instrumental work, consisting of seven adagio movements, and in this form was produced in London by the composer himself as a "Passione instrumentale." He afterwards introduced solos and choruses, and divided it into two parts, separating them by a largo movement for wind instruments. It was then given at Eisenstadt in 1797, and four years later was published in the new form, with the following preface by the composer himself: —

About fifteen years ago I was applied to by a clergyman in Cadiz, and requested to write instrumental music to the seven words of Jesus on the cross. It was then customary every year, during Lent, to perform an Oratorio in the Cathedral at Cadiz, the effect of which the following arrangements contributed to heighten. The walls, windows, and columns of the church were hung with black cloth, and only one large lamp, hanging in the centre, lighted the solemn and religious gloom. At noon all the doors were closed, and the music began. After a prelude, suited to the occasion, the bishop ascended the pulpit, pronounced one of the seven words, which was succeeded by reflections upon it. As soon as these were ended he descended from the pulpit and knelt before the altar. The pause was filled by music. The bishop ascended and descended again a second, a third time, and so on ; and each time the orchestra filled up the intervals in the discourse.

My composition must be judged on a consideration of these circumstances. The task of writing seven adagios, each of which was to last about ten minutes, to preserve a connection between them, without wearying the hearers, was none of the lightest, and I soon found that I could not confine myself within the limits of the time prescribed.

The music was originally without text, and was printed in that form. It was only at a later period that I was induced to add the text. The Oratorio entitled "The Seven Words of our Redeemer on the Cross," as a complete and, as regards the vocal parts, an entirely new work, was first published by Messrs. Breitkopf and Härtel, of Leipsic. The partiality with which this work has been received by scientific musicians leads me to hope that it will not be without effect on the public at large.

JOSEPH HAYDN.

VIENNA, March 1, 1880.

As the various movements are all of the same general tone and character, though varied with all that skill and mastery of instrumental effect for which Haydn was so conspicuous, it is needless to describe each separately. By many of the musicians of his day it was considered one of his most sublime productions ; and Bombet declares that Haydn on more than one occasion, when he was asked to which of his works he gave the preference, replied, "The Seven Words."

It opens with an adagio for full orchestra, of a very sorrowful but impressive character. Then follow each of the Seven Words, given out in simple chorale form, followed by its chorus, namely: —

I.

PATIENCE.

"Father, forgive them; for they know not what they do."
Chorus: "Lamb of God! Surely Thou hast borne our sorrows."

II.

THE PENITENT FORGIVEN.

"Verily I say unto thee, this day shalt thou be with me in Paradise."
Chorus: "Lord, have mercy on me after Thy great goodness."

III.

THE MOURNERS.

"Woman, behold thy Son. Son, behold Thy mother."
Chorus: "Daughters of Jerusalem, weep not for Me."

IV.

DESOLATION.

"Eli, Eli, lama sabacthani?"
Chorus: "O my God, look upon Me."

V.

THE BITTER CUP.

" I thirst."
Chorus: " He treadeth the winepress of the fierceness and wrath."

VI.

COMPLETE OBEDIENCE.

" It is finished."
Chorus: " He came down from Heaven."

VII.

THE GREAT OBLATION.

"Father, into Thy hands I commend my spirit."
Chorus: " Into Thy hands, O Lord."

Following immediately after the last number the whole spirit of the music changes with the chorus, " The Veil of the Temple was rent in twain," a presto movement, sung fortissimo, describing the darkness, the quaking of the earth, the rending of the rocks, the opening of the graves, and the arising of the bodies of the saints who slept, with all that vividness in imitation and sublimity of effect which characterize so many of the composer's passages in " The Creation " and " The Seasons." ·Haydn was by nature a deeply religious man, and that he felt the inspiration of the solemn subject is shown by the manner in which he conceived it, and by the exalted devotion of the music which accompanies the last words of the Man of Sorrows. The lines which Bombet quotes from Dante in this connection are hardly exaggerated : —

> "He with such piety his thought reveals,
> And with such heavenly sweetness clothes each tone,
> That hell itself the melting influence feels."

Ariadne.

The cantata "Ariana a Naxos" was written in 1792, and is for a single voice with orchestra. As an illustration of the original cantata form, it is one of the most striking and perfect. Its story is an episode familiar in mythology. When Minos, King of Crete, had vanquished the Athenians, he imposed upon Ægeus, their king, the severe penalty that seven youths should be annually sent to Crete to be devoured by the Minotaur. In the fourth year the king's son, Theseus, was among the number. He was more fortunate than his predecessors, for he slew the Minotaur and was rescued from the labyrinth by following the thread of Ariadne, daughter of Minos, who had conceived a violent passion for the handsome warrior, conqueror of Centaurs and Amazons. Upon his return to Athens she accompanied him as far as the island Naxos, where the ungrateful wretch perfidiously left her. It is this scene of desertion which Haydn chose for his cantata.

Ariadne is supposed to have just awakened from sleep and reclines upon a mossy bank. The first number is a recitative and largo in which she hopefully calls upon Theseus to return. The melody is noble and spirited in style, and yet tender and fervent in its expression of love for the absent one. In the next number, a recitative and andante ("No one listens! My sad Words Echo but repeats"), hopefulness turns to anxiety. The contrast between the blissful longing of the one and the growing solicitude expressed in the other number is very striking. The next melody, an *allegro vivace*, —

"What see I? O heavens! Unhappy me!
Those are the sails of the Argosy! Greeks are those yonder!
Theseus! 'T is he stands at the prow," —

is remarkable for its passionate intensity and dramatic strength. The clouds of despair close over her, and she calls down the vengeance of the gods upon the deserter. In the next two numbers, an adagio ("To whom can I turn me?"), and an andante ("Ah! how for Death I am longing"), the melodies closely follow the sentiment of the text, accompanied by very expressive instrumentation. An *allegro presto*, infused with the very spirit of hopeless gloom and despair, ends the cantata: —

"Woe's me! deceived, betrayed!
Earth holds no consolation."

In the mythological version, however, consolation came; for Bacchus, "ever young," and full of pity for lorn maids, married her, and gave her a crown of seven stars, which after her death was placed among the constellations. The music presents many difficulties for a singer, as it requires the noblest style of declamation, peculiar refinement of sentiment, and rare musical intelligence, as well as facility in execution to give expression to its recitative and strongly contrasting melodies, which have no unity of key, but follow the varying sentiments, with their changes of tone-color, as closely as Theseus followed his thread.

HILLER.

FERDINAND HILLER, one of the most eminent of modern German composers, and a writer of more than ordinary ability, was born at Frankfort-on-the-Main, Oct. 24, 1811. His musical talent displayed itself so early that in his tenth year he appeared in concerts. In 1825 he began his studies with Hummel, and two years afterwards accompanied him on a concert-tour to Vienna, where he published his first work, a piano-forte quartet. He next went to Paris, where he remained until 1835, occupying for a time the position of professor in Choron's " Institution de Musique," but principally devoting himself to piano-playing, composition, and concerts. In 1836 he returned to Frankfort, and for more than a year conducted the concerts of the Cœcilienverein. He then went to Milan, where he met Rossini, and with his assistance brought out his opera "Romilda" at La Scala, but without much success. About the same time he began his oratorio "The Destruction of Jerusalem," one of his most important works. In 1841 he made a second journey to Italy and gave particular attention to church music. On his return he first resided at Frankfort, but was soon in Leipsic, where he conducted the Gewandhaus concerts (1843-44), and after that time in Dresden, where he produced two more operas, "Traum in der Christ-nacht" and "Conradin." In 1847 he was appointed municipal capellmeister at Düsseldorf, and three years later took a similar position at Cologne, where he organized the Conservatory. In that city he exercised a widespread influence, not alone by his teaching, but also by his direction of the famous Lower Rhine festivals. He also made many musical tours which increased his fame. In 1852-53 he conducted opera in Paris; in 1870, gave a series of successful concerts in St. Petersburg; and in 1871-72 visited England, where he produced his works both in public concerts and festivals. His compositions are very numerous, including among the most prominent, five operas, four overtures, a festival march for the opening of the Albert Hall, the Spring Symphony, the oratorios "Destruction of Jerusalem" and "Saul," and the cantatas "Heloise," "Night," "Loreley," "O weint um Sie," "Ver sacrum," "Nala and Damajanti," "Song of Victory," "Song of the Spirits over the Water," "Prometheus," and "Rebecca." He has also enriched musical literature with many important works, among them, "Aus dem Tonleben unserer Zeit" (1867), "Personalisches und Musikalisches" (1876), "Recollections of Mendelssohn" (1874), and "Letters to an Unknown" (1877). He died in May, 1885.

Song of Victory.

The "Song of Victory," a cantata for soprano solo, chorus, and orchestra, was first produced at the Cologne Festival of 1871, and was written to celebrate the victorious conclusion of the Franco-German war of 1870. It consists of eight numbers, all of which are sacred in character, though their purpose is to express gratitude and joy over the triumph of the German arms.

The opening number is a vigorous, jubilant chorus ("The Lord great Wonders for us hath wrought"). It begins with a slow movement in massive chords, gathering animation as it proceeds, and closing pianissimo on the words, "There is none that searcheth or understandeth." The second number is a soprano solo and chorus ("Praise, O Jerusalem, praise the Lord") declamatory in style. The third ("The Heathen are fallen in the Pit") is assigned to chorus, and is the most dramatic in the work, describing as it does the terrors of war. In the fourth ("See, it is written in the Book of the Righteous"), a short soprano solo, the melody is a tender lament for the dead. The fifth ("He in Tears that soweth") is a soprano solo with chorus of first and second sopranos and altos. In this number lamentation gives way to hope and gladness, leading up to the last three numbers, —

the six-part chorus ("Mighty is our God"), full of effective sustained harmony, and the soprano solos and choruses of praise and hallelujah which resume the triumphant style of the opening chorus with increased power and enthusiasm.

HOFMANN.

HEINRICH KARL JOHANN HOFMANN was born Jan. 13, 1842, at Berlin. In his younger days he was a scholar at the Kullak Conservatory, and studied composition with Grell, Dehn, and Wüerst. Prior to 1873 he devoted himself to private instruction, but since that time he has been engaged exclusively in composition. Among his works which first attracted public attention by their intrinsic excellence as well as by the knowledge of orchestration which they displayed, were an "Hungarian Suite" and the "Frithjof Symphony." Among his piano compositions are the following four-handed pieces, which have been remarkably popular: "Italienische Liebesnovelle," "Liebesfrühling," "Trompeter von Säckingen," "Steppenbilder," and "Aus meinem Tagebuch." His choral works are "Nonnengesang," "Die Schöne Melusine," "Aschenbrödel," and "Cinderella." Among his operas are "Cartouche" (1869), "Armin" (1878), and "Annchen von Tharau" (1878). He has also written several works for mixed chorus and männerchor, piano pieces, songs, duets, a violoncello concerto, piano trios and quartets, and a string sextet.

Melusina.

The beautiful story of Melusina has always had an attraction for artists and musicians. Moritz von Schwind, the painter, has illustrated it in a cycle of frescos; Julius Zellner has told it for us in a series of orchestral tone-pictures; and Mendelssohn has chosen it as the subject of one of his most charming overtures. The version which Hofmann uses in his cantata entitled "The Fable of the Fair Melusina" (written in 1875) runs as follows: Melusina, the nymph of a beautiful fountain in the Bressilian forest, and Count Raymond have fallen in love with each other. They declare their passion in the presence of her nymphs, and plight their troth. Melusina engages to be his dutiful wife the first six days of the week, but makes Raymond promise never to inquire or seek to discover what she does on the seventh, which, she assures him, shall "never see her stray from the path of duty." On that day she must assume her original form, half fish and half woman, and bathe with her nymphs. Raymond promises, calls his hunters, introduces his bride to them, and the wedding cortège moves joyfully on to the castle. In the second part Raymond's mother, Clotilda, and her brother, Sintram, intrigue against Melusina. They denounce her as a witch, and the accusation seems to be justified by a drought which has fallen upon the land since the marriage. The suffering people loudly clamor for the surrender of the " foul witch." After long resistance Raymond is induced to break into the bathing-house which he had erected over the fountain. Melusina and her nymphs, surprised by him, call upon the king of the water-spirits to avenge his treason. The king appears and consigns him to death. Seized with pity, Melusina intercedes for him, and the king agrees to spare his life upon condition that they shall separate. Raymond once more embraces her, neither of them knowing that it will be fatal to him, dies in her arms, and the sorrowing Melusina returns to the flood.

The prologue describes Melusina's fountain, and contains a leading motive which characterizes Raymond. The chorus part is very romantic in its style, and is set to a graceful, poetical accompaniment. The opening number introduces Melusina and her nymphs in a chorus extolling their watery abode ("For the Flood is life-giving"). In the second number she describes the passion she feels when thinking of Raymond. The song is interrupted by horn signals indicating the approach of her lover and his hunters, who join in a fresh, vigorous hunting-song and then disperse. In the fourth number Raymond gives expression to his love for Melusina, followed by a fervid duet between them, in which the lovers interchange vows of constancy. The sixth number, describing their engagement in presence of the nymphs, and concluding with a stirring chorus of nymphs and hunters, closes the first part.

The second part begins with a theme from the love-duet, followed by a significant theme in the minor, ominous of approaching danger. In the eighth number the people clamor in furious chorus for the witch. In the ninth, a trio and chorus, Clotilda warns her son of the misery he has brought upon his house and people, and urges him to discover what his wife does on the seventh day. The next number introduces Melusina and her nymphs in the bath, the former singing a plaintive song ("Love is freighted with Sorrow and Care"). A noise is heard at the gate, and the nymphs join in a chorus in canon form ("Hark! hark! Who has come to watch"). As Raymond appears, the scene grows very dramatic. The king of the water-spirits is summoned; but before he rises from the water Melusina, in very melodious recitative, laments her lover's treason. The scene culminates in the sentence, "Let Death be his lot." He is spared by her intercession, but she is commanded to return to the flood. Raymond appeals for forgiveness, and a part of the love-duet is repeated. The final embrace is fatal to him, and he dies in her arms. The chorus repeats the melody of the opening number ("For the Flood is life-giving"), and she bids her dead lover a last farewell, and disappears with the nymphs and water-spirits, singing, "Forget with the Dwellers on Earth all earthly Woe." The epilogue is substantially the same as the prologue.

LESLIE.

HENRY DAVID LESLIE was born in London, June 18, 1822, and in his sixteenth year began his musical studies with Charles Lucas, a famous violoncellist and for a long time principal of the Royal Academy of Music. Like his master, Leslie played the violoncello several years in the concerts of the Sacred Harmonic Society, subsequently becoming its conductor,— a position which he held until 1861. In 1855 he organized the famous Leslie choir of one hundred voices, which took the first prize at the international competition of 1878 in Paris. In 1863 he was chosen conductor of the Herefordshire Philharmonic Society, and in the following year became principal of the National College of Music. In 1874 he was appointed conductor of the Guild of Amateur Musicians in London. He has been a prolific and very popular composer, among his works being the following: Te Deum and Jubilate in D (1846); symphony in F (1847); anthem, "Let God arise" (1849); overture, "The Templar" (1852); oratorio, "Im-manuel" (1853); operetta, "Romance, or Bold Dick Turpin" (1857); oratorio, "Judith," written for the Birmingham Festival (1858); cantata, "Holyrood" (1860); cantata, "The Daughter of the Isles" (1861); and the opera "Ida" (1864). In addition to these he has written a large number of songs, anthems, part songs, madrigals, and piano pieces, besides music for his choir.

Holyrood.

"Holyrood" was written in 1861, and was first produced in February of that year at St. James's Hall, London. Leslie's collaborator was the accomplished scholar Chorley, who has certainly prepared one of the most refined and attractive librettos ever furnished a composer. The story represents an episode during the period of Queen Mary's innocent life, overshadowed in the close by the dismal prophecy of the terrible fate so rapidly approaching her. The characters are Queen Mary (soprano), Mary Beatoun (Beton), her maid of honor (contralto); Rizzio, the ill-fated minstrel (tenor); and John Knox (bass). The scene is laid in a court of the palace of Holyrood, and introduces a coterie of the court ladies and gentlemen engaged in one of those joyous revels of which Mary was so fond. In the midst of the pleasantry, however, the Queen moves pensively about, overcome with sadness, as if her thoughts were far away. Her favorite maid tries in vain to rouse her from her melancholy with a Scotch ballad. The minstrel Rizzio is then urged to try his skill. He takes his lute and sings an Italian canzonet which has the desired effect. The sensuous music of the South diverts her. She expresses her delight, and seizing his lute sings her new joy in a French romance. It is interrupted by a Puritan psalm of warning heard outside. The revellers seek to drown it; but it grows in power, and only ceases when the leader, John Knox, enters with stern and forbidding countenance. The Queen is angry at first, but bids him welcome provided his mission is a kindly one. He answers with a warning. As he has the gift of prophecy, she orders him to read her future. After the bridal, the murder of the bridegroom; after the murder, battle; after the battle, prison; after the prison, the scaffold, is the tragic fate he foresees. The enraged courtiers call for his arrest and punishment, but the light-hearted Queen bids him go free: —

> "Let him go, and hear our laughter!
> Mirth to-day, whate'er come after."

The cantata opens with a chorus for female voices in three divisions, with a contralto solo, in the Scotch style: —

> "The mavis carols in the shaw,
> The leaves are green on every tree,
> And June, whose car the sunbeams draw,
> Is dropping gold on bank and lea;
> The hind is merry in the mead,
>   The child that gathers gowan flower,
> The Thane upon his prancing steed,
>   The high-born lady in her bower, —
>   Gay, gay, all are gay,
>   On this happy summer day."

After a short recitative passage in which Mary Beatoun appeals to the revellers to lure the Queen from her loneliness, and their reply ("O Lady, never sit alone"), the maid sings a very characteristic and engaging Scotch ballad:—

> "There once was a maiden in Melrose town
>   (Oh! the bright Tweed is bonny to see!)
> Who looked on the best in the country down,
>   Because she had lovers, one, two, three.
> The first was a lord with his chest of gold,
>   The second a ruddy shepherd so tall,
> The third was a spearsman bluff and bold,—
>   But Pride, it goeth before a fall.
>
> "One hour she smilèd, the next she wept
>   (Oh! the bright Tweed is bonny to see!)
> And with frowns and blushes a chain she kept
>   Round the necks of her hapless lovers three.
> For the lord in her lap poured wide his gold,
>   And the shepherd ran at her beck and call,
> And the spearsman swore she was curst and cold,
>   But Pride, it goeth before a fall.
>
> "At last it fell out on a bleak March day
>   (Oh! the bright Tweed is bonny to see!)
> There sate at her window the maiden gay
>   And looked o'er the frost for her lovers three.
> But the lord had to France sailed forth with his gold,
>   And the shepherd had married her playmate small,
> And the spearsman in battle lay stark and cold,—
>   So Pride, it goeth before a fall."

As might have been expected, this mournful ditty fails to rouse the Queen from her melancholy, whereupon Rizzio takes his lute and sings the canzonet "Calla stagion novella," a very slow and graceful movement, closing with a sensuous allegro, written in the genuine Italian style, though rather Verdi-ish for the times of Rizzio. The canzonet has the desired effect, and is followed by a delightful French romance, sung by the Queen, in which a tender minor theme is set off against a fascinating waltz melody, closing with a brilliant finale : —

> "In my pleasant land of France
>   There is gladness everywhere;
> In the very streams a dance,
>   Full of life, yet debonair,
> Ah, me ! ah, me !
>   To have left it was a sin,
> Even for this kind countrie.
>   But we will not mourn to-day,
>   Bid the harp and rebec play,
>   Merrilie, merrilie,
> Sing and smile, and jocund be ;
> If my father's land is dear,
> Mirth and valor still are here ;
> Maidens faithful, champions gay,
> France has melted far away
>   Beyond the sea."

At the close of the pretty romance, the revel begins with a stately minuet and vocal trio ("Fal, lal, la") for the Queen, Mary Beatoun, and Rizzio. It is interrupted by the unison psalm-tune of the Puritans, a stern, severe old melody set to a "moving bass" accompaniment : —

> "O thou who sittest on the throne
>   And wilt exalt thine horn on high,
> While captive men in prison groan,
>   And women poor of hunger die,
> Beware ! albeit a Haman proud,
>   Served by thy slaves on bended knee,
> The heaven can speak in thunder loud
>   And rend to dust both them and thee."

There is a temporary pause in the revels, but at the Queen's command they are resumed with a quickstep introduced by the pipes and full of the genuine Scotch spirit and bustle, the "Fal lal" trio and chorus still accompanying it. It is interrupted afresh by a repetition of the psalm ("A Hand of Fire was on the Wall"), after which John Knox enters. With his entrance the gay music closes and the work assumes a gloomy tragic cast as the dialogue proceeds and the terrible incidents of the prophecy are unfolded. It is a relief when they join in a hopeful duet ("E'en if Earth should wholly fail me") which is very quiet and melodious. It leads to the Queen's farewell, a quaintly-written bit, with an old-fashioned cadenza, followed by the final chorus, which takes up a theme in the same joyous spirit as the opening one: —

> "Hence with evil omen,
> Doleful bird of night,
> Who in tears of women
> Takest chief delight!
> Think not to alarm her,
> As with mystic power;
> Nought shall ever harm her,
> Scotland's lily flower."

LISZT.

FRANZ LISZT, the most eminent pianist of his time, who also obtained world-wide celebrity as a composer and orchestral conductor, was born at Raiding, Hungary, Oct. 22, 1811. His father was an accomplished amateur, and played the piano and violoncello with more than ordinary skill. He was so impressed with the promise of his son that he not only gave him lessons in music, but also devoted himself to his artistic progress with the utmost assiduity. In his ninth year Liszt played for the first time in public at Oedenburg. His performances aroused such enthusiasm that several Hungarian noblemen encouraged him to continue his studies, and guaranteed him sufficient to defray the expenses of six years' tuition. He went to Vienna at once and studied the piano with Czerny, besides taking lessons in composition of Salieri and Randhartinger. It was while in that city that his first composition, a variation on a waltz of Diabelli, appeared. In 1823 he went to Paris, hoping to secure permission to enter the Conservatory; but Cherubini refused it on account of his foreign origin, though Cherubini himself was a foreigner. Nothing daunted, young Liszt continued his studies with Reicha and Paer, and two years afterwards brought out a two-act opera entitled "Don Sancho," which met with a very cordial reception. The slight he received from Cherubini aroused popular sympathy for him. His wonderful playing attracted universal attention and gained him admission into the most brilliant Parisian salons. He was a favorite with every one, especially with the ladies. For two or three years he made artistic tours through France, Switzerland, and England, accompanied by his father, and everywhere met with the most brilliant success. In 1827 the father died, leaving him alone in the world; but good fortune was on his side. During his stay in Paris he had made the friendship of Victor Hugo, George Sand, Lamartine, and other great lights in literature and music, and their influence prepared the way for his permanent success. From 1839 to 1847 he travelled from one city to another, arousing the most extraordinary enthusiasm; his progress was one continued ovation. In 1849 he went to Weimar and accepted the post of conductor at the Court Theatre. He made that city the musical centre of Europe. It was there that his greatest compositions were written, that the school of the music of the future was founded, and that Wagner's operas first gained an unprejudiced hearing; and it is from Weimar that his distinguished pupils, like Von Bülow, Tausig, Bendel, Bronsart, Klindworth, Winterberger, Reubke, and many others date their success. In 1859 he resigned his position and after that time resided at Rome, Pesth, and Weimar, working for the best interest of his beloved art, and encouraging young musicians to reach the highest standards. Few men of this century have had such a powerful influence upon music, or have done so much to elevate and purify it. His most important works were the "Divina Commedia" and "Faust" symphonies, the twelve symphonic poems, the six Hungarian rhapsodies, the "Graner Mass," the "Hungarian Coronation Mass," and the oratorios "Christus" and "The Legend of the Holy Elizabeth." Besides these he wrote a large number of orchestral pieces, songs, and cantatas, and a rich and varied collection of piano-forte solos, transcriptions, and arrangements. He died July 31, 1886.

Prometheus.

Liszt's cantata " Prometheus," composed in 1850, is based upon the poem of the same name, written by Johann Gottfried von Herder, the court preacher of Weimar. The poem closely follows the well-known legend of Prometheus' punishment for stealing fire from heaven, and his ultimate rescue by Hercules from the vulture which preyed upon his vitals. The poet pictures the victim in the midst of his sufferings, consoled by the knowledge that he has been a benefactor to the human race. The spirits of the ocean mock and menace him, but the harvesters and tillers of the soil praise him for the bounteous gifts he has given to the earth. Ceres and Bacchus, protectors of the soil and its products, also pay their tribute of sympathy to him and thank him for the blessing of fire. Hercules at last releases him from his torture by killing the vulture and breaking the chains which bind him to his rock. The sufferer is brought before Themis, who announces that the divine wrath has been appeased by his long punishment, and that the gods forgive him.

In building up his cantata Liszt has introduced several prologues from the poem without music, which serve as narrators explaining the situations, linking and leading up to the musical numbers, which are mainly choral. Thus the opening prologue pictures the sufferings of Prometheus, the crime for which he is forced to endure such a terrible penalty, and the patience, hope, and heroism of the victim. The closing lines, —

> "Now through the hush of night burst well-known voices
> Upon his ear. From out the slumbering ocean,
> Fanning his cheek with breath of the sea waves,
> The daughters of Oceanus approach," —

introduce the opening chorus of sea-nymphs ("Prometheus, Woe to thee"), for female voices, arranged in double parts, and set to a restless, agitated accompaniment, expressive of fear and despair. The second prologue, reciting the wrath of Oceanus " on his swift-winged ocean steed," that mortals should have dared to vex his peaceful waters, and the reply of Prometheus that " on the broad earth each place is free to all," introduces the choruses of Tritons and Oceanides. The first is a mixed chorus full of brightness and spirit ("Freedom! afar from Land upon the open Sea"). Their exultant song is followed by a fascinating melody ("Hail! O Prometheus, hail!") for female chorus, with short but expressive solos for soprano and alto ("When to our Waters the golden Time shall come"), the number closing with double chorus in full rich harmony ("Holy and grand and free is the Gift of Heaven"). Thereupon follows the third prologue: —

> "Scarcely has ceased the Ocean's song of joy,
> Which, breathing peace unto Prometheus' soul,
> Wakens within his breast long-buried hope,
> When once again the sound of lamentation
> Bursts on his ear and fills the air with sighs.
> Seated within a lion-drawn chariot comes
> The founder of his race — Gæa herself —
> With her a train of wood-nymphs, loudly weeping."

It introduces a chorus of Dryads ("Woe to thee, Prometheus") of the same general character as the opening chorus of sea-nymphs, and containing a very dramatic and declamatory alto solo ("Deserted stand God's sacred Altars in the old Forest"). A dialogue follows between Gæa and Prometheus, in which the latter bravely defends his course. As the Dryads disappear, Prometheus soliloquizes: —

> "'This is, in truth, the noblest deed
> Mortal has ever dared. Beat high, my heart!
> On this foundation built I up my race, —
> On deathless friendship and fraternity.
> Courage, Alcides! Bravely fight thy fight.
> Conquer, and thou shalt free me.' From his dreams,
> Roused is the Titan by a song of joy.
> Before him, crowned with the rich harvest, stands
> Ceres with her train of reapers."

A mixed chorus of gleaners follows ("With the Lark sweetly singing"), which can hardly be excelled for grace and loveliness of melody. In the next prologue Ceres consoles Prometheus, and while she is speaking a shout of gladness rises and Bacchus appears. He smites the rock, and at his touch a bower of grape-vines and ivy boughs interlaces over the head of the Titan and shadows him. This serves to introduce the chorus of Vine-dressers ("Hail to the Pleasure-giver"), a lively strain for male voices with an effective solo quartet. As Prometheus resumes his soliloquy, Hermes approaches, leading Pandora, and seeks to allure him from his purpose by her enchantments, but in vain : —

> "The Titan conquers, and he feels the hour —
> The fated hour — draw near. Above his head
> The vulture hovers, fearing to approach;
> While the earth trembles, and the rocks are shaken.
> Voices are heard from out the gloomy depths."

The voices are those of the spirits in the lower regions singing a very melodramatic chorus ("Woe! woe! the sacred Sleep of the Dead has been disturbed"). An *allegro moderato* for orchestra follows, preluding the approach of Hercules, who bends his giant bow and kills the vulture, strikes the fetters off and bids him "Go hence unto thy Mother's Throne." The scene introduces the seventh number ("All human Foresight wanders in deepest Night"), an expressive and stately male chorus with solo quartet. The last prologue describes the scene at the throne of Themis, the pardon of Prometheus, and her assurance that "Henceforth Olympus smiles upon the Earth." Pallas presents him with a veiled figure as the reward of his heroism, "who will bring to thy race the richest blessing, — Truth." The goddess unveils her and declares her name "Agathea. She brings to man the purest, holiest gift, — Charity." The closing chorus of the Muses follows: —

> "Of all bright thoughts that bloom on earth,
> That raise poor mortals high as heaven,
> The holiest, the blessedest is Charity.
> Hail, Prometheus! Hail to mankind!"

The Bells of Strasburg.

"Die Glocken des Strassburger Münsters" ("The Bells of Strasburg Cathedral") was written in 1874, and is dedicated to the poet Longfellow, from whose "Golden Legend" the composer took his theme for musical treatment. The cantata, however, does not deal with the beautiful legend itself as related by the old minnesinger, Hartmann von Aue, which Longfellow has told so powerfully in his "Christus," but simply with the prologue, describing the futile attempt of Lucifer and the Powers of the Air to tear down the cross of the Strasburg Cathedral during the night storm. It was a subject peculiarly attractive to Liszt, as it offered him free scope for his fancies and unlimited opportunity for the display of his unique and sometimes eccentric orchestration. The work is written for barytone solo and mixed chorus, and is divided into two parts, — a short prelude which is entitled "Excelsior" (*andante maestoso*), and in which this word is several times repeated by the chorus with gradually increasing power from piano to fortissimo; and "The Bells," which comprises the principal part of the work.

The second part opens with a massive introduction (*allegro agitato assai*), in which the bells, horns, and trumpets play an important part, leading up to the furious invocation of Lucifer: —

> "Hasten! Hasten!
> O ye spirits!
> From its station drag the ponderous
> Cross of iron that to mock us
> Is uplifted high in air!"

Without a break comes the response of the spirits, first and second sopranos, altos, and tenors ("Oh! we cannot, for around it"), followed by the Latin chant of the bells sung by tenors and basses, with a soft tremolo accompaniment: —

> "Laudo Deum verum!
> Plebem voco!
> Congrego clerum!"

Again with increasing power Lucifer shouts his command: —

> "Lower! Lower!
> Hover downward!
> Seize the loud, vociferous bells, and
> Clashing, clanging to the pavement,
> Hurl them from their windy tower!"

As before, the chorus responds in a sweet harmonious strain ("All thy Thunders here are harmless"), again followed by the slow and sonorous chant of the bells: —

> "Defunctos ploro!
> Pestem fugo!
> Festa decoro!"

Lucifer reiterates his command with constantly increasing energy: —

> "Shake the casements
> Break the painted
> Panes that flame with gold and crimson;
> Scatter them like leaves of autumn,
> Swept away before the blast."

In its response this time the chorus is full of energy and impetuosity as it shouts with great power, "O, we cannot! the Archangel Michael flames from every window." The chant of the bells is now taken by the basses alone: —

> "Funera plango!
> Fulgura frango!
> Sabbato pango!"

Lucifer makes his last appeal with all the strength that voice and orchestra can reach: —

> "Aim your lightnings
> At the oaken
> Massive, iron-studded portals!
> Sack the house of God, and scatter
> Wide the ashes of the dead."

In the choral response ("The Apostles and the Martyrs wrapped in Mantles") the sopranos and altos are in unison, making with the first and second tenors a splendid effect. For the last time the first and second basses sing the chant of the bells: —

> "Excito lentos!
> Dissipo ventos!
> Paco cruentos!"

With no abatement of vigor the baffled Lucifer sounds his signal for retreat, and the voices reply, sopranos and altos in unison: —

> "Onward! onward!
> With the night-wind,
> Over field and farm and forest,
> Lonely homestead, darksome hamlet,
> Blighting all we breathe upon."

As the voices die away, choir, organ, and orchestra join with majestic effect in the intonation of the Gregorian chant: —

> "Nocte surgentes
> Vigilemus omnes!
> Laudemus Deum verum."

The cantata shows Liszt's talent rather than his genius. It is a wonderful mosaic-work of fancies, rather than an original, studied composition with definite purpose. Its motives, while not inspired, are finely conceived, and are presented not only gracefully, but in keeping with the spirituality of the subject.

MACFARREN.

GEORGE ALEXANDER MACFARREN, one of the most prominent of modern English composers, was born in London, March 2, 1813. He began the study of music under the tuition of Charles Lucas in 1827. Two years later he entered the Royal Academy of Music, and in 1834 became one of its professors. The latter year dates the beginning of his career as a composer, his first work having been a symphony in F minor. During the next thirty years his important works were as follows: overture, "Chevy Chace" (1836); "Devil's Opera," produced at the Lyceum (1838); "Emblematical Tribute on the Queen's Marriage" and an arrangement of Purcell's "Dido and Æneas" (1840); editions of "Belshazzar," "Judas Maccabæus," and "Jephthah," for the Handel Society (1843); the opera "Don Quixote" (1846); the opera "Charles II." (1849); serenata, "The Sleeper Awakened," and the cantata "Lenora" (1851); the cantata "May Day," for the Bradford Festival (1856); the cantata "Christmas" (1859); the opera "Robin

Hood" (1860); the masque "Freya's Gift" and opera "Jessy Lea" (1863); and the operas "She Stoops to Conquer," "The Soldier's Legacy," and "Helvellyn" (1864). About the last year his sight, which had been impaired for many years, failed. His blindness, however, did not diminish his activity. He still served as professor in the Royal Academy, and dictated compositions, — indeed some of his best works were composed during this time of affliction. In 1873 appeared his oratorio "St. John the Baptist," which met with an enthusiastic reception at the Bristol Festival of that year. In 1875 he was elected professor of music at Cambridge, to fill the vacancy occasioned by the death of Sterndale Bennett, and in the same year was also appointed principal of the Royal Academy of Music. In 1876 his oratorio "The Resurrection" was performed at the Birmingham Festival, and in 1877 the oratorio "Joseph" at Leeds, besides the cantata "The Lady of the Lake" at Glasgow. Grove catalogues his other compositions as follows: a cathedral service, anthems, chants, psalm-tunes, and introits for the Holy Days and Seasons of the English Church (1866); "Songs in a Cornfield" (1868); "Shakspeare Songs for Four Voices" (1860–64); songs from Lane's "Arabian Nights," and Kingsley's and Tennyson's poems; overtures to "The Merchant of Venice," "Romeo and Juliet," "Hamlet," and "Don Carlos;" symphonies, string quartets, and a quintet; a concerto for violin and orchestra; and sonatas for piano-forte alone, and in combination with other instruments. As lecturer, writer, and critic, Sir George Macfarren also holds a high place, among his important works being "Rudiments of Harmony" (1860); six Lectures on Harmony (1867); analyses of oratorios for the Sacred Harmonic Society (1853-57), and of orchestral works for the Philharmonic Society (1869-71); and a "Musical History," being a reprint of an article on this subject contributed by him to the Encyclopædia Britannica.

Christmas.

"Christmas," the poem by John Oxenford, was written in 1859, and was first performed at one of the concerts of the Musical Society of London, on the 9th of May 1860. The poem itself contains no story. It is merely a tribute to the season; but at the same time it is not destitute of incident, so that it possesses considerable dramatic interest.

After a short instrumental introduction the cantata opens with a double chorus in antiphonal style, in which both the bright and the dark sides of winter are celebrated. The second choir takes up the theme:—

> "The trees lift up their branches bare
>   Against the sky:
> Through the keen and nipping air
>   For spring's return they seem to cry,
> As the winds with solemn tone
> About them sadly moan;"

and the first choir replies : —

> "Old Winter's hand is always free,
>   He scatters diamonds round;
> They dart their light from every tree,
>   They glisten on the ground.
> Then who shall call the branches bare,
> When gems like those are sparkling there?"

The two then join and bring their friendly contest to a close : —

2d Choir. — "Come in, and closely shut the door
  Against the wintry weather;
Of frost and snow we'll think no more,
  While round the fire we sit together."

1st Choir. — "Rush out from every cottage door,
  'T is brave and bracing weather;
A madder throng ne'er met before,
  Than those which now have come together."

This double number, which is very effective, is followed by a soprano recitative and romance ("Welcome, blest Season"), tender and yet joyous in character, which celebrates the delight of friendly reunions at Christmas tide, and the pleasure with which those long absent seek "the old familiar door." In the next number, an old English carol ("A Blessing on this noble House and all who in it dwell"), Christmas is fairly introduced. It is sung first in unison by full chorus, then changes to harmony, in which one choir retains the melody, and closes with a new subject for orchestral treatment, the united choirs singing the carol. Christmas would not be complete without its story; and this we have in the next number for contralto solo and chorus, entitled "A Christmas Tale." It is preceded by recitative, written in the old English style, and each verse closes with a refrain, first sung as a solo, and then repeated in full harmony by the chorus: —

"A bleak and kindless morning had broke on Althenay,
  Where shunning Danish foemen the good King Alfred lay;
'In search of food our hunters departed long ago,
I fear that they have perished, embedded in the snow.'
While thus he sadly muses, an aged man he sees,
With white hair on his forehead like frost upon the trees.
An image of the winter the haggard pilgrim stands,
And breathing forth his sorrows, lifts up his withered hands:
      'The Heavenly King, who reigns on high,
      Bless him who hears the poor man's cry.'

"'Our hearts are moved with pity, thy sufferings we deplore,'
  Said Alfred's queen, the gentle, 'but scanty is our store;
One loaf alone is left us.' 'Then give it,' said the King,
'For He who feeds the ravens, yes, He will fresh abundance bring.'
The wind was roaring loudly, the snow was falling fast,
As from the lofty turret the last, last loaf he cast.
An image of the winter, the haggard pilgrim stands,
And Alfred's welcome pittance he catches with his hands.
      'The Heavenly King, who reigns on high,
      Bless him who hears the poor man's cry.'

"The snow is thickly falling, the winter wind is loud,
  But yonder in the distance appears a joyous crowd.
The hunters bring their booty, the peasants bring their corn,
And cheering songs of triumph along the blast are borne.
Before another morning down-stricken is the foe,
And blood of Danish warriors is red upon the snow.
Amid the conquering Saxons the aged pilgrim stands,
And like a holy prophet exclaims with lifted hands,
      'The Heavenly King, who reigns on high,
      Bless him who hears the poor man's cry.'"

A graceful little duet for female voices ("Little Children, all rejoice"), picturing the delights of childhood and its exemption from care, follows the Saxon story and leads up to the finale, which is choral throughout, and gives all the pleasant details of Christmas cheer, — the feast in the vaulted hall, the baron of beef, the boar with the lemon in his jaw, the pudding, "gem of all the feast," the generous wassail, and the mistletoe bough with its warning to maids. In delightfully picturesque old English music the joyous scene comes to an end: —

> "Varied sports the evening close,
>   Dancers form in busy rows:
>   Hoodwink'd lovers roam about,
>   Hope to find the right one out,
> And when they fail how merry is the shout!
>   Round yon flickering flame of blue
>   Urchins sit, an anxious crew;
>   Dainties rich the bold invite,
> While from the fire the timid shrink with fright.
>   Welcome all, welcome all.
>   'T is merry now in the vaulted hall,
>   The mistletoe is overhead,
>   The holly flaunts its berries red,
>   The wassail-bowl goes gayly round,
>   Our mirth awakes the echoes sound,
>   All eyes are bright, all hearts are gay;
>   Thus ends our Christmas day."

MACKENZIE.

ALEXANDER C. MACKENZIE, one of the very few successful Scotch composers, was born at Edinburgh, in 1847. His father was a musician, and recognizing his son's talent, sent him to Germany at the age of ten. He began his studies with Ulrich Eduard Stein at Schwartzburg-Sondershausen, and four years later entered the ducal orchestra as violinist. He remained there until 1862, when he went to England to study the violin with M. Sainton. In the same year he was elected king's scholar of the Royal Academy of Music. Three years later he returned to Edinburgh and established himself as a piano-teacher. The main work of his life, however, has been composition, and to this he has devoted himself with assiduity and remarkable success. Grove catalogues among his works: "Cervantes," an overture for orchestra; a scherzo, for ditto; overture to a comedy; a string quintet, and many other pieces in MS.; piano-forte quartet in B., op. 11; Trois Morceaux pour Piano, op. 15; two songs, op. 12; besides songs, part-songs, anthems, and pieces for the piano. This catalogue can now be increased by four of the most important works he has produced: a Scotch Rhapsody, introduced into this country by the Theodore Thomas orchestra; the oratorio "Rose of Sharon" (1884); an opera, "The Troubadour" (1885), and the cantata, "The Story of Sayid" (1886), which forms the subject of the subjoined sketch.

The Story of Sayid.

"The Story of Sayid," a dramatic cantata in two parts, the libretto by Joseph Bennett, was first produced at the Leeds Triennial Festival, Oct. 13, 1886. Its story is founded upon that of a poem in Edwin Arnold's "Pearls of the Faith," and embodies a myth which is current among nearly all Oriental nations. The characters are Ilmas, daughter of Sâwa (soprano); Sayid, an Arab chief (tenor); Sâwa, a Hindoo prince (barytone); a watchman (tenor or barytone); and a horseman (barytone). The opening scene pictures the desolation of the land of Sâwa, caused by the invasion of an Arab band, led by their chieftain, Sayid. In the midst of the popular lamentations a messenger announces the defeat of the Arabs and the capture of their leader, who is brought to the city and sentenced to death on the spot. As Sayid prepares to meet his fate, he is recognized by Sâwa as his rescuer at a time when he was hunting in the hills and perishing with thirst. He offers him any boon he may ask except that of life. Sayid entreats that he may be allowed to visit his aged father, promising to return afterwards and suffer his fate. When Sâwa asks who will be hostage for him, his own daughter, Ilmas, offers herself. Moved to pity for the Arab, she persists in her offer, and her father at last reluctantly consents. The second scene opens in Ilmas's palace, and we discover that pity has grown into passion for Sayid during his absence. She is interrupted in her meditations by Sâwa, who enters with his counsellors, and announces that lightnings have flashed from the altars of Siva, and that the gods have demanded that the hostage must suffer in the absence of Sayid. Ilmas bids her attendants array her in bridal robes, and in the next scene appears in an open space near the city gate, surrounded by the court retinue and soldiers, and accompanied by her maidens, strewing flowers in her path. Ilmas is led to the centre of the space and kneels down, the executioner standing over her and awaiting the signal to be given by the watchman when the sun sets. Before that time comes the latter excitedly announces the rapid approach of an Arab horseman. While the crowd stand eagerly waiting his arrival, Sayid gallops through the gateway and presents himself to the Prince. He then turns to Ilmas, who warmly receives him, and affirms that whatever fate may overtake him she shall always cherish his memory. Sâwa relents, bids the Arab live and be his friend, and we infer the happiness of the lovers from the invocation of "Love the Conqueror," which brings the Damon and Pythias story to a close.

A very brief orchestral prelude introduces the opening chorus with solos : —

> "Alas! our land is desolate,
>   The children cry for bread;
> Around, fierce fire and sword devour,
>   Our women wail their dead.
>
> "We pray for vengeance on the foe,
>   To death consign them all;
> Siva, arise and fight for us,
>   Or see thine altars fall."

As the expressive chorus comes to a close, an allegro movement leads to a dialogue between the people and the watchman, and subsequently with the horseman, who announces the approach of the victorious army, followed by a second chorus of the people invoking Siva ("Vishnu, Vishnu, thou hast heard our Cry!"). The scene is very dramatic throughout, and is accompanied by vigorous and suggestive music. The next number is a triumphal march, remarkable for its local color, and gradually increasing in power and effect as the army approaches the city. It is followed by an excited dialogue between Sâwa and Sayid, with choral responses, and leads up to a beautiful melody for Sayid : —

> "Where sets the sun adown the crimson west
>   My native valley lies;
> There by a gentle stream that murmurs rest
>   My father's tents arise.

> "Fearing no harm, the happy peasant tills,
>   The woolly flocks increase;
> The shepherd's pipe is heard upon the hills,
>   And all around is peace."

Another dramatic scene follows, in which Sâwa consents to Sayid's return to his father, and accepts Ilmas as his bondswoman, which leads to a very spirited and elaborate melody for the latter ("First of his Prophet's Warriors he"). The first part closes with the departure of Sayid and a repetition of the choral invocation of Siva.

The second part opens in an apartment of Sâwa's palace, and discloses Ilmas sitting with her maidens, as a thunderstorm dies away in the distance. The latter join in a graceful chorus, which is one of the most beautiful numbers in the cantata: —

> "Sweet the balmy days of spring,
>   And blushing roses that they bring;
>   But sweeter far is love."

Ilmas answers them in a broad and exultant strain ("Ay, sweet indeed is Love"). As the song ends, Sâwa and attendants enter, and the scene closes with a very dramatic chorus and solos, accompanying the preparations for death. The second scene opens with a solemn march for orchestra, preparing the way for the climax, and leading up to a chorus and solo for Ilmas ("What have these Sounds to do with bridal Robes?"). As she kneels, awaiting her fate, an orchestral interlude, set to the rhythm of the gallop, indicates the rapid approach of Sayid. A short and agitated dialogue follows between the watchman and the people. Sayid declares his presence, and a graceful duet with Ilmas ensues ("Noble Maiden, low before thee Sayid bows"), leading to a powerful choral finale ("Never before was known a Deed like this"), closing with a stirring outburst for all the voices: —

> "O Love, thy car triumphal
> Rolls round the subject world
> More glorious than the chariot
> Of the sun.
>
> "We hail thee, Love victorious!
> Ride on with strength divine,
> And quench all mortal passion
> In thine own."

Jubilee Ode.[1]

This work, upon which Dr. Mackenzie has been engaged for some time past, is now complete, and on its way to several distant parts of the Empire, where arrangements are making to perform it in celebration of the Jubilee. Primarily, as our readers know, the Ode was intended for the Crystal Palace only, but it will be given also in Canada, Australia,

---

[1] As the score of Mr. Mackenzie's Ode has not yet reached this country, the author has taken the liberty of transferring the above analysis of it to his work from the London "Musical Times" for May, 1887. Although its local character may preclude its performance here, it is not improbable that the composition of a composer so eminent will attract attention among American musicians.

Trinidad, Cape Colony, etc.; thus standing out from all its fellows as in some sort an Imperial work.

Without anticipating the criticism which will follow upon performance, we may here give some idea of the scope and character of the Ode. Mr. Joseph Bennett, the writer of the words, has kept strictly in view the exigencies of a musical setting. He has obviously prepared, not a short poem for readers, but one for musical hearers. Hence a variety of rhythm and structure which otherwise would certainly not have been ventured upon. From the same cause arises also the manner in which the subject is laid out, with a view to contrast of musical effect. We may indicate the nature of this arrangement. In the first vocal number, a chorus, the news of the Jubilee is proclaimed, and its diffusion throughout the Empire called for. The second number, a tenor solo, conveys to the Queen the affectionate greetings of her home-lands, declaring that, to keep the feast with unanimity, all weapons of party warfare are laid aside. In the third number the Colonies and Dependencies pay their homage, the idea worked out being that of a procession passing before the throne. First comes the Dominion, followed by Australia, the smaller colonies and islands, and, lastly, by India. Each of these divisions has a section of the chorus to itself. The fifth number, a soprano solo, dwells upon the personal virtues of the Sovereign; while the sixth, and last, opening with a choral prayer for the Empire, continues with lines leading to the National Anthem, for which a new second verse has been written. How far the writer has been guided by consideration for musical opportunities need not, after this outline sketch, be indicated. The spirit in which Mr. Bennett has approached his theme best appears, perhaps, in the opening verses: —

> " For fifty years our Queen !
> Victoria ! hail !
> Take up the cry, glad voices,
> And pass the strain
> O'er hill and plain,
> Peaceful hamlet, roaring city, flowing river,
> Till all the land rejoices.
> Wild clanging bells and thund'rous cannon
> With your loudest shock the air, and make it quiver
> From Dee to Tamar, Thames to Shannon.
>
> " For fifty years our Queen!
> Victoria ! hail !
> Take up the cry, old ocean,
> And hoarsely shout
> The words about.
> British ships and world-wide British lands will cheer them,
> Rouse an Empire's full devotion.
> O blowing wind, come hither, bearing
> Answering voices, loud acclaiming. Hark ! we hear them.
> They our loyal pride are sharing."

In setting the words to music, Dr. Mackenzie has necessarily to consider the place of performance and the number of performers. This, however, was an amiable and fortunate obligation, since the result has been to give us a work built upon broad lines, and marked by plainness of structure to an extent unusual with the composer. We think that the music will be found to have a true festive ring, and a majestic solidity befitting the occasion. In the solos, with their more subdued expression, Dr. Mackenzie has kept contrast in view, without sacrifice of simplicity; but it is in the choruses that he best shows himself a master of bold and striking effects. Every bar goes straight to the point, while avoiding the commonplaces that naturally suggest themselves in the writing of festive music. The procession chorus is, in this respect, most noteworthy of all, and may be found no mean rival of that in the "Rose of Sharon."

MASSENET.

JULES ÉMILE FRÉDÉRIC MASSENET, a composer as yet but little known in this country, was born at Montaud, France, May 12, 1842. His musical education was obtained in the Paris Conservatory, in which between the years 1859 and 1863 he carried off two first prizes and one second. After leaving the Conservatory, he went to Italy for a time and pursued his studies in composition. On his return to Paris one of his operas, "La Grand Tante," was produced at the Opéra Comique (1867) through the influence of Ambroise Thomas, and this performance called attention to the works of the rising young musician. In 1872 he brought out "Don Cæsar de Bazan," an opéra comique in three acts, and in the following year incidental music to the tragedy "Les Erinnyes," after Æschylus. Among his works written since that time are "Le Roi de Lahore" (1877); "Herodiade" (1882); "Manon" (1885); "Le Cid" (1885); the cantata "Paix et Liberté" (1867); "Marie Magdaleine" (1873); "Eve," a mystery (1875); "La Vierge," sacred legend; and "Narcisse," antique idylle (1878).

Among his orchestral works the best known are "Suites d'orchestre;" "Scenes Hongroises;" "Scenes Pittoresques;" "Scenes Dramatiques;" overture "Phèdre;" and "Pompeia," fantasia-symphony. He has also written numerous songs and piano-forte pieces. His operas thus far have been his most successful works, though several of his large concert pieces have been very favorably received. He now occupies a position in the Paris Conservatory, and is regarded as one of the most promising members of the modern French school.

Mary Magdalen.

"Mary Magdalen" was written in 1873, and was first performed at the Odéon, Paris, in that year, with Mmes. Viardot and Vidal and MM. Bosquin and Petit in the solo parts. It is styled by its composer a sacred drama, and is divided into three acts, the first entitled "The Magdalen at the Fountain;" the second, "Jesus before the Magdalen;" the third, "Golgotha," "The Magdalen at the Cross," and "The Tomb of Jesus and the Resurrection;" the first two scenes in the last act being included in one tableau, and the third in another. The characters represented are Mary Magdalen, Martha, Jesus, and Judas, the chorus parts being assigned to the Disciples, Pharisees, Scribes, publicans, soldiers, servants, holy women, and people.

After a short introduction, pastoral in character, the work begins with a scene representing Mary at the fountain of Magdala near sunset, among women, publicans, Scribes, and Pharisees, strolling along the banks of the little stream that flows from it. The women sing a short chorus full of Oriental color anticipating the approach of the beautiful Nazarene. A group of young Magdalens pass along singing blithely of love and gay cavaliers ("C'est l'heure où conduisant de longues Caravanes"), and the song of the women blends with it. Next follows a chorus of the Scribes, discussing this Stranger, and pronouncing Him an impostor, and again the young Magdalens take up their strain. The second number is a pathetic aria by Mary ("O mes Sœurs"), which is full of tender beauty. The women shrink back from her and join in a taunting chorus ("La belle Pécheresse oublie"). Next, Judas appears upon the scene, and servilely saluting Mary counsels her to abandon sadness and return to love, in an aria which is a good illustration of irony in music. It is followed by a powerful and mocking chorus of women, Pharisees, and Scribes ("Vainement tu pleures"), in which she is taunted with her shame, despite her sad appeals for pity. The next scene is an aria and trio. Jesus appears in their midst, and in a calm impressive aria ("Vous qui flétrissez les Erreurs des autres") rebukes them. Mary prostrates herself at His feet and implores pardon, and the scene closes with a trio for Jesus, Mary, and Judas, leading up to a strong concerted finale closing the act, in which

Jesus bids the Magdalen rise and return to her home, whither He is about to repair.

The second act opens in the Magdalen's house, which is richly decorated with flowers and redolent with perfume. It begins with a sensuous female chorus ("Le Seuil est paré de Fleurs rares") followed by Martha's admonition to the servants that He who is more powerful than earthly kings cares not for vain shows. The chorus resumes its song, and at its close Judas appears and a long dialogue follows in which Martha rebukes his hypocrisy. As he departs, Mary and Martha in a very graceful duet discourse of the Saviour's coming, which is interrupted by His presence and invocation of blessing. After a duet between Jesus and Mary, in which He commends her to the Good Shepherd, the act closes with a powerful and very dramatic finale containing Jesus' rebuke to Judas and His declaration of the coming betrayal, after which the Disciples join in a simple but very effective prayer ("Notre Père, loué soit Nom radieux").

The third act is divided into two tableaux. In the first we have the scene of the crucifixion, the agitated choruses of the groups about the Cross, the mocking strains of the Pharisees bidding Him descend if He is the Master, the sorrowing song of Mary ("O Bien-aimé sous la sombre Couronne"), and the final tragedy. The second is devoted to the resurrection and apparition, which are treated very dramatically, closing with an exultant Easter hymn ("Christ est vivant, ressuscité").

In the first two acts the music is full of rich Oriental color and is gracefully melodious and well adapted to the situation; but in the last act the awful solemnity of the tragedy is somewhat lost in the theatrical manner of its treatment. Indeed it was hardly necessary that the composer should have disclaimed the title of oratorio which some have assigned to the work. His division of it into acts and tableaux was sufficient to indicate that he had the stage in mind when he was writing; or at least that his scheme was operatic in style.

MENDELSSOHN.

FELIX MENDELSSOHN BARTHOLDY, the son of a Berlin banker, was born at Hamburg, Feb. 3, 1809, and, unlike almost all other composers, was reared in the lap of luxury. He enjoyed every advantage which wealth could procure, with the result that he became highly educated in the other arts as well as in music. His teachers in music were Zelter and Ludwig Berger, and he made such progress that in his ninth year he appeared in public as a pianist in Berlin and afterwards in Paris. The first of his compositions to attract general notice were the overture to Shakspeare's "Midsummer Night's Dream" and the little opera "The Marriage of Camacho," which were brought out in Berlin in 1827. After several concert-tours, in which he met with great success, he resided for some time in Düsseldorf. In 1835 he went to Leipsic as director of the famous Gewandhaus concerts, — which are still given in that city. Two years later he married Cécile Jeanrenaud, the beautiful daughter of a minister of the Reformed Church in Frankfort, and shortly afterwards went to Berlin as general director of church music. In 1843 he returned to his former post in Leipsic, and also took a position in the newly established Conservatory, where he spent the remainder of his days in company with his family, to whom he was closely attached. He has left a large and rich collection of musical works, which are favorites the world over. His three great oratorios are the "Hymn of Praise," catalogued as a symphony-cantata, "St. Paul," and "Elijah." Besides these oratorios, the exquisite music to the "Midsummer Night's Dream," which is familiar the world over, and his stately dramatic music to "Antigone," he has left five symphonies, of which the "Scotch," the "Italian," and the "Reformation" are best known; four beautiful overtures, "Ruy Blas," "Calm Sea and Prosperous Voyage," "Hebrides," and "Melusina;" the very dramatic cantata, "The Walpurgis Night;" a long list of songs for one or more voices; the incidental music to Racine's "Athalia;" a very large collection of sacred music, such as psalms, hymns, anthems, and cantatas; several trios and other specimens of chamber music; and the lovely "Songs without Words," which are to be found upon almost every piano, the beauty and freshness of which time has not impaired. Mendelssohn never wrote a grand opera, owing to his fastidiousness as to a libretto; though he finally obtained one from Geibel on the subject of the "Loreley" which suited him. He had begun to write it, and had finished the finale to the first act, when death interrupted his work, Nov. 4, 1847. In addition to the subjoined compositions selected for description, the following may be mentioned as possessing the cantata characteristics: op. 31, the 115th Psalm, for solo, chorus, and orchestra; op. 46, the 95th Psalm, for chorus and orchestra; op. 51, the 114th Psalm, for double chorus and orchestra; op. 78, three Psalms for solo and chorus; op. 91, the 98th Psalm, for double chorus and orchestra; and op. 96, Hymn ("Lass, O Herr mich") for alto solo, chorus, and orchestra.

The Walpurgis Night.

It was during his Italian travels in 1831 that Mendelssohn composed the music to Goethe's poem "The First Walpurgis Night." His letters throw much and interesting light upon the composition and his ideas while writing it. In a letter written at Rome, Feb. 22, 1831, he says:—

"Listen and wonder! Since I left Vienna I have partly composed Goethe's 'First Walpurgis Night,' but have not yet had courage to write it down. The composition has now assumed a form and become a grand cantata, with full orchestra, and may turn out well. At the opening there are songs of spring, etc., and plenty others of the same kind. Afterwards, when the watchmen with their 'Gabeln, und Zacken, und Eulen,' make a great noise, the fairy frolics begin, and you know that I have a particular foible for them; the sacrificial Druids then appear with their trombones in

C major, when the watchmen come in again in alarm; and here I mean to introduce a light, mysterious, tripping chorus, and lastly to conclude with a grand sacrificial hymn. Do you not think that this might develop into a new style of cantata? I have an instrumental introduction as a matter of course, and the effect of the whole is spirited."

On the 27th of April ensuing he refers to it again: —

"I must however return to my witches, so you must forgive my not writing any more to-day. This whole letter seems to hover in uncertainty, or rather I do so in my 'Walpurgis Night,' whether I am to introduce the big drum or not. 'Zacken, Gabeln, und wilde Klapperstöcke' seem to force me to the big drum, but moderation dissuades me. I certainly am the only person who ever composed for the scene on the Brocken without employing a piccolo-flute, but I can't help regretting the big drum; and before I can receive Fanny's[1] advice, the 'Walpurgis Night' will be finished and packed up."

On his way back to Germany he writes from Milan, July 13, 1831, to the artist and operatic director, Eduard Devrient: —

"I have been writing a large composition that perhaps will one day make some effect, — 'The First Walpurgis Night' of Goethe. I began it simply because it pleased and excited me; I did not think of any performance. But now that it is finished, I see that it is well suited for a large concert piece, and in

---

[1] His sister.

my first subscription concert in Berlin you shall sing the bearded Druid, — the chorus sung by ——, kindly assisted by ——. I have written the part of the Druid into your throstle (by permission), and you will have to sing it out again."

It was several years before the "Walpurgis Night" was publicly performed, and meanwhile it underwent several changes. On the 28th of November, 1842, he writes to his mother: —

" I am really anxious to make the 'Walpurgis Night' into a symphony-cantata, for which it was originally intended, but did not become so from want of courage on my part."

On the 11th of December of the same year he writes her: —

" My 'Walpurgis Night' is to appear once more in the second part, in a somewhat different garb indeed from the former one, which was somewhat too richly endowed with trombones, and rather poor in the vocal parts; but to effect this I have been obliged to rewrite the whole score from A to Z, and to add two new arias, not to mention the rest of the clipping and cutting. If I don't like it now, I solemnly vow to give it up for the rest of my life."

The cantata was first publicly performed in Leipsic, Feb. 2, 1843, at a concert, in which it occupied the second part of the programme. It had to stand a severe test of comparison, for the first part was very brilliant, including a Haydn symphony, a Mozart aria, Beethoven's " Choral Fantasie," the piano part played by Madame Schumann, the overture from "Euryanthe," and the chorus from Weber's "Lyre and Sword;" but it made a success, and was received with great enthusiasm.

The subject of the cantata is a very simple one. The witches of the Northern mythology were supposed to hold their revels on the summit of the Brocken on the eve of the 1st of May (Walpurgis Night), and the details of their wild and infernal "Sabbath" are familiar to every reader of "Faust." In his separate poem Goethe seeks to go back to the origin of the first Walpurgis Night. May-day eve was consecrated to Saint Walpurgis, who converted the Saxons from Druidism to Christianity, and on that night the evil spirits were said to be abroad. Goethe conceived the idea that the Druids on that night betook themselves to the mountains to celebrate their rites without interference from the Christians, accomplishing their purpose by disguising their sentinels as demons, who, when the Christians approached, ran through the woods with torches, clashed their arms, uttered hideous noises, and thus frightened them away, leaving the Druids free to finish their sacrifices.

The cantata begins with an overture in two movements, an *allegro con fuoco* and an *allegro vivace*, which describes in vivid tone-colors the passing of the season from winter to spring. The first number is a tenor solo and chorus of Druids, which are full of spring feeling, rising to religious fervor in the close : —

> "Now May again
>   Breaks winter's chain,
> The buds and bloom are springing;
>   No snow is seen,
>   The vales are green,
> The woodland choirs are singing!
>   Yon mountain height
>   Is wintry white;
> Upon it we will gather, —
>   Begin the ancient holy rite;
> Praise our Almighty Father."

The next number is an alto solo, the warning of an aged woman of the people, which is very dramatic in its style: —

> "Know ye not a deed so daring
> Dooms us all to die despairing?
> Know ye not it is forbidden
> By the edicts of our foemen?"

The warning is followed by a stately exhortation from the Druid priest ("The man who flies our sacrifice"), leading up to a short chorus of a very stirring character in which the Druids resolve to go on with their rites. It is followed by a pianissimo chorus of the guards whispering to each other to "secure the passes round the glen." One of them suggests the demon scheme for frightening the enemy, which leads to the chorus: —

> "Come with torches brightly flashing;
> Rush along with billets clashing;
> Through the night-gloom lead and follow,
> In and out each rocky hollow.
>   Owls and ravens,
> Howl with us and scare the cravens."

In this chorus the composer has given the freest rein to his fancy, and presents the weird scene in a grotesque chaos of musical effects, both vocal and instrumental, which may fairly be called infernal, and yet preserves form and rhythm throughout. It is followed by an exalted and impressive hymn for bass solo and chorus, which is a relief after the diablerie of the preceding number : —

> " Restrained by might
> We now by night
> In secret here adore Thee.
> Still it is day
> Whene'er we pray,
> And humbly bow before Thee.
> Thou canst assuage
> Our foemen's rage
> And shield us from their terrors.
> The flame aspires !
> The smoke retires !
> Thus clear our faith from errors !
> Our customs quelled,
> Our rights withheld,
> Thy light shall shine forever."

Following this impressive hymn comes the terrified warning of the Christian guard (tenor) and the response of his equally terrified comrades : —

> " Help, my comrades ! see a legion
> Yonder comes from Satan's region !
> See yon group of witches gliding
> To and fro in flames advancing ;
> Some on wolves and dragons riding,
> See, ah, see them hither prancing !
> What a clattering troop of evil !
> Let us, let us quickly fly them !

> Imp and devil
> Lead the revel;
> See them caper,
> Wrapt in clouds of lurid vapor."

As the Christians disappear, scared by the demon *ruse*, the Druids once more, led by their priest, resume their rites, closing with another choral hymn of praise similar in style to the first.

Antigone.

Mendelssohn wrote incidental music to four great dramas, — the "Antigone" of Sophocles (1841); the "Œdipus at Colonos" of Sophocles (1843); the "Athalia" of Racine (1843); and the "Midsummer Night's Dream" of Shakspeare (1843), the overture to which was written by him in 1826. The latter is mainly instrumental. Of the other three, the music to "Antigone" and "Œdipus" is most frequently performed, and for that reason has been selected for description.

In June, 1841, the King of Saxony invited Mendelssohn to become his Capellmeister. Frederick William IV. of Prussia had made him a similar offer about the same time. He accepted the latter and removed to Berlin, and the first duty imposed upon him by the King was the composition of music to the "Antigone" of Sophocles. With the assistance of the poet Tieck, who helped arrange the text, the work was accomplished in the short space of eleven days, and was given on the Potsdam

Court stage October 28, to a private audience. It was first performed in public at Leipsic, March 5, 1842. It is written for male chorus and orchestra, and includes seven numbers; namely, 1. Introduction and maestoso ("Strahl des Helios schönstes Licht"); 2. Andante con moto ("Vieles Gewaltige lebt"); 3. Moderato ("Ihr Seligen deren"); 4. Adagio ("O Eros, Allsieger im Kampf"); 5. Recitative and chorus ("Noch toset des Sturmes Gewalt"); 6. Allegro maestoso ("Vielnamiger! Wonn' und Stolz"); 7. Andante alla marcia ("Hier Kommt er ja selbst").

The following extracts will give a comprehensive view of this powerful and felicitous music. Lampadius, writing of the first public performance, says:—

"On the 5th of March the 'Antigone' of Sophocles, translated by Donner and set to music by Mendelssohn, was brought out at the Leipsic theatre before a full audience. The composer directed, and was received with great applause. The music indeed was not antique, if to be so it must be played on the σύριγξ, the σάλπιγξ, and the φόρμιγξ, or if the composer must confine himself to that Greek type of melody and harmony of which all we know is that it was extremely simple, and, according to our ideas, meagre; but it was antique completely, in its being filled with the fire of the tragedy and making its spirit intelligible to us moderns, strengthening the meaning of the words, and giving a running musical commentary on them. . . . With us at Leipsic, as indeed everywhere, the Eros Chorus, with its solemn awe in the presence of the divine omnipotence of love, and the Bacchus Chorus, which, swinging the thyrsus, celebrates the praise of the Theban maiden's son in joyous strains, as well as the melodramatic passages, where Antigone enters, wailing, the chamber where her dead lover lay, and whither Creon has borne in his son's corpse, had an imposing effect. The impression of the whole piece, taken by itself, was very powerful. With amazement our modern world realized the sublimity of the ancient tragic muse, and recognized the 'great, gigantic fate which exalts man while grinding him to powder.'"

Devrient, the director of the opera at Carlsruhe, in his "Recollections of Mendelssohn," has left a delightful sketch of the composition of the work. He says: —

"Felix did not enter upon his task without the fullest consideration. The first suggestion was to set the chorus in unison throughout, and to recitative interspersed with solos; and as nearly as possible to intone or recite the words, with accompaniment of such instruments only as may be supposed in character with the time of Sophocles, — flutes, tubas, and harps, in the absence of lyres. I opposed to this plan that the voice parts would be intolerably monotonous, without the compensatory clearness of the text being attained. . . .

"Nevertheless Felix made the attempt to carry out this view, but after a few days he confessed to me that it was impracticable; that I was right in maintaining the impossibility of making the words clear in choral singing, except in a few places that are obviously suited for recitative;[1] that the chanting of a chorus would

[1] The passages, "But see, the son of Menœtius comes," etc., and "See, Hæmon appears," etc., are examples.

be vexatiously monotonous, tedious, and unmusical; and that accompaniments for so few instruments would give so little scope for variety of expression that it would make the whole appear as a mere puerile imitation of the ancient music, about which, after all, we knew nothing. He concluded therefore that the choruses must be sung, as the parts must be recited, not to assimilate themselves with the usages of Attic tragedy (which might easily lead us into absurdity) but as we would now express ourselves in speech and song. . . . With this I fully concurred; and Felix set, so vigorously to work, that in a few weeks he played me sketches, and by the end of September nearly the whole chain of choruses was completed. Besides my delight at the beauty of these choruses, they confirmed me in the certainty that Felix's genius was eminently dramatic. They not only gave the key to every scene, the expression to each separate verse, from the narrow complacency of the Theban citizens to their heartful and exalted sympathy, but also a dramatic accent soaring far beyond the words of the poet. I allude particularly to the dithyrambus that occurs between Creon's attempt to rescue Antigone and the relation of its terrible failure. This song of praise really consists entirely of glorifying appeals to Bacchus, and its dramatic application lies only in the verse : —

> 'She was its pride,
> Who, clasping the Thunderer, died;
> And now, seeking its lost repose,
> We pray thee to come and heal its woes.
> Oh, hither bend;
> From thy Parnassian heights descend.'

"To raise this chorus to be the terrible turning-point of the action; to bring here to its culmination the tension excited by the awful impending doom; to give this continually gathering power to the invocation, 'Hear us, Bacchus!' till it becomes a cry of agony; to give this exhaustive musical expression to the situation, marks the composer to have a specially dramatic gift. And this is betokened no less in the melodramatic portions. The idea of adding rhythmical accompaniments to spoken words may have been suggested by a few well-set passages in the music to 'Faust' by Prince Radziwill. It is to be regretted that the public is scarcely able to appreciate how exquisitely Mendelssohn has done this, since the representatives of Antigone and of Creon are seldom sufficiently musical to enter completely into the composer's intention; besides that in two passages of the accompanied dialogue of Antigone the words are not correctly set under the music."

Of the private performance before the King and Court, Oct. 28, 1841, the same writer says:—

"We had two more rehearsals on the following day, the evening one in the presence of the King, and the performance itself took place on the 28th, before the Court and all the invited celebrities of art and science. It produced a very great sensation. The deep impression that the revival of an ancient tragedy could produce in our theatrical life promised to become an influence; it has purified our musical atmosphere, and it is certain that to Mendelssohn must be ascribed great and important merit in the cause.

"Although the learned, of whom each expected the ancient tragedy to be put upon the stage according to his peculiar conception of it (which would of course be totally different in every case) might find the music too modern, too operatic, in fact, not sufficiently philological, it is undeniable that Mendelssohn's music has made the tragedy of Sophocles accessible to the sympathies of the general public, without in any wise violating the spirit and aroma of the poem, but rather lending it new life and intelligibility."

Œdipus at Colonos.

The story of "Œdipus Tyrannus" is told in this work in connection with Professor Paine's composition. The "Œdipus at Colonos," to which Mendelssohn set music, is the continuation of Sophocles' tragedy, describing the banishment of the blind hero, the loving care of his daughters, his arrival at Attica, and his death in the gardens of the Eumenides at Colonos, absolved by the fate which had so cruelly pursued him.

The music to "Œdipus" was written at the command of the King of Prussia in 1843, and was first produced at Potsdam, Nov. 1, 1845. It contains a short introduction and nine choral numbers. The first and second choruses describe the entrance of Œdipus and Antigone into the grove of the Eumenides, their discovery by the people, the story of his sorrows which he relates to them, his meeting with his daughter Ismene, and the arrival of Theseus the King. The third number is the gem of the work, and is often given on the concert-stage. The free translation of the text for this beautiful double chorus is as follows: —

"*Strophe.* — Thou hast come, O stranger, to the seats of this land, renowned for the steed; to seats the fairest on earth, the chalky Colonos; where the vocal nightingale, chief abounding, trills her plaintive note in the green dells, tenanting the dark-hued ivy and the leafy grove of the god, untrodden, teeming with fruits, impervious to the sun, and unshaken by the winds of every storm; where Bacchus, the reveller, ever roams attending his divine nurses.

"*Antistrophe.* — And ever day by day the narcissus, with its beauteous clusters, bursts into bloom by heaven's dew, the ancient coronet of the mighty goddesses, and the saffron with golden ray; nor do the sleepless founts of Cephisus that wander through the fields fail, but ever each day it rushes o'er the plains with its limpid wave, fertilizing the bosom of the earth; nor have the choirs of the muses loathed this clime; nor Venus, too, of the golden reign.

"*Strophe.* — And there is a tree, such as I hear not to have ever sprung in the land of Asia, nor in the mighty Doric island of Pelops, a tree unplanted by hand, of spontaneous growth, terror of the hostile spear, which flourishes chiefly in this region, the leaf of the pale gray olive that nourishes our young. This shall neither any one in youth nor in old age, marking for destruction, and having laid it waste with his hand, bring to nought; for the eye that never closes of Morian Jove regards it, and the blue-eyed Minerva.

"*Antistrophe.* — And I have other praise for this mother-city to tell, the noblest gift of the mighty divinity, the highest vaunt, that she is the great of chivalry, renowned for the steed and famous on the main; for thou, O sovereign Neptune, son of Saturn, hast raised her to this glory, having first, in these fields, founded the bit to tame the horse; and the well-rowed boat, dashed forth by the hand, bounds marvellously through the brine, tracking on the hundred-footed daughters of Nereus."

The first strophe is begun by one choir in unison after a short but graceful introduction which is repeated at the end of the strophe in another form, and then the second choir begins the antistrophe, set to the same beautiful melody. At its close the music changes in character and grows vigorous and excited as the first choir sings the second strophe, with which shortly the second choir joins in splendid eight-part harmony. The latter takes up the strain again in the second antistrophe, singing the praise of "the mother-city," and the number closes with the united invocation to Neptune, — an effect which has hardly been excelled in choral music. The fourth chorus, which is very dramatic in its effect, tells of the assault of Creon upon Œdipus, and the fifth, his protection by Theseus, who comes to the rescue. In this number the double choirs unite with magnificent effect in the appeal to the gods ("Dread Power, that fillest Heaven's high Throne") to defend Theseus in the conflict. The sixth number ("When the Health and Strength are gone") is a pathetic description of the blind hero's pitiful condition, and prepares the way for the powerful choruses in which his impending fate is foreshadowed by the thunderbolts of Jove which rend the heavens. The eighth and ninth choruses are full of the mournful spirit of the tragedy itself, and tell in notes as eloquent as Sophocles' lines of the mysterious disappearance of the Theban hero, ingulfed in the opening earth, and the sorrowful lamentations of the daughters for the father whom they had served and loved so devotedly.

As the Hart Pants.

The music to the Forty-second Psalm, familiarly known by the caption which forms the title of this sketch, was first performed at the tenth subscription Gewandhaus concert in Leipsic in 1838, Claar Novello taking the soprano part. Though not constructed upon the large scale of the "Hymn of Praise," or even of the "Walpurgis Night," it is a work which is thoroughly artistic, and just as complete and symmetrical in its way. It contains seven numbers. After a slow and well-sustained introduction, the work begins with a chorus ("As the Hart pants after the Water Brooks, so panteth my soul for Thee, O God") which is a veritable prayer in its tenderness and expression of passionate longing. After the chorus a delicate and refined soprano solo ("For my Soul thirsteth for God") continues the sentiment, first given out in an oboe solo, and then uttered by the voice in a beautifully melodious adagio. The third number is a soprano recitative ("My Tears have been my Meat") leading to a chorus in march time by the sopranos and altos ("For I had gone with the Multitude; I went with them to the House of God"). Then follows a full chorus beginning with male voices in unison ("Why, my Soul, art thou cast down?"), answered by the female voices ("Trust thou in God"). Again the soprano voice is heard in pathetic recitative ("O my God! my Soul is cast down within me; all Thy Waves and thy Billows are gone over me"). A beautiful quartet of male voices with string accompaniment replies: "The Lord will command His Loving-kindness in the Day-time; and in the Night His Song shall be with me, and my Prayer unto the God of my Life." The response is full of hope and consolation; but through it all runs the mournful strain of the soprano (forming a quintet at the end), coming to a close only when the full chorus joins in a repetition of the fourth number ("Trust thou in God"), this time elaborated with still greater effect, and closing with a stately ascription of praise to the God of Israel.

The Gutenberg Fest-Cantata.

The occasion for which the short festival cantata known as the "Gutenberg" was written, was the fourth centennial celebration of the art of printing, which was observed at Leipsic in 1840 by the unveiling of Gutenberg's statue in the public square, and other ceremonies. The direction of the musical part of the festivity was intrusted to Mendelssohn. The text for the hymn to be sung at the unveiling, which occurred on the morning of

June 24, immediately after the public service in Church, was furnished by Adolphus Prölsz, a teacher in the Gymnasium at Freiberg. Lampadius, in his Life of Mendelssohn, says of the performance: —

"Mendelssohn arranged it with trombone accompaniment. When the opening words, 'Fatherland! within thy Confines broke the dawning Light,'— so the opening ran, if my memory is correct, — were heard in the Music Hall at the first rehearsal, the heartiest applause arose among the performers as well as the invited guests. Nothing so simple, powerful, joyous, and unconstrained had been heard for a long time. . . . Many will remember how, on the very day of the public performance, the slight form of Mendelssohn was seen moving nervously around to find just the right place for the trombonists, and how nearly he came to a fall from the platform. During that performance the singers were divided into two choirs, which sat at some distance from each other; one of them was conducted by David, and the other by Mendelssohn."

The cantata opens with a stately chorale ("With solemn Hymn of Praise") set to the old tune "Honor to God alone," followed by the song in memory of Gutenberg ("Fatherland! within thy Confines"), which has been separately arranged and printed as a solo. The third number is a quick, spirited movement for tenors ("And God said, 'Let there be Light'") followed by another effective chorale ("Now, thank God all"), which brings the work to a close. On the afternoon of the same day Mendelssohn's much more important work, "The Hymn of Praise," was given. A sketch of this has already appeared in the "Standard Oratorios."

Lauda Sion.

The "Lauda Sion," or sequence sung at High Mass on the Feast of Corpus Christi, was chosen by Mendelssohn as the subject of one of his most beautiful cantatas, for four solo voices, chorus, and orchestra. The majestic rhythm of Saint Thomas Aquinas's verses loses none of its stateliness in this musical setting. The work was composed for the celebration of this Festival by the Church of St. Martin at Liège, and was first performed there June 11, 1846. Chorley, the English critic who accompanied Mendelssohn on that occasion, has left us in his "Modern German Music" an interesting sketch of its first production. He says:—

"The early summer of 1846 was a great year for the Rhine Land and its adjacent district; since there the Lower Rhenish Festival at Aix-la-Chapelle was conducted by Mendelssohn, and starred by Mlle. Jenny Lind; and within a fortnight afterwards was celebrated at Liège the ' Fête Dieu,' for which his ' Lauda Sion ' was written. . . .

"It was a pity that those who had commissioned such a composer to write such a work had so entirely miscalculated their means of presenting it even respectably. The picturesque old Church of St. Martin is one of those buildings which swallow up all sound, owing to the curve of the vaults and the bulk of the piers; the orchestra was little more powerful, when heard from below, than the distant scraping of a Christmas serenade far down the street; the chorus was toneless, and out of tune; and only one solo singer, the soprano, was even tolerable. On arriving at Liège with the purpose of conducting his work, Mendelssohn gave up the matter in despair. 'No! it is not good, it cannot go well, it will make a bad noise,' was his greeting to us. . . .

"We drove with him that afternoon up to St. Martin's Church, to hear, as he merrily styled it, 'the execution of his music.' The sight of the steep, narrow, winding street, decked out with fir-trees and banners and the escutcheons of the different towns of Belgium, pleased him, for he was as keen a lover of a show as a child, and had a true artist's quick sense of the picturesque. . . .

"Not envy's self could have helped being in pain for its composer, so slack and tuneless and ineffective was the execution of this clear and beautiful work, by a scrannel orchestra, and singers who could hardly be heard, and who evidenced their nationality by resolutely holding back every movement. But in the last verse, *alla breve* —

'Ecce panis angelorum' —

there came a surprise of a different quality. It was scenically accompanied by an unforeseen exposition of the Host, in a gorgeous gilt tabernacle, that slowly turned above the altar, so as to reveal the consecrated elements to the congregation. Incense was swung from censers, and the evening sun, breaking in with a sudden brightness, gave a fairy-like effect to the curling fumes as they rose; while a very musical bell, that timed the movement twice in a bar, added its charm to the rite. I felt a quick grasp on my wrist, as Mendelssohn whispered to me, eagerly, 'Listen! how pretty that is! it makes amends for all their bad playing and singing, — and I shall hear the rest better some other time.' That other time I believe never came for the composer of the 'Lauda Sion,' — since this was only the year before his death."

The work is composed in seven numbers. After a short introduction the voices give out the theme, "Lauda Sion," followed by a chorus, "Laudis Thema," full of devotional spirit. The soprano then enunciates in the "Sit Laus plena" phrases repeated by the chorus, followed by a beautifully accompanied quartet, "In hac Mensa." The fifth number is a solemn chorale in unison, leading to a soprano solo in the arioso style, "Caro cibus," which is exquisitely beautiful. The work concludes with a very dramatic solo and chorus, "Sumit unus," set to the words "Bone pastor," and the closing verses of the hymn itself. Short as the cantata is, it is one of the most felicitous of all Mendelssohn's settings of the ritual.

MOZART.

JOHANN CHRYSOSTOMUS WOLF-GANG AMADEUS MOZART, one of the most remarkable of musical geniuses, and the only one of his contemporaries whose operas still hold the stage with unimpaired freshness, was born at Salsburg, Jan. 27, 1756. 'He was the son of Leopold Mozart, the Salzburgian Vice-Capellmeister, who gave him and his sister Nannerl their earliest instruction in music, and with such good results that the children travelled and gave concerts with great success. Before he was seven years of age he had composed several pieces for piano and violin, his earliest having been written at the age of five. At twelve he became court capellmeister in Salzburg. After his musical travels he went to Vienna, and there began his period of classic activity, which commenced with "Idomeneus," reached its culmination in "Don Giovanni," and closed with the "Requiem," — the "swan-song" of his wonderful career. In his brief life Mozart composed more than fifty great works, besides hundreds of minor ones in every possible form of musical writing. His greatest compositions may be classed in the following order : "Idomeneus" (1780); "Entführung aus dem Serail" (1781); "Figaro's Hochzeit" ("The Marriage of Figaro"), (1785); "Don Giovanni" (1787); "Cosi fan Tutti," "Zauberflöte" ("The Magic Flute"), and "Titus" (1790); and the "Requiem" (1791, the year of his death). The catalogue of Mozart's works is an immense one, for his period of productivity was unusually long. From the age of five to his death there was not a year that was not crowded with his music. Besides his numerous operas, of which only the more famous are given above, he wrote a large number of symphonies (of which the "Jupiter" is now the best known), sonatas, concertos, for all kinds of instruments, even to musical-glasses, trios, quartets, quintets, and sextets for all possible combinations of instruments, marches, fugues, masses, hymns, arias of extraordinary brilliancy, liturgies, cantatas, songs and ballads, and indeed every form of music that is now known. His style was studied by Beethoven, and so closely imitated that the music of his first period, if published without autograph, would readily be attributed to Mozart. His style was so spontaneous and characteristic that it has been well said there is but one Mozart. The distinguishing trait of his music is its rich melodic beauty and its almost ravishing sweetness. His melody pours along in a bright unbroken stream that sometimes even overflows its banks, so abundant is it. It is peculiarly the music of youth and spring-time, exquisite in form, graceful in technique, and delightful in expression. It was the source where all his immediate successors went for their inspiration, though it lacked the maturity, majesty, and emotional depths which were reached by such a Titan as Beethoven. Old as it is, and antiquated in form, especially as compared with the work of the new schools, its perennial freshness, grace, and beauty have made it immortal.

King Thamos.

The historical drama, "Thamos, King of Egypt," was written by Freiherr von Gebler. Otto Jahn, in his Life of Mozart, gives the following sketch of its story: —

"Menes, King of Egypt, has been deposed by a usurper, Rameses, and, as it is thought, assassinated; but he is living, under the name of Sethos, as high priest of the Temple of the Sun, the secret being known only to the priest Hammon and the general Phanes. After the death of Rameses, his son Thamos is heir to the throne. The day arrives when Thamos attains majority, is to be invested with the diadem, and to select a bride. The friends of Menes seek in vain to persuade him to dispute the throne. He will not oppose the noble youth, whom he loves and esteems. But Pheron, a prince and confidant of Thamos, has, in conjunction with Mirza, the chief of the Virgins of the Sun, organized a conspiracy against Thamos, and won over a portion of the army. Tharsis, daughter of Menes, who is believed by all, even her father, to be dead, has been brought up by Mirza under the name of Sais. It is arranged that she shall be proclaimed rightful heir to the throne, and, as she will then have the right to choose her consort, Mirza will secure her beforehand for Pheron. When she discovers that Sais loves Thamos, and he her, she induces Sais to believe that Thamos prefers her playmate Myris, and Sais is generous enough to sacrifice her love and her hopes of the throne to her friend. Equally nobly Thamos rejects all suspicions against Pheron, and awards him supreme command. As the time for action draws near, Pheron discloses to Sethos, whom he takes for a devoted follower of Menes, and consequently for an enemy to Thamos, the secret of Sais' existence and his own plans. Sethos prepares secretly to save Thamos. Sais also, after being pledged to silence by an oath, is initiated into the secret by Mirza and Pheron, and directed to choose Pheron. She declines to give a decided answer, and Pheron announces to Mirza his determination to seize the throne by force in case of extremity. Sais, who believes herself not loved by Thamos, and will not therefore choose him as consort, but will not deprive him of the throne, takes the solemn and irrevocable oath as Virgin of the Sun. Thamos enters, and they discover, to their sorrow, their mutual love. Sethos, entering, enlightens Thamos as to the treachery of Pheron, without disclosing the parentage of Sais. Pheron, disturbed by the report that Menes is still living, comes to take council of Sethos, and adheres to his treacherous design. In solemn assembly Thamos is about to be declared king, when Mirza reveals the fact that Sais is the lost Tharsis, and heiress to the throne. Thamos is the first to offer her his homage. When she is constrained to choose between Thamos and Pheron she declares herself bound by her oath, and announces Thamos as the possessor of the throne. Then Pheron calls his followers to arms, but Sethos steps forward and discloses himself as Menes; whereupon all fall at his feet in joyful emotion. Pheron is disarmed and led off; Mirza stabs herself; Menes, as father and ruler, releases Sais from her oath, unites her with Thamos, and places the pair on the throne. A message arrives that Pheron has been struck with lightning by Divine judgment, and the piece ends."

To this drama Mozart composed the incidental music in 1779 and 1780 at Salzburg, where it was produced under Böhm and Shickaneder's direction. The play did not keep the stage long. Mozart refers to this circumstance in a letter to his father, written Feb. 15, 1783:—

"I regret much not being able to make use of the music for 'Thamos,' for not having pleased here, it is included among the tabooed pieces, no longer to be performed. For the sake of the music alone it might possibly be given again, but it is not likely. It is really a pity."

The music consists of five entr'actes and three choruses constructed in a large and majestic style and specially adapted to ceremonial performance. The first is a responsive chorus of maidens and priests ("Before thy Light, Sun-god, thy Foe the Darkness takes Wing") sung in the temple of the sun at Heliopolis. The second ("Godhead, throned in Power eternal") is also sung in the temple before Thamos' coronation, at the beginning of the fifth act, and contains short snatches of solos for a priest and maiden, leading to a close in full harmony for the voices, and an instrumental finale of soft music during which the priest offers sacrifice upon the altar. The third opens with a majestic bass solo for the high priest ("Ye Children of Dust, come, with Trembling, adore ye") and closes with a stately strain for all the voices ("We Children of Dust in our Reverence tremble").

Although the play was shelved, the music was not lost. Mozart subsequently set the choruses to Latin and German words, and they were adapted as hymns and motets for church use. They are now familiar to musicians as "Splendente te Deus," "Deus tibi Laus et Honor," and "Ne Pulvis et Cinis." Nohl says of them: —

"A certain solemnity pervades them such as few of his sacred works possess, and an elevation of feeling only surpassed in the 'Flauto Magico.' But the composer has relied on theatrical effect; and thus, in spite of his graver intentions, we find more worldly pomp than religious depth in these choruses, which Mozart worked out with all love and care, even in their most minute details, and which manifest the thoughtful mood that absorbed his soul."

Davidde Penitente.

The cantata "Davidde Penitente" was the outcome of a work of love. Before his marriage with Constance Weber, Mozart vowed that when he brought her to Salzburg as his wife he would write a mass for the occasion and have it performed there. In a letter written to his father, Jan. 4, 1783, he says: "As a proof of the fulfilment of this vow, the score of a 'half-mass' is now lying by, in hopes of some day being finished." Holmes, in his admirable Life of Mozart, says: —

"To exercise his pen in the grand contrapuntal style of church music was at all times agreeable to him; and he was now free from the local restrictions under which he had written his numerous masses at Salzburg, where neither the style, the length of the pieces, nor their instrumentation was left to his own discretion; hence, making due allowance for the effect of some few years in developing the composer's genius, the great superiority of 'Davidde Penitente,' by which title this mass was in the sequel better known over all the earlier masses, as well for breadth of style as in true ecclesiastical solemnity."

The "half-mass" which Mozart brought to Salzburg in fulfilment of his vow comprised only the Kyrie, Gloria, Sanctus, and Benedictus. The remaining numbers were supplied from another mass, and in this form the work was produced at St. Peter's Church, Aug. 25, 1783, his wife taking the solo part. The original work is described as exceedingly majestic and beautiful, particularly the " Gratias " for five, and the " Qui Tollis " for eight-voiced chorus. Jahn says of them that the same wonderful and mysterious impression of the supernatural conveyed by the most beautiful numbers in his Requiem characterizes these choruses.

The " half-mass " was destined to undergo still more radical changes. In the spring of 1785 the committee of the society for the relief of the widows and orphans of musicians at Vienna wished to celebrate their annual festival with some new work, and commissioned Mozart to write a cantata. As the time was very short, he took the Kyrie and Gloria of the mass, set Italian words to them, and added four new numbers, in which form it was produced under the title of " Davidde Penitente " at the Burg-theatre, March 13, the solo singers being Fraulein Cavalieri,[1] Fraulein Distler, and Herr Adamberger.[2] The cantata comprises ten numbers. The first number is a chorus (" Alzai le flebile voci ") taken from the " Kyrie " of the mass ; the second, an allegro chorus (" Cantiam le lodi "), from the " Gloria ; " the third, a soprano solo (" Lungi le

[1] Catharina Cavalieri, born in 1761, died June 30, 1801. She was a singer in Italian and German opera in Vienna from 1775 to 1783; but as she never left that city her reputation was purely local. Mozart wrote for her the part of Constanza in his opera " Die Entführung."

[2] Valentin Adamberger was born at Munich, July 6, 1743, and was famed for his splendid tenor voice. Mozart composed for him the part of Belmont in the " Entführing," and highly esteemed him as a friend and adviser. He died Aug. 24, 1804.

cure"), from the "Laudamus;" the fourth, an adagio chorus ("Sii pur sempre") from the "Gratias;" the fifth, a very melodious soprano duet ("Sorgi o Signore"), from the "Domine Deus;" the sixth, a beautiful tenor aria ("A te fra tanti affanni"), written for Adamberger; the seventh, a double chorus ("Se vuoi, puniscimi"); the eighth, a bravura aria for soprano ("Fra le oscure Ombre"), written for Mademoiselle Cavalieri; the ninth, a terzetto ("Tutti le mie speranze"); and the tenth, a final chorus and fugue which, by general consent of the critics of the time, was called the "queen of vocal fugues." Notwithstanding the introduction of specially-written arias, and the brilliant music assigned to the soprano, the cantata is regarded as one of the purest examples of Mozart's church style.

The Masonic Cantatas.

Mozart became a member of the Masonic fraternity shortly after his arrival in Vienna in 1784, and devoted himself to its objects with all the ardor of his nature. In the following year his father visited him and was also persuaded to join, though not without considerable entreaty on the son's part. He was a devoted member of the Church and entertained a deep reverence for its forms. The Church then, as now, was hostile to all secret orders, and was particularly inimical to the

Masons because they had attacked certain alleged abuses in the cloisters. His prejudices were overcome, however, and he soon became as ardent a devotee of Masonry as his son. It formed one of the principal subjects of their correspondence; but unfortunately all these letters were destroyed by the cautious father a short time before his death, which occurred May 28, 1787. In only one letter do we find reference to the subject, and that in a guarded manner. On the 3d of April of that year Mozart heard of his father's illness, and the next day he writes to him: —

"I have this moment heard tidings which distress me exceedingly, and the more so that your last letter led me to suppose you were so well; but I now hear that you are really ill. I need not say how anxiously I shall long for a better report of you to comfort me, and I do hope to receive it, though I am always prone to anticipate the worst. As death (when closely considered) is the true goal of our life, I have made myself so thoroughly acquainted with this good and faithful friend of man, that not only has its image no longer anything alarming to me, but rather something most peaceful and consolatory; and I thank my Heavenly Father that He has vouchsafed to grant me the happiness, *and has given me the opportunity (you understand me), to learn that it is the key to our true felicity.*"

Mozart's membership in the order began at an opportune time for him. Though at the height of his fame he was at the very lowest depth of his finances; and both in 1787 and 1789, though he was Imperial Chamber Musician and his opera "Don Giovanni" was having a successful run, he was obliged to apply repeatedly to his friend and brother Mason, the merchant Puchberg of Vienna, for loans, and also to Herr Hofdämmel, who was about to become a Mason upon Mozart's solicitation. During the short remainder of his life he was devotedly attached to the order, and he was buried in the dress of the brotherhood; but, strange to say, not one of the members accompanied their illustrious associate to the grave.

Four of Mozart's works were directly inspired by Masonry. In 1785 he wrote a simple but beautiful lodge song for voice, with piano accompaniment ("Die ihr einem neuen Grade"). This was followed by the wonderfully beautiful "Freemason's Funeral Music" for orchestra, written upon the occasion of the death of two brothers in the fraternity, of which Jahn says: —

"Mozart has written nothing more beautiful, from its technical treatment and finished effect of sound, its earnest feeling and psychological truth, than this short adagio. It is the utterance of a resolute, manly character, which, in the face of death, pays the rightful tribute to sorrow without being either crushed or stunned by it."

In the same year he composed a small cantata, "Die Maurerfreude," for tenor and chorus, in honor of Herr Born, the master of the lodge to which he belonged in Vienna, which is full of true feeling combined with graceful melody.

The second cantata, catalogued in Köchel "Eine Kleine Freimaurer Cantate, 'Laut verkünde unsre Freude,'" better known by its title "Lob der Freundschaft" ("Praise of Friendship") is notable as the last work written by Mozart. Its date is Nov. 15, 1791, only three weeks before his death. At this time he was engaged in finishing up his "Requiem," which had such a depressing effect upon him that he was ordered by his physician to lay it aside. The rest he thus secured had such a good effect that by the middle of November he was able to attend a Masonic meeting and produce the little cantata which he had just written for them. On reaching home after the performance he said to his wife, "O Stänerl, how madly they have gone on about my cantata! If I did not know that I had written better things, I should have thought this my best composition." It is constructed upon a larger scale than the cantata of 1785, and is very pleasing and popular, but lacks the spirit and earnestness of the förmer. It has six numbers: 1. Chorus, "Laut verkünde unsre Freude;" 2. Recitative, "Zum ersten Male;" 3. Tenor aria, "Dieser Gottheit Allmacht;" 4. Recitative, "Wohlan, ihr Brüder;" 5. Duet, "Lange sallen diese Mauern"; 6. Chorus, "Lasst uns mit geschlungen Händen." It was Mozart's swan-song. Two days after its performance he was stricken down with his last illness.

PAINE.

JOHN K. PAINE, one of the very few really eminent American composers, was born at Portland, Me., Jan. 9, 1839. He studied the piano, organ, and composition with Kotzschmar in that city, and made his first public appearance as an organist, June 25, 1857. During the following year he went to Germany, and studied the organ, composition, and instrumentation with Haupt and other masters in Berlin. He returned to this country in 1861, and gave several concerts, in which he played many of the organ works of the best writers for the first time in the United States. Shortly after his return he was appointed instructor of music in Harvard University, and in 1876 was honored with the elevation to a professorship and given a regular chair. He is best known as a composer, and several of his works have been paid the rare compliment of performance in Germany, among them his Mass in D and all his symphonies. The former was given at the Berlin Singakademie in 1867, under his own direction. Among his principal compositions are the oratorio "St. Peter," the music to "Œdipus," the cantatas,

"Nativity," "The Realm of Fancy," and "Phœbus, Arise;" the Mass in D; the Centennial Hymn, set to Whittier's poem, and sung at the opening of the Philadelphia Centennial Exhibition; the overture to "As You Like It;" "The Tempest," in the style of a symphonic poem; the symphony in C minor, and "Spring" symphony; besides numerous sonatas, fantasias, preludes, songs, and arrangements for organ and piano. His larger orchestral works have been made familiar to American audiences by Mr. Theodore Thomas's band, and have invariably met with success. His style of composition is large, broad, and dignified, based upon the best classic models, and evinces a high degree of musical scholarship.

Œdipus Tyrannus.

The first public performance of the "Œdipus Tyrannus" of Sophocles in this country was given at the Sanders Theatre (Harvard College), Cambridge, Mass., May 17, 1881, for which occasion Mr. Paine composed the music incidental to the world-famous tragedy. The performance was a memorable one in many ways. The tragedy was given in the original language. It was the first event of the kind in America. The audience was a representative one in culture, education, and social brilliancy. The programme was also unique, being printed in Greek, and translated into English was as follows: —

TO ALL THE SPECTATORS GREETING.

[The college seal.]

Six verses from the Eumenides of Æschylus:

" Hail people of the city
That sit near to Zeus,
Friends of the friendly goddess,
Wise in your generation,
Ye whom under the wings of Pallas
The father guards."

THE ŒDIPUS TYRANNUS OF SOPHOCLES

WILL BE REPRESENTED IN THE THEATRE OF HARVARD UNIVERSITY

on the 17th of May (Θαργηλιών), 1881, and again on the 19th, 20th, and 21st.

DRAMATIS PERSONÆ.

Œdipus, King of Thebes . . . . GEORGE RIDDLE.
Priest of Zeus . . . . WILLIAM HOBBS MANNING.
Creon, Jocasta's brother . . . . HENRY NORMAN.
Teiresias, the blind seer . . . . CURTIS GUILD.
Jocasta, Queen of Thebes . LEONARD ECKSTEIN OPDYCKE.
Messenger, from Corinth . ARTHUR WELLINGTON ROBERTS.
Servant of Laius . . . . . . GARDINER MARTIN LANE.
Messenger from the Palace . . . . OWEN WISTER.

ATTENDANTS.

Attendants on Œdipus . . J. R. COOLIDGE, E. J. WENDELL.
Attendants on Jocasta . J. J. GREENOUGH, W. L. PUTNAM.
Attendants on Creon . . . . G. P. KEITH, J. LEE.
Boy guide of Teiresias . . . . C. H. GOODWIN.
Antigone . . . . E. MANNING.
Ismene . . . . .J. K. WHITTEMORE.
Suppliants. — G. P. KEITH, G. D. MARKHAM (priests), W. H. HERRICK, J. LEE, E. LOVERING, H. PUTNAM, L. A. SHAW, C. M. WALSH (chosen youths), C. H. GOODWIN, E. MANNING, R. MANNING, W. MERRILL, E. R. THAYER, J. K. WHITTEMORE (boys).

CHORUS OF THEBAN OLD MEN.

Coryphæus . . . . LOUIS BUTLER MCCAGG.
Assistant to the chorus in the third
    stasmon, with solo . . . . . GEORGE LAURIE OSGOOD.

MEMBERS OF THE CHORUS.

N. M. BRIGHAM,	MORRIS EARLE,
FREDERICK R. BURTON,	PERCIVAL J. EATON,
HENRY G. CHAPIN,	GUSTAVUS TUCKERMAN,
SUMNER COOLIDGE,	CHARLES S. HAMLIN,
EDWARD P. MASON,	JARED S. HOW,
MARSHALL H. CUSHING,	HOWARD LILIENTHAL,
WENDELL P. DAVIS,	CHARLES F. MASON.

Leader of the chorus and composer
    of the music . . . . JOHN KNOWLES PAINE.
Prompter . . . . GEORGE L. KITTREDGE.

The scene is laid in front of the palace in Boetian Thebes. The chorus is composed of Theban old men. Œdipus speaks first. The managers request all the spectators to remain sitting until the postlude is ended. Immediately after the last chorus has been sung there will be a pause for those who wish to go out. After this the doors will be closed.

After the play, horse-cars (ἄμαξαι ἱπποσιδηροδρομικαί) will be ready for those who want to go to the city.

Wilsons, printers. (Οὐιλσῶνες τύποις ἔγαψαν.)

The story of the Theban hero, his ignorance of his own parentage, his dismay at the revelation of the oracle that he would kill his father and marry his mother, his quarrel with the former, resulting in the very tragedy he was seeking to avoid, his solution of the riddle of the sphinx, the reward of the Queen's hand which Creon had promised, leading to the unfortunate marriage with his mother, Jocasta, thus completing the revelation of the oracle, does not need description in detail. The marriage was followed by a pestilence that wasted Thebes, and at this point the plot of the drama begins. It concerns itself with the efforts of Œdipus to unravel the mystery of the death of his father, Laius, which lead to the discovery that he himself was the murderer, and that he had been guilty of incest with his own mother. Jocasta hangs herself, and Œdipus, rushing frantically into the palace, beholds her, and overwhelmed with horror at the sight and the fulfilment of the oracle, seizes her brooch-pin and blinds himself. In the Œdipus at Colonos the sequel is told. The hero dies in the gardens of the Eumenides, happy in the love of his daughters and the pardon which fate grants him.

The music to the tragedy is thoroughly classical in spirit, and has all the nobility, breadth, dignity, and grace characteristic of the Greek idea. The principal lyric movements of the chorus, the choral odes, of which there are six, comprise the scheme of the composer. The melodramatic practice of the orchestra accompanying spoken dialogue only appears to a limited extent in the third ode; and the chorus, as narrator, is accompanied by music only in the seven last lines of the play, which form the postlude. The orchestral introduction, which is treated in a very skilful and scholarly manner, epitomizes the spirit of the work. The odes are divided as usual into strophes and antistrophes, assigned alternately to a male chorus of fifteen and full chorus. The first ("Oracle sweet-tongued of Zeus"), which has the genuine antique dignity and elevation, is a description of the sufferings of the people from the pestilence which has wasted Thebes since the unnatural marriage of Œdipus and Jocasta, and a fervent prayer to the gods for aid. The second ("Thou Delphic Rock, who can he be?") concludes the scene where the blind prophet Teiresias arrives upon the summons of Creon and accuses Œdipus of the crime, accompanying the accusation with dark hints of further guilt. In this ode, which is specially noticeable for its rich and graceful treatment, the chorus expresses its disbelief of the charges. In the third scene, Creon enters to protest against the accusations of Œdipus, but a quarrel ensues between them, which results in the menace of death to the former. Jocasta appears, and upon her intercession Creon is allowed to depart. In the ode, the chorus joins in this appeal to Œdipus, — a strong, vigorous number, the effect of which is heightened by the intervening spoken parts of Creon, Œdipus, and Jocasta, with musical accompaniment. The fourth ode ("O may my Life be spent in Virtue") is a vigorous denunciation of the impiety of Jocasta in speaking scornfully of the oracles. The fifth ode ("If I the Prophet's Gift possess") is full of idyllic grace and sweetness, realizing in a remarkable degree the old Grecian idea of sensuous beauty. It is a speculation upon the divine origin of Œdipus, after the messenger relates the story of the King's exposure in his childhood upon Mount Cithæron, and contains a charming tenor solo. The last ode ("O Race of mortal

Men ") bewails the vicissitudes of fortune, and is full of the tragic significance of impending fate. The work comes to a close with the postlude : —

" Ye who dwell in Thebes our city, fix on Œdipus your eyes,
Who resolved the dark enigma, noblest liver and most wise.
Glorious like a sun he mounted, envied of the popular throng,
Now he sinks in seas of anguish, quenched the stormy waves among.
Therefore I await the final hour, to ancient wisdom known,
Ere I 'call one mortal happy. Never shall that thought be shown,
Till he end his earthly being, scathless of a sigh or groan."

Six public performances of the " Œdipus " were given in 1881, and every season since that time selections from the music have been performed in New York, Boston, and other cities. As the most important and scholarly work an American composer has yet produced, it cannot be heard too often.

The Nativity.

The text of "The Nativity," for chorus, solo voices, and orchestra, is taken from the hymn in Milton's ode " On the Morning of Christ's Nativity," and is composed in three parts. The first part includes the first, third, fourth, fifth, sixth, and seventh ; the second, a combination of the eighth and ninth ; and the third, the thirteenth, fourteenth, and fifteenth verses. After a short instrumental introduction, which works up to an effective climax, the cantata begins with a chorus ("It was the Winter wild "), introduced by the soprano, developing to full harmony at the words, "Nature in Awe to Him," and closing pianissimo. After a short soprano solo ("But He her Fears to cease") the chorus resumes ("With Turtle Wing the amorous Clouds dividing"). A succession of choral passages follows, admirably suggestive of the sentiment of the poem, — a vigorous, stirring allegro, "No War or Battle's Sound was heard the World around;" "And Kings sat still with awful Eye," broadly and forcibly written; and a tender, graceful number, "But peaceful was the Night." They are followed by another soprano solo ("And though the shady Gloom"), full of brightness and animation, which leads directly to a majestic chorus ("He saw a greater Sun appear"), which closes the first part.

The second part, a quartet and chorus, is pastoral in character, and reflects the idyllic quiet and beauty of the text. The quartet, "The Shepherds on the Lawn," is introduced by short tenor, bass, and alto solos, and also contains a very melodious and graceful solo for soprano ("When such Music sweet their Hearts and Ears did greet"), after which the full quartet leads up to a vigorous chorus ("The Air such Pleasure loath to lose"), closing the part.

The third part is choral, and forms an effective climax to the work. It opens with the powerful chorus, "Ring out, ye crystal Spheres," emphasized by the organ bass with stately effect, and moves on majestically to the close, —

> "And Heaven as at some festival
> Will open wide the gates of her high palace hall."

The Realm of Fancy.

"The Realm of Fancy" is a short cantata, the music set to Keats's familiar poem: —

> "Ever let the fancy roam,
> Pleasure never is at home:
> At a touch sweet pleasure melteth,
> Like to bubbles when rain pelteth."

With the exception of a dozen lines, the dainty poem is used entire, and is set to music with a keen appreciation of its graceful beauty. A short allegretto fancifully trips along to the opening chorus ("Ever let the Fancy roam"), which is admirable for its shifting play of musical color. A soprano solo ("She will bring in spite of Frost"), followed by a very expressive barytone solo ("Thou shalt at a Glance behold the Daisy and the Marigold"), leads up to a charming little chorus ("Shaded Hyacinth, always Sapphire Queen"). A short instrumental passage, in the time of the opening allegretto, introduces the final chorus ("O Sweet Fancy, let her loose"), charmingly worked up, and closing in canon form. The cantata is very short; but rarely have poem and music been more happily wedded than in this delightful tribute to fancy.

Phoebus, Arise.

Mr. Paine's ripe scholarship is shown to admirable advantage in his selection of the poem " Phœbus, Arise " from among the lyrics of the old Scottish poet, William Drummond, of Hawthornden, and the characteristic old-style setting he has given to it. Like " The Realm of Fancy," it is very short; but like that cantata, also, it illustrates the versatility of his talent and the happy manner in which he preserves the characteristics of the poem in his music. Drummond, who has been called " the Scottish Petrarch," and whose poems were so celebrated that even Ben Jonson could find it in his way to visit him, was noted for the grace and lightness of his verse, and the pensive cast with which it was tinged. It has little of the modern poetic style, and the composer has clothed his poem in a musical garb to correspond.

The cantata is written for tenor solo, male chorus, and orchestra, and opens with a brilliant chorus (" Phœbus, arise, and paint the sable Skies with azure, white, and red "), closing with a crescendo in the old style. An expressive and somewhat pensive tenor solo follows : —

> " This is that happy morn
> And day, long-wishèd day,
> Of all my life so dark
> (If cruel stars have not my ruin sworn
> And fates my hope betray),
> Which purely white deserves
> An everlasting diamond should it mark.
> This is the morn should bring unto the grove
> My love, to hear, and recompense my love."

A short choral passage with tenor solo ("Fair King, who all preserves") leads to a full rich chorus ("Now, Flora, deck thyself in fairest Guise"). In the next number the chorus returns to the opening theme ("Phœbus, Arise"), and develops it with constantly increasing power to the close.

PARKER.

HORATIO W. PARKER, a young American composer of more than ordinary promise, was born at Auburndale, Mass., Sept. 15, 1863. After his fifteenth year he began the study of music, taking his earlier lessons of the three Boston teachers, Stephen A. Emery, John Orth, and G. W. Chadwick. In 1882 he went to Munich and studied the organ and composition with Josef Rheinberger, for three years. In the spring of 1885 he wrote the cantata "King Trojan," and it was produced for the first time in that city with success during the summer of the same year. Since then it has been given in this country by Mr. Jules Jordan, of Providence, R. I., Feb. 8, 1887. His string quartet in F major was played at a concert of the Buffalo Philharmonic Society in January, 1886; and a short scherzo was performed by the Van der Stücken orchestra in New York City in the same year. Besides these compositions, he has written three overtures, quite a number of songs and pieces for the piano-forte, and a symphony in C, and ballade for chorus and orchestra, both of which were played in Munich last year. In 1886 he accepted the professorship of music at the Cathedral School of St. Paul, Garden City, L. I., and in February, 1887, went to New York, where he now resides, to take charge of a boy choir in St. Andrew's Church, Harlem.

King Trojan.

"King Trojan," composed for chorus, solos, and orchestra, was written in March, 1885, and first performed in July of the same year, at Munich. Its story is the poem of the same name, by Franz Alfred Muth, the English version being a free and excellent translation by the composer's mother, Mrs. Isabella G. Parker, of Auburndale, Mass.

After a short and graceful introduction, the cantata opens with a solo describing the quiet beauty of a summer night, daintily accompanied by wind instruments and harp. A second voice replies ("O Summer Night"), and then the two join in a very vigorous duet ("O fill thou Even with Light of Heaven"). A short solo for third voice leads up to a chorus which gives us a picture of King Trojan's castle gleaming in the moonlight. It is followed by a very effective solo for the King ("The Horse is neighing, O Page of mine"), in which he bids his Page saddle his steed for a night ride to visit his distant love. The chorus intervenes with a reflective number ("What thinks she now?"), which is very dramatic in style, describing the mutual longing of the lovers to be together.

The second scene opens with a short solo by the Page ("Up, up, O King, the Horses wait"), followed by the chorus as narrator, describing the ride of the King and his companion through the greenwood, with which is interwoven Trojan's solo ("How sweet and cool is yet the Night"). In the next number, a vivacious allegro, the story of the ride is continued by the chorus, with a characteristic accompaniment, and again Trojan sings a charming tribute to the summer night, which is followed by responsive solos of the King and the Page, in the allegro and penseroso style, — the one singing of the raptures of night, the other of the gladness of day and sunlight. A passionate bit of recitative ("Now swift, ye Horses") by Trojan reveals the secret of the King's haste. He is King of the night, and the morning ray will be fatal to him. A short choral number ("And forward fly they") brings the first part to a close with the arrival of the riders at the Queen's castle.

The second part opens with a beautiful solo, quartet, and chorus ("Good-Night, the Lindens whisper"), which describes the meeting of the lovers, while

> "Beneath the lofty castle gate
> Slumbers the page who so long must wait.
> Then crows the cock, the hour is late."

At this note of warning the Page appeals to his master to fly, for the sunlight will bring him pain and harm. The dallying King replies, "Hark! how the Nightingale yet sings." A small chorus intervenes with the warning, "Love is so fleeting, Night is so fair." The Queen appeals to him, "What seest thou, O King?" To which Trojan replies with agitation, "The ruddy Morning, it is my Death." Again comes the Page's warning. The King springs up in alarm and hastens to his steed. In a choral presto movement the ride back is described. The King conceals himself in a dark thicket, hoping to escape, but the night has vanished and the day has begun. Its beams penetrate his refuge, and with a last despairing cry ("Accursed Light, I feel thee now") he expires. A short choral passage, with harp accompaniment, brings this very dramatic and fanciful composition to a close: —

> "And from his horse the king now falls,
> He was but king of the night;
> The sunlight sparkles, the sunlight shines,
> But death comes with morning light."

PARKER.

AMES C. D. PARKER, an American composer, was born at Boston, Mass., June 2, 1828. He received his primary education in the schools of that city, was graduated from Harvard University in 1848, and immediately thereafter began the study of law. His love for music, however, was irresistible, and he soon dropped law-books and entered upon a thorough course of musical instruction, at first in Boston, and afterwards at the Conservatory in Leipsic, where he finished the regular course. He returned to Boston in 1854, and at once devoted himself to musical work in which he took a prominent part, and made an excellent reputation as pianist, organist, and teacher, as well as composer, though he has not as yet attempted any very large or ambitious works. In 1862 he organized an amateur vocal association under the name of the Parker Club, which has performed several works by Gade, Mendelssohn, Berlioz, Schumann, and others, with success. His most important composition is the "Redemption Hymn," which he wrote for the Boston Handel and Haydn Society during the period he was its organist. He has also held the position of organist and choir-director of Trinity Church in that city, and of Professor of the College of Music connected with the Boston University. During his unostentatious career he has earned an enviable reputation as an earnest, honest musician deeply devoted to his art.

The Redemption Hymn.

"The Redemption Hymn," for alto solo and chorus, was written for the Fourth Triennial Festival of the Handel and Haydn Society, and was first given on that occasion, May 17, 1877, Anna Louise Cary-Raymond taking the solo. The words are taken from Isaiah li. 9–11.

CHORUS:— "Awake, put on strength, O arm of the Lord!
"Awake as in the ancient days, in the generations of old.
"Art thou not it that hath cut Rahab and wounded the dragon?
   Awake, put on strength, O arm of the Lord!
SOLO AND CHORUS:— "Art thou not it that hath dried the sea, the waters of the great deep, that hath made the depths of the sea a way for the ransomed to pass over? Therefore the redeemed of the Lord shall return and come with singing unto Zion, and everlasting joy shall be upon their head; they shall obtain gladness and joy, and sorrow and mourning shall flee away."

The work opens with a brief but spirited orchestral introduction, which leads to an exultant chorus ("Awake, O Arm of the Lord"), changing to a well-written fugue in the middle part ("Art thou not it?"), and returning to the first theme in the close. The next number is an effective alto solo ("Art thou not it which hath dried the Sea?") alternating with chorus. It is followed by a slow movement for alto solo and chorus ("Therefore the Redeemed of the Lord shall return"), which closes very gracefully and tenderly on the words, "Sorrow and Mourning shall flee away." This little work has become a favorite with singing societies, by the scholarly and effective manner in which it is written.

RANDEGGER.

ALBERTO RANDEGGER was born at Trieste, April 13, 1832, and began the study of music at an early age with Lafont and Ricci. In his twentieth year he had written numerous minor pieces of church music, several masses and two ballets which were produced with success in his native city. From 1852 to 1854 he was engaged as a conductor in the theatres of Fiume, Zera, Brescia, and Venice. In the latter year he brought out a grand opera in Brescia, called "Bianca Capello," shortly after which he went to London, where he has since resided and made a world-wide reputation as a teacher. In 1857 he conducted Italian opera at St. James's Theatre; in 1864 brought out a comic opera, "The Rival Beauties," at the Theatre Royal, Leeds; in 1868 was appointed Professor of Singing at the Royal Academy of Music, in which he has since become a director; in 1879-80 was conductor for the Carl Rosa English Opera Company at Her Majesty's Theatre, London; and has since been appointed conductor of the Norwich Festival in the place of Benedict. His principal works, besides those already mentioned, are : "Medea," a scena, sung by Madame Rudersdorff at the Gewandhaus, Leipsic (1869) ; the One hundred and fiftieth Psalm, for soprano solo, chorus, orchestra, and organ (1872) ; cantata, "Fridolin" (1873) ; soprano scena, "Saffo" (1875) ; funeral anthem for the death of the Prince Consort ; and a large number of songs which are great favorites on the concert-stage.

Fridolin.

"Fridolin, or the Message to the Forge" was written for the Birmingham Triennial Musical Festival of 1873. The words, by Mme. Erminia Rudersdorff, are founded on Schiller's ballad, " Der Gang nach dem Eisenhammer." The *dramatis personæ* are Waldemar, Count of Saverne ; Eglantine, Countess of Saverne ; Fridolin, page to the Countess ; and Hubert, squire to the Count. The story closely follows that of Schiller. The preface to the piano score gives its details as follows : —

"Fridolin and Hubert are in the service of the Count of Saverne. Hubert, aspiring to win the affections of his beautiful mistress, conceives a violent hatred of Fridolin, whom he regards as an obstacle in his path. Taking advantage of Fridolin's loyal devotion to the Countess, Hubert excites the jealousy of the Count, and prompts a stern revenge. The Count forthwith writes to some mechanic serfs, ordering that whoever comes asking a certain question shall be at once thrown into their furnace. Fridolin, innocent of wrong and unconscious of danger, receives the 'message to the forge;' but, ere setting out, he waits upon his mistress for such commands as she might have to give. The Countess desires him to enter the chapel he would pass on his way and offer up a prayer for her. Fridolin obeys, and thus saves his own life; but vengeance overtakes the traitor Hubert, who, going to the forge to learn whether the plot has succeeded, himself asks the fatal question, 'Is obeyed your lord's command?' and himself becomes the victim. Fridolin subsequently appears, and is about to perish likewise, when the Count and Countess, between whom explanations have taken place, arrive on the scene, to preserve the innocent and to learn the fate of the guilty."

The cantata opens with a short but stirring prelude, introducing the declamatory prologue-chorus:—

> "A pious youth was Fridolin,
>   Who served the Lord with zeal,
> And did his duty faithfully,
>   Come thereby woe or weal.
> For this when subtle foe conspired
>   And sought o'er him to boast,
> About his path in direst need
>   Kept guard the angel host."

The cantata proper opens with a recitative by Fridolin ("Arising from the Lap of star-clad Night"), leading up to the quiet, dreamy air, "None but holy, lofty Thoughts." It is followed by a bass scena for Hubert ("Proceed thou, hateful Minion, on thy Path") which opens in an agitated manner, but grows more reposeful and tender in style as the subject changes in the passage, " For one kind Glance from out those Eyes divine." Again the scena changes and becomes vigorous in the recitative, " Dispelled by jealous Rage is Hope's fond Dream," set to an imposing accompaniment, and leading to a brilliant fiery allegro (" A thousand hideous Deaths I 'd make him die "). The next number is a very graphic and spirited hunting-chorus (" Hark ! the Morn awakes the Horn "), introduced and accompanied by the horns, and full of breezy, out-door feeling. A long dialogue follows between Hubert and the Count, somewhat gloomy in character, in which the former arouses his master's jealous suspicions. The gloom still further deepens as Hubert suggests the manner of Fridolin's death (" Mid yon gloomy Mountains "). Then follows the message to the forge by the Count in monotone phrases (" Mark, ye Serfs, your Lord's Commands ") and the scene closes with a very dramatic duet (" Death and Destruction fall upon his Head "). In striking contrast with these stormy numbers comes the charming, graceful chorus of the handmaidens (" Calmly flow the equal Hours "), followed by a very expressive song for the Countess (" No Bliss can be so great "). A short scene in recitative leads up to a tender duet (" Above yon Sun, the Stars above ") for Fridolin and the Countess, closing with a powerful quartet for the four principal parts (" Now know I, Hubert, thou speakest true ").

The ninth scene is admirably constructed. It opens with an animated and picturesque dance and chorus of villagers ("Song is resounding, Dancers are bounding"), which swings along in graceful rhythm until it is interrupted by a solemn phrase for organ, introduced by horns, which prepares the way for a chorale ("Guardian Angels sweet and fair"), closing with Fridolin's prayer at the shrine, interwoven with a beautiful sacred chorus ("Sancta Maria, enthroned above"). In a recitative and ballad ("The wildest Conflicts rage within my fevered Soul") the Count mourns over what he supposes to be the infidelity of his wife, followed by a long and very dramatic scene with the Countess ("My Waldemar, how erred thine Eglantine?"). The last scene is laid at the forge, and after a short but vigorous prelude opens with a chorus of the smiths ("Gift of Demons, raging Fire"), in which the composer has produced the effect of clanging anvils, roaring fire, and hissing sparks with wonderful realism. The chorus closes with passages describing the providential rescue of Fridolin and the fate of Hubert, and an *andante religioso* ("Let your Voices Anthems raise"). The epilogue is mainly choral, and ends this very dramatic work in broad flowing harmonies.

RHEINBERGER.

JOSEPH GABRIEL RHEINBERGER was born at Vaduz, in Lichtenstein, March 17, 1839, and displayed his musical talent at a very early age. He studied the piano in his fifth year, and in his seventh was organist in the church of his native place. At the age of twelve he entered the Munich Conservatory, where he remained as a scholar until he was nineteen, when he was appointed one of its teachers; at the same time he became organist at the Hofkirche of St. Michael, and afterwards director of the Munich Oratorio Society. In 1867 he was appointed professor and inspector of the Royal Music School, and since 1877 has been the royal Hofkapellmeister, directing the performances of the Kapellchor, an organization similar to that of the Berlin Domchor. He is a very prolific composer, nearly two hundred works having proceeded from his pen. Among them are the "Wallenstein" and "Florentine" symphonies; a Stabat Mater; two operas, "The Seven Ravens" and "Thürmer's Töchterlein;" incidental music to a drama of Calderon's; a symphony-sonata for piano; a requiem for the dead in the Franco-German war; theme and variations for string quartet; a piano concerto; five organ sonatas; the choral works, "Toggenburg," "Klärchen auf Eberstein," "Wittekind," and "Christophorus;" and a large number of songs and church pieces, besides much chamber music.

Christophorus.

"Christophorus," a legend, as Rheinberger calls it, was written in 1879, and is composed for barytone, soprano, and alto solos, chorus, and orchestra. Its subject is taken from the familiar story of the giant who bore the infant Christ across the flood. The chorus acts the part of narrator, and in its opening number relates the legend of Christophorus' wanderings and his arrival before the castle whose master he would serve. He offers his services, but when they are accepted as an offering from the gods he haughtily declares that he only serves "for fame and chivalry." A voice thereupon in an impressive solo ("Trust not this loud-voiced Stranger") warns him away as an envoy of Satan, and the chorus repeats the warning. The giant departs with the intention of drawing his sword in Satan's cause, —

> "For he alone must be lord of all,
> Whose name doth so valiant a monarch appall."

In a very picturesque number the chorus describes his wanderings among the mountain crags and rocks where Satan weaves his spells about him; and then suddenly changing to a tender, delicate strain ("Over us Stars shine") anticipates the Voice, which in a sensuous aria ("Who is the sovereign Lord of the Heart?") sings the power of love. In graceful chorus the spirits taunt him, whereupon he once more resolves to fly and to abandon the cause of Satan, but is thwarted by them. A weird chorus closes the first part ("Satan a-hunting is gone"), ending with an impressive strain: —

> "Stormily falleth the night:
> Frightened maidens fleeing,
> Demon hordes all around.
> 'A cross, see, upraised!
> Fly, master! too far we have come.
> Hallowed is the ground.'"

The second part opens with a reflective soliloquy by the giant, followed by a plaintive chorus ("All now is lone and silent") describing the suffering of our Saviour on the cross and the sadness of a hermit gazing upon the scene. The giant approaches the latter, and a dialogue ensues between them, in which the identity of the victim on the cross is revealed. Having found the King of the universe, Christophorus determines to devote himself to His cause, and inquires how he may serve Him. He is informed he must go to the swiftly-rolling river and carry the pilgrims across. A charming chorus ("As flows the River seawards, so onward glide the Years") describes the work of the faithful toiler. Then comes a voice calling him, and he beholds an

Infant waiting for him. He takes Him upon his shoulders and bears Him into the flood, but as he advances, bends and struggles beneath his load "as though the whole world he bore." He inquires the meaning, and the Voice replies: —

> "Thou bear'st the world and bearest its Creator:
> This Child is Jesus, God's own Son.
> Soldier of Christ!
> Thine arms were charity and mercy,
> The arms of love.
> Now mayst rejoice:
> The prize of thy faith is won."

A joyful, exultant chorus, ("Blessed of Rivers, the Child embrace") closes this very graceful little "legend."

Toggenburg.

"Toggenburg," a cycle of ballads, was written in 1880. The music is for solos and mixed chorus, the ballads being linked together by motives, thus forming a connected whole. The story is a very simple one. The bright opening chorus ("At Toggenburg all is in festive Array") describes the pageantry which has been prepared to welcome the return of Henry, Knight of Toggenburg, with his fair young Suabian bride, the Lady Etha. The chorus is followed by a duet and alto or barytone solo, which indicate the departure of the Knight for the wars, and the Lady Etha's loss of the wedding ring. The next number, a solo quartet and chorus ("Ah! Huntsman, who gave thee the Diamond Ring?"), is very dramatic in its delineation of the return of the victorious Knight, who, observing the ring on the finger of the huntsman, slays him, and then in a fit of jealousy hurls the Lady Etha from the tower where she was waving his welcome. The next number is a female chorus ("On mossy Bed her gentle Form reposes"), very slow in its movement and plaintive in character. It is followed by a weird and solemn chorus ("Through the Night rings the Horn's Blast with Power"), picturing the mad ride of the Knight through the darkness, accompanied by the dismal notes of ravens and mysterious sounds like "greetings from the dead," which only cease when he discovers the corpse of his lady with the cross on its breast. A short closing chorus, funereal in style, ends the mournful story :—

> "Toggenburg all is in mourning array,
>   The banners wave, the gate stands wide,
> Count Henry returns to his home this day,
>   In death he anew has won his bride.
> Once more for their coming the hall is prepared,
>   Where flickering tapers are ranged around,
> And far through the night in the valley are heard
>   The chants of the monks with their mournful sound."

Though the work has somewhat both of the Schumann and Mendelssohn sentiment in it, it is nevertheless original and characteristic in treatment. The melodies are pleasing throughout, and cover a wide range of expression, reaching from the tenderness of love to the madness of jealousy, and thence on to the elegiac finale.

ROMBERG.

ANDREAS ROMBERG was born April 27, 1767, at Vechte, near Münster. At a very early age he was celebrated as a violinist. In his seventeenth year he made a *furor* by his playing at the Concerts Spirituels, Paris. In 1790, with his cousin Bernhard, who was even more celebrated as a violoncellist (indeed the Rombergs, like the Bachs, were all musicians), he played in the Elector's band, and also went with him to Rome, where the cousins gave concerts together under the patronage of one of the cardinals. During the next four years Andreas travelled in Austria and France, and during his stay at Vienna made the acquaintance of Haydn, who was very much interested in his musical work. In 1800 he brought out an opera in Paris which made a failure. He then left for Hamburg, where he married and remained many years. In 1820 he was appointed court capellmeister at Gotha, and died there in the following year. Among his compositions are six symphonies; five operas, "Das graue Ungeheuer," "Die Macht der Musik,"

"Der Rabe," "Die Grossmuth des Scipio," and "Die Ruinen zu Paluzzi;" and several cantatas, quartets, quintets, and church compositions. Of all his works, however, his "Lay of the Bell" is the best known. A few years ago it was the stock piece of nearly every choral society in Germany, England, and the United States; and though now relegated to the repertory of old-fashioned music, it is still very popular.

Lay of the Bell.

The "Lay of the Bell" was composed in 1808, the music being set to Schiller's famous poem of the same name, whose stately measures are well adapted to musical treatment. It opens with a bass solo by the Master, urging on the workmen:—

> "In the earth right firmly planted,
> Stands well baked the mould of clay:
> Up, my comrades, be ye helpful;
> Let the bell be born to-day."

The full chorus responds in a rather didactic strain ("The Labor we prepare in Earnest"), and as it closes the Master gives his directions for lighting the fire in the furnace and mixing the metals. In this manner the work progresses, the Master issuing his orders until the bell is ready for the casting, the solo singers or chorus replying with sentiments naturally suggested by the process and the future work of the bell. The first of these responses is the chorus, "What in the Earth profoundly hidden," a smoothly flowing number followed by a soprano solo (" For with a Burst of joyous Clangor "), a pleasantly-rippling melody picturing the joys of childhood, and a spirited tenor solo ("The Youth, Girl-playmates proudly leaving") indicating the dawn of the tender passion which broadens out into love, as the two voices join in the charming duet, " O tender Longing, Hope delightsome." The bass still further emphasizes their delight in the recitative, " When stern and gentle Troth have plighted," leading up to a long but interesting tenor solo ("Though Passion gives way") which describes the homely joys of domestic life. The male chorus thereupon takes up the story in a joyful strain ("And the good Man with cheerful Eye"), and tells us of the prosperity of the happy pair and the good man's boast, —

"Firm as the solid earth,
Safe from misfortune's hand,
Long shall my dwelling stand;"

to which comes the ominous response of the female chorus : —

"Yet none may with Fate supernal
Ever form a league eternal;
And misfortune swiftly strides."

The Master now gives the signal to release the metal into the mould, whereupon follows a stirring and picturesque chorus ("Right helpful is the Might of Fire") describing the terrors of fire, the wild alarm, the fright and confusion of the people, the clanging bells and crackling flames, and the final destruction of the homestead, closing the first part.

The second part opens with the anxious orders of the Master to cease from work and await the result of the casting. The chorus takes up a slow and stately measure ("To Mother Earth our Work committing") which closes in a mournful finale describing the passing funeral train, followed by a pathetic soprano solo which tells the sad story of the death of the good man's wife, while "To the orphaned Home a Stranger comes unloving Rule to bear." The scene now changes from a desolate to a happy home as the Master bids the workmen seek their pleasure while the bell is cooling. A soprano solo takes up a cheery strain ("Wends the weary Wanderer"), picturing the harvest home, the dance of the youthful reapers, and the joys of evening by the fireside, followed by a tribute to patriotism, sung by tenor and bass, the pleasant scene closing with an exultant full chorus ("Thousand active Hands combining"). The Master then gives the order to break the mould, and in contemplation of the ruin which might have been caused had the metal burst it, the chorus breaks out in strong, startling phrases picturing the horrors of civil strife ("The Master's Hand the Mould may shatter"). The work, however, is complete and successful, and in the true spirit of German Gemüthlichkeit the Master summons his workmen : —

> "Let us, comrades, round her pressing,
> Upon our bell invoke a blessing.
> 'Concordia,' let her name be called:
> In concord and in love of one another,
> Where'er she sound, may brother meet with brother."

The cantata closes with a last invocation on the part of the Master, followed by a jubliant chorus ("She is moving, She is moving").

SCHUBERT.

FRANZ PETER SCHUBERT was born in Vienna, Jan. 31, 1797, and received his first musical lessons from his father and his elder brother Ignaz. In his eleventh year he sang in the Lichtenthal choir and shortly afterwards entered the Imperial Convict School, where for the next three or four years he made rapid progress in composition. In 1813 he returned home, and to avoid the conscription entered his father's school as a teacher, where he remained for three years, doing drudgery but improving his leisure hours by studying with Salieri and devoting himself assiduously to composition. His life had few events in it to record. It was devoted entirely to teaching and composition. He wrote in almost every known form of music, but it was in the Lied that he has left the richest legacy to the world, and in that field he reigns with undisputed title. Unquestionably many of these songs were inspirations, like the "Erl King," for instance, which came to him in the midst of a carousal. The most famous of them are to be found in the cycluses "Müllerlieder,"

"Die Gesänge Ossians," "Die Geistlichen Lieder," "Die Winterreise," and "Der Schwanengesang." They are wonderful for their completeness, their expression of passion, their beauty and grace of form, the delicacy of their fancy, and their high artistic finish. Among the other great works he has left are the lovely "Song of the Spirits over the Water," for male voices; "Die Allmacht;" "Prometheus;" "Miriam's War Song;" the eight-part chorus "An den Heiligen Geist;" the "Momens Musicale;" impromptus and Hungarian fantasies for piano; the sonatas in C minor and B flat minor; nine symphonies, two of them unfinished; the trios in B flat and E flat; the quartets in D minor and G major; the quintet in C; two operas, "Alfonso and Estrella" and "Fierrabras;" the mass in G, which he wrote when but eighteen years of age, and the mass in E flat, which was his last church composition. His catalogued works number over a thousand. He died Nov. 19, 1828, and his last wish was to be buried by the side of Beethoven, who on his deathbed had recognized "the divine spark" in Schubert's music. Three graves only separate the great masters of the Symphony and the Lied in the cemetery of Währing.

Miriam's War Song.

The majestic cantata, "Miriam's War Song," was written in March, 1828, the last year of Schubert's life, — a year which was rich, however, in the productions of his genius. The beautiful symphony in C, the mass in E flat, the string quartet in C, the three piano sonatas dedicated to Schumann, the eight-voiced "Hymn to the Holy Ghost," the 92d Psalm, a "Tantum Ergo," and several songs, among them "Am Strom," "Der Hirt auf den Felsen," and a part of the "Schwanengesang," all belong to this year. The authorities differ as to the time of the first performance of " Miriam's War Song." Nottebohm in his catalogue says that it was first sung at a concert, Jan. 30, 1829, given for the purpose of raising funds to erect a monument in memory of the composer, who died on the 19th of the previous November. Others assert that Schubert was induced to give a concert, March 26, 1828, the programme being composed entirely of his own music, and that it was first heard on that occasion.

The work is for soprano solo and chorus, the words by the poet Grillparzer, and the accompaniment, for the piano, as Schubert left it. He had intended arranging it for orchestra, but did not live to complete it. The work, however, was done a year or two afterwards by his friend Franz Lachner, at that time officiating as Capellmeister at the Kärnthnerthor Theatre in Vienna.

The theme of the cantata is Miriam's hymn of praise for the escape of the Israelites, and the exultant song of victory by the people, rejoicing not alone at their own delivery but at the destruction of the enemy. It opens with a spirited and broad harmony, "Strike the Cymbals," changing to a calm and graceful song, describing the Lord as a shepherd leading his people forth from Egypt. The next number, depicting the awe of the Israelites as they passed through the divided waters, the approach of Pharaoh's hosts, and their destruction, is worked up with great power. As the sea returns to its calm again, the opening chorus is repeated, closing with a powerful fugue. The cantata is short, but it is a work of imperishable beauty.

SCHUMANN.

ROBERT SCHUMANN was born at Zwickau, in Saxony, June 8, 1810. In his earliest youth he was recognized as a child of genius. His first teacher in music was Baccalaureus Kuntzch, who gave him piano instruction. He studied the piano with Wieck, whose daughter Clara he subsequently married, now world-famous as a pianist. In 1830, in which year his artistic career really opened, he began the theoretical study of music, first with Director Kupsch in Leipsic and later with Heinrich Dorn, and at the same time entered upon the work of composition. Schumann was not only a musician but an able critic and graceful writer; and in 1834, with Schunke, Knorr, and Wieck, he founded the " Neue Zeitschrift für Musik," which had an important influence upon musical progress in Germany, and in which the great promise of such musicians as Chopin and Brahms was first recognized. He married Clara Wieck in 1840, after much opposition from her father; and in this year appeared some of his best songs, including the three famous cycluses, " Liederkreis," "Woman's Life and Love," and "Poet's Love," which now have a world-wide fame. In the following year larger works came from his pen, among them his B minor symphony, overture, scherzo, and finale in E major, and the symphony in D minor. During this period in his career he made many artistic journeys with his wife, which largely increased the reputation of both. In 1843 he completed his great "romantic oratorio," "Paradise and the Peri," set to Moore's text, and many favorite songs and piano compositions, among them the "Phantasiestücke" and "Kinderscenen," and his elegant piano quintet in E flat. In 1844, in company with his wife, he visited St. Petersburg and Moscow, and their reception was a royal one. The same year he abandoned his "Zeitschrift," in which "Florestan," "Master Raro," "Eusebius," and the other pseudonyms had become familiar all over Germany, and took the post of director in Düsseldorf, in the place of Ferdinand Hiller. During the last few years of his life he was the victim of profound melancholy, owing to an affection of the brain, and he even attempted suicide by throwing himself into the Rhine. He was then removed to an asylum at Endenich, where he died July 20, 1856. The two men who exercised most influence upon Schumann were Jean Paul and Franz Schubert. He was deeply pervaded with the romance of the one and the emotional feeling of the other. His work is characterized by genial humor, a rich and warm imagination, wonderfully beautiful instrumentation, especially in his accompaniments, the loftiest form of expression, and a rigid adherence to the canons of art.

Advent Hymn.

In a letter to Strakerjan, Schumann writes : —

"To apply his powers to sacred music is the artist's highest aim. But in youth we are all very firmly rooted to earth, with its joys and sorrows; in old age the twigs tend upwards. And so I hope that that day may not be too far distant from me."

The first of his works indicated in the above words to his friend was the "Advent Hymn," written in 1848, based upon Rückert's poem. It was followed later by a requiem and a mass, these comprising his only sacred music.

The "Advent Hymn" describes the entry of Christ into Jerusalem, reflectively considers his peaceful career as compared with that of earthly kings, and appeals to His servants to bear tidings of Him throughout the world, closing with a prayer that He will bring His peace to all its people. It is a hymn full of simple devotion and somewhat narrow in its limitations; but Schumann has treated it with all the dignity and breadth of the oratorio style. It opens with a melodious soprano solo ("In lowly Guise thy King appeareth"), with choral responses by sopranos and altos, leading to an effective five-part chorus ("O King indeed, though no Man hail Thee"), begun by first and second tenors and basses, and closing in full harmony with the added female voices. The soprano voice again announces a subject ("Thy Servants faithful, Tidings bearing"), which is taken up by full chorus, in somewhat involved form, though closing in plain harmony. The third number ("When Thou the stormy Sea art crossing") is given out by the soprano and repeated by the female chorus with a charming pianissimo effect. A few bars for male chorus ("Lord of Grace and Truth unfailing") lead into full chorus. The fifth number ("Need is there for Thyself returning"), also choral, is very elaborately treated with interchanging harmonies and bold rhythms, leading up to the final choruses, which are very intricate in construction, but at the close resolve into a double chorus of great power and genuine religious exaltation.

There are other works of Schumann's which are more or less in the cantata form, such as "The King's Son," op. 116, set to a ballad of Uhland's; "The New Year's Song," op. 144, poem by Rückert; "The Luck of Edenhall," op. 143, poem by Uhland; "Of the Page and the King's Daughter," op. 140, poem by Geibel; the "Spanish Love Song," op. 138; the "Minnespiel," op. 101; and the "Ritornelle," op. 65.

The Pilgrimage of the Rose.

"The Pilgrimage of the Rose," for solo and chorus, with piano accompaniment, twenty-four numbers, was written in the spring of 1851, and was first performed May 6, 1852, at a Düsseldorf subscription concert. The story is taken from a somewhat vapid fairy-tale by Moritz Horn, and has little point or meaning. It turns upon the commonplace adventures of a young girl whose origin is disclosed by a rose which was never to fall from her hand.

The principal numbers are the opening song, a joyous hymn to spring, in canon form, for two sopranos; the dancing choruses of the elves, for two sopranos and alto; the male chorus, "In the thick Wood," which is very effective in harmony; the exultant bridal songs, "Why sound the Horns so gayly?" and "Now at the Miller's;" the duet, "In the smiling Valley, 'mid the Trees so green;" the Grave Song; the quartet, "Oh, Joy! foretaste of Heaven's Rest;" and the duet, "I know a blushing Rosebud."

The work as a whole has never attained the popularity of his "Paradise and the Peri," though detached numbers from it are frequently given with great success. The inadequacy of the poem has much to do with this; and it must also be remembered that it was written at a time when Schumann's powers had begun to weaken under the strain of the mental disorder which finally proved fatal. Reissmann, in his analysis of the work, says: —

"The man who had hitherto refused to allow even the simplest composition to flow from any but a distinct idea, who constantly strove to enter into relations with some distinct movement of the heart or the imagination, here grasped at a poem utterly destitute of any rational fundamental idea, and so arbitrary in execution, so tasteless in parts, that the musical inspiration it offered could never have moved any other composer to set it to music."

The Minstrel's Curse.

"The Minstrel's Curse," for solo voice, chorus and orchestra, was written in 1852, and first performed in the same year. Its text is based upon Uhland's beautiful ballad of the same name, which was adapted for the composer by Richard Pohl. The libretto shows numerous variations from the original text. Some of the verses are literally followed, others are changed, and many new songs and motives are introduced. Several of Uhland's other ballads are assigned to the minstrel, the youth, and the queen, among them "Die Drei Lieder," "Entsagung," and "Hohe Liebe," as well as extracts from "Rudello," "Lied des Deutschen Sängers," "Gesang und Krieg," and "Das Thal." Instead of the beautiful verse in the original poem: —

> "They sing of spring and love, of happy golden youth,
> Of freedom, manly worth, of sanctity and truth.
> They sing of all emotions sweet the human breast that move,
> They sing of all things high the human heart doth love.
> The courtly crowd around forget to sneer and nod,
> The king's bold warriors bow before their God.
> The queen, to pleasure and to melancholy willing prey,
> Down to the singers casts the rose which on her bosom lay," —

THE MINSTREL'S CURSE. 323

which leads up to the tragedy, it is the singing of the "Hohe Liebe" which is made the motive by Pohl, who from this point on follows the story as told by Uhland.

The work contains fourteen numbers. The first two verses, describing the castle and its haughty monarch, are sung by the narrator, and are followed by an alto solo, very bright and joyous in style, which tells of the arrival of the two minstrels. The fourth number is a Provençal song, full of grace and poetical feeling, sung by the youth, followed by full chorus. The King angrily interposes in the next number, "Enough of Spring and Pleasure," whereupon the harper sings a beautiful ballad interpolated by the librettist. The queen follows with a quiet, soothing strain, appealing for further songs, and in reply the youth and harper once more sing of spring. The youth's powerful song of love, which changes to a trio in the close, the queen and harper joining, indicates the coming tragedy, and from this number on the chorus follows the story as told by Uhland, with great power and spirit. The general style of the work is declamatory, but in many of its episodes the ballad form is used with great skill and effect.

SINGER.

OTTO SINGER was born in Saxony, July 26, 1833, and attended the Leipsic Conservatory from 1851 to 1855, studying with Richter, Moscheles, and Hauptmann. In 1859 he went to Dresden and for two years thereafter studied with Liszt, of whom he was not only a favorite scholar but always a most zealous advocate. In 1867 he came to this country to take a position in the Conservatory at New York, then under the direction of Theodore Thomas and William Mason. In 1873, upon Mr. Thomas's suggestion, he went to Cincinnati and became the assistant musical director of the festival chorus of that city, a position which he filled with eminent ability for several years. At the festival of 1878 he conducted the first performance of Liszt's "Graner Mass" in this country, and also his own "Festival Ode" set to a poem by F. A. Schmitt, and written to commemorate the dedication of the new Music Hall. In the same year the Cincinnati College of Music was organized, and he was engaged as one of the principal instructors, a position which he still holds, and in which he has displayed signal ability. Mr. Singer has written many compositions for piano and orchestra, and besides his "Festival Ode," the cantata "Landing of the Pilgrims" (1876).

The Landing of the Pilgrims.

"The Landing of the Pilgrims," written in 1876, was Mr. Singer's Centennial offering to the patriotic music of that year. The text of the cantata is the familiar poem written by Mrs. Felicia Hemans, which was first set to music by her own sister, Miss Browne, though in somewhat different style from this work of the modern school.

The cantata opens with an instrumental prelude which gives out the principal motive as we afterwards find it set to the words, "With their Hymns of lofty Cheer;" and truly lofty cheer it is, that antique, strong melody. Breathed softly at first, as from afar, it is repeated after a rapid crescendo with the whole weight of the orchestra, to melt away again on an organ point in more subdued tone-color. In the second movement (andante) it appears in quadruple time, augmented in its cadence by a chromatic harmony which serves well to enrich the working-up of this fine piece of orchestral writing. A short interlude containing the germ of a second theme, which afterwards appears at the words, "This was their Welcome Home," now prepares the entrance of the voices. To the words, "The breaking Waves dashed high," the basses and tenors give out the first motive, and after declaiming the stormy opening lines of the poem break forth in unison with "When a Band of Exiles moored their Bark on the wild New England Shore." The time again changing, the composer very happily contrasts the phrases, "Not as a Conqueror comes" and "They the true-hearted came." Soon, however, the ever-pliable principal theme falls into a martial stride, and a very effective setting of the words, "Not with the Roll of stirring Drums," concludes the opening male chorus. Here follows the Centennial Hymn as given out in the beginning, sung first by an alto voice, and repeated by the full chorus of mixed voices. After the close, the orchestra, dreaming along in the spell, as it were, seems to spiritualize the sturdy Pilgrim Fathers into meek Pilgrims of the Cross, — a piece of exquisite tenderness, Liszt-Wagnerish, and yet beautiful. After some alto recitatives and short choral phrases, the leading theme once more enters with heavy martial step to the words, "There was Manhood's Brow," etc. The musical setting of the question, "What sought they?" etc., is cast in simpler form, and the response, "They sought a Faith's pure Shrine," is given in six measures, *a capella*, for five voices. This brings us to the last movement, *andante maestoso*. The leading motive, now contracted into one measure, is tossed about in the double basses as on the waves of a heavy surf until it reaches the climax on the words "Freedom to worship God." The cantata forms a valuable addition to our musical literature, and was first sung by the Cincinnati Harmonic Society, of which Mr. Singer was leader at the time.

SMART.

HENRY SMART, one of the most prominent of the modern English composers, was born in London, Oct. 26, 1813. Though almost entirely self-taught, he soon made his mark as a musician of more than ordinary ability. For many years he was principally known as an organist and organ-writer. He wrote numerous compositions for that instrument, which are still largely in use, and from 1836 to 1864 was famous in London for his contributions to the church service. In 1855 his opera, "Bertha, or the Gnome of Hartzburg," was produced with success in that city. Among his festival works were the cantatas, "The Bride of Dunkerron," for Birmingham (1864); "King René's Daughter" and "The Fishermaidens," for female voices (1871); the sacred cantata "Jacob," for Glasgow (1873); and two anthems for solos, chorus, and organ, for the London Choral Choirs' Association Festivals of 1876 and 1878. As a writer of part-songs he has also achieved a wide reputation. Grove states that he also was " a very accomplished mechanic, and had he taken up engineering instead of music, would no doubt have been successful. As a designer of organs he was often employed." Shortly after 1864 he lost his sight and thereafter composed entirely by dictation. His services for music secured him a government pension in June, 1879, but he did not live to enjoy it, dying July 6 of the same year.

The Bride of Dunkerron.

"The Bride of Dunkerron," words by Frederick Enoch, was written for the Birmingham Festival of 1864, and is based upon a tradition, the scene located at the Castle of Dunkerron, on the coast of Kerry, which has also been made the subject of a ballad by Crofton Croker. The story is a very simple one. The Lord of Dunkerron becomes enamoured of a sea-maiden, and as she is unable to leave her element he follows her to her abode. She seeks the Sea-King to obtain his consent to their union, but returns to her lover with the sad message that she is doomed to death for loving a mortal. He in turn is driven from the Sea-King's realm, and is cast back by the tempest to the shores of the upper world; and the work closes with the laments of the sea-spirits for the maiden, and of the serfs for their master.

After an expressive orchestral introduction the cantata opens with a chorus of the serfs (tenors and basses) ("Ere the Wine-cup is dry"), followed by a very romantic chorus of sea-maidens, the two at times interwoven and responsive, — the one describing Lord Dunkerron's nightly vigils on the seashore, and the other the melody of the maidens which tempts him. A charming orchestral intermezzo, full of the feeling of the sea, ensues, and is followed by recitative and aria ("The full Moon is beaming") for Dunkerron, which is very simple in style but effective as a song, even apart from its setting. It leads up to another chorus of the sea-maidens ("Let us sing, the moonlit Shores along") and a long love dialogue between Dunkerron and the Maiden. The next number is a very spirited and picturesque chorus ("Down through the Deep") describing the passage of the lovers to the Maiden's home, which is followed by a sturdy, sonorous recitative and aria for bass voice ("Oh, the Earth is fair in Plain and Glade") sung by the Sea-King. Two very attractive choruses follow, the first ("O Storm King, hear us") with a solo for the Sea-King, and the second ("Hail to thee, Child of the Earth") by the sea-maidens. Another graceful melody, "Our Home shall be on this bright Isle," is assigned to the Maiden, leading to a duet with Dunkerron, in which she announces her departure to obtain the Sea-King's consent to their union. A chorus of the storm-spirits ("Roar, Wind of the Tempést, roar") indicates her doom and leads up to the finale. A powerful trio for the Maiden, Dunkerron, and Sea-King, followed by the angry commands of the latter ("Hurl him back!"), tells of the death of the lovers, and the work closes as it opened, with the intermingled choruses of serfs and sea-maidens, this time, however, full of lamentation over the sad tragedy.

King René's Daughter.

"King René's Daughter," a cantata for female voices only, the poem by Frederick Enoch, was written in 1871. The story is freely adapted from Henrik Hertz's lyric drama. Iolanthe, the daughter of King René, Count of Provence, was betrothed in her infancy to the son of the Count of Vaudemont. When but a year old she was stricken with blindness. She has been reared in ignorance of her affliction by a strict concealment from her of all knowledge of the blessings of sight. A wandering magician agrees to cure her by the use of an amulet, provided she is first informed of the existence of the missing sense; but her father refuses permission. Her betrothed has never seen her, but wandering one day through the valley of Vaucluse, singing his troubadour lays, he beholds her, and is captivated by her beauty. His song reveals to her the faculty of which she has been kept in ignorance, and the magician, his condition thus having been fulfilled, restores her to sight.

The work is divided into thirteen numbers, the solo parts being Iolanthe (soprano), Martha (mezzo-soprano), and Beatrice (contralto). In the third number another soprano voice is required in a trio and chorus of vintagers; and in the sixth number, a soprano and contralto in the quartet, which acts the part of narrator, and tells of the troubadour's rose song to Iolanthe. It is unnecessary to specify the numbers in detail, as they are of the same general character, — smooth, flowing, and graceful in melody throughout. The most striking of them are No. 3, trio and chorus ("See how gay the Valley shines"); No. 5, arietta for Martha ("Listening to the Nightingales"); No. 6, quartet ("Who hath seen the Troubadour?"); No. 8, Iolanthe's song ("I love the Rose"); No. 11, duet and chorus ("Sweet the Angelus is ringing"); and the finale, with the jubilant chorus: —

"René the king will ride forth from the gate
With his horsemen and banners in state;
And the trumpets shall fanfaron ring
To René, to René, the king.
Then with rebec and lute and with drum
The bride in her beauty will come;
And the light of her eyes, they will say, has surpassed
The diamonds that shine at her waist, —
The diamonds that shine in her long golden hair, —
King René's daughter the fair."

SULLIVAN.

ARTHUR SEYMOUR SULLIVAN was born in London, May 13, 1842. His father, a band-master and clarinet-player of distinction, intrusted his musical education at first to the Rev. Thomas Hilmore, master of the children of the Chapel Royal. He entered the chapel in 1854 and remained there three years, and also studied in the Royal Academy of Music under Goss and Sterndale Bennett, during this period, leaving the latter institution in 1858, in which year he went to Leipsic. He remained in the Conservatory there until 1861, when he returned to London and introduced himself to its musical public, with his music to Shakspeare's "Tempest," which made a great success. The enthusiasm with which this was received, and the favors he gained at the hands of Chorley, at that time musical critic of the "Athenæum," gave him a secure footing. The cantata "Kenilworth," written for the Birmingham Festival, the music to the ballet "L'Île enchantée," and an opera, "The Sapphire Necklace," were produced in 1864. In 1866 appeared his first symphony and an overture, "In Memoriam," a tribute to his father, who died that year. The next year his overture "Marmion" was first performed. In 1869 he wrote his first oratorio, "The Prodigal Son," in 1873 "The Light of the World," and in 1880 "The Martyr of Antioch;" the first for the Worcester, the second for the Birmingham, and the third for the Leeds festival. The beautiful "Overture di Ballo," so frequently played in this country by the Thomas orchestra, was written for Birmingham in 1870, and the next year appeared his brilliant little cantata, "On shore and Sea." On the 11th of May, 1867, was first heard in public his comic operetta, "Cox and Box." It was the first in that series of extraordinary successes, really dating from "The Sorcerer," which are almost without parallel in the operatic world, and which have made his name, and that of his collaborator, Gilbert, household words. He has done much for sacred as well as secular music. In addition to his oratorios he has written numerous anthems, forty-seven hymn tunes, two Te Deums, several carols, part-songs, and choruses, and in 1872 edited the collection of "Church Hymns with Tunes" for the Christian Knowledge Society. His latest works are the opera "Ruddygore" and the cantata "The Golden Legend," both written in 1886. He received the honorary degree of Doctor of Music from Cambridge in 1876, and from Oxford in 1879, and in 1883 was knighted by the Queen.

On Shore and Sea.

The cantata "On Shore and Sea" was written for the London International Exhibition of 1871. The solo parts are allotted to La Sposina, a Riviera woman, and Il Marinajo, a Genoese sailor. The action passes in the sixteenth century, at a port of the Riviera and on board of a Genoese and Moorish galley at sea. The cantata opens with a joyous sailors' chorus and the lament of the mothers and wives as the seamen weigh anchor and set sail. The scene then changes to the sea. On board one of the galleys, in the midnight watch, the Marinajo invokes the protection of Our Lady, Star of the Sea, for the loved one left behind. The scene next changes to the return of the fleet, triumphant in its encounters with the Moorish vessels. The women throng to the shore, headed by La Sposina, to welcome the sailors back, but the galley on board which her lover served is missing. It has been captured by the Moors, and in a pathetic song she gives expression to her sorrow. In the next scene we find him toiling at the oar at the bidding of his Moorish masters. While they are revelling he plans a rising among his fellow-captives which is successful. They seize the galley and steer back to the Riviera, entering port amid choruses of rejoicing. The cantata is full of charming melodies, the instrumentation is Oriental in color, and the choruses, particularly the closing ones, are very stirring.

The Golden Legend.

"The Golden Legend" was first produced at the Leeds Musical Festival, Oct. 16, 1886. The story of the legend has already been told in the description of Mr. Buck's cantata by the same name, which took the Cincinnati Festival prize in 1880. The adaptation of Mr. Longfellow's poem for the Sullivan cantata was made by Joseph Bennett, who while omitting its mystical parts, except the prologue, has confined himself to the story of Prince Henry and Elsie. All the principal scenes, though sometimes rearranged to suit the musical demands of the composer, have been retained, so that the unity of the legend is preserved.

The prologue, representing the effort of Lucifer and the spirits of the air to tear down the cathedral cross, is used without change. The part of Lucifer is assigned to the barytone voice, the spirits of the air to the sopranos and altos, and the bells to the tenors and basses, the whole closing with the Gregorian Chant. The orchestral accompaniment is very realistic, particularly in the storm music and in the final number, where the organ adds its voice to the imposing harmony. The first scene opens with the soliloquy of Prince Henry in his chamber ("I cannot sleep"), followed by a dramatic duet with Lucifer, describing the temptation, and closes with a second solo by the Prince, accompanied by a warning chorus of angels. The second scene opens before the cottage of Ursula at evening, with a short alto recitative ("Slowly, slowly up the Wall") with pastoral accompaniment, followed by a very effective choral hymn ("O Gladsome Light") sung by the villagers ere they depart for their homes, the Prince's voice joining in the Amen. The remainder of the scene includes a dialogue between Elsie and her mother, in which the maid expresses her determination to die for the Prince, and a beautiful prayer ("My Redeemer and my Lord") in which she pleads for strength to carry out her resolution, closing with her noble offer to the Prince, which he accepts, the angels responding Amen to the blessing he asks for her.

The third scene opens with Elsie, the Prince, and their attendants on the road to Salerno where the cure is to be effected by her sacrifice. They fall in with a band of pilgrims, among whom is Lucifer in the disguise of a monk. The two bands part company, and as night comes on the Prince's attendants encamp near the sea. The continuity of the narrative is varied by a simple, graceful duet for the Prince and Elsie ("Sweet is the Air with budding Haws"); the Gregorian music of the pilgrims in the distance ("Cujus clavis lingua Petri"); the mocking characteristic song of Lucifer ("Here am I too in the pious Band"), interwoven with the chant; the song of greeting to the sea by the Prince ("It is the Sea"); and a very effective solo for Elsie ("The Night is calm and cloudless"), which is repeated by full chorus with soprano obligato dwelling upon the words "Christe Eleison." The fourth scene opens in the Medical School at Salerno, and discloses Lucifer disguised as the physician Friar Angelo, who receives Elsie and takes her into an inner apartment, notwithstanding the protests of the Prince, who suddenly resolves to save her, and finally effects her rescue. The music to this scene is very dramatic, and it also contains a short but striking unaccompanied chorus ("O Pure in Heart").

The fifth scene is short. It passes at the door of Ursula's cottage, where a forester brings the mother the news of Elsie's safety and of the Prince's miraculous cure. The dialogue is followed by a prayer of thanksgiving ("Virgin, who lovest the Poor and Lowly"). The last scene opens on the terrace of the castle of Vautsberg. It is the evening of the wedding day, and amid the sound of bells heard in the distance the Prince relates to Elsie the story of Charlemagne and Fastrada, at the close of which the happy pair join in an exultant duet. The cantata ends with a choral epilogue, worked up to a fine fugal climax in which Elsie's "deed divine" is compared to the mountain brook flowing down from "the cool hills" to bless "the broad and arid plain."

WAGNER.

RICHARD WAGNER, who has been sometimes ironically called the musician of the future, and whose music has been relegated to posterity by a considerable number of his contemporaries, was born at Leipsic, May 22, 1813. After his preliminary studies in Dresden and Leipsic, he took his first lessons in music from Cantor Weinlig. In 1836 he was appointed musical director in the theatre at Magdeburg, and later occupied the same position at Königsberg. Thence he went to Riga, where he began his opera "Rienzi." He then went to Paris by sea, was nearly shipwrecked on his way thither, and landed without money or friends. After two years of hard struggling he returned to Germany. His shipwreck and forlorn condition suggested the theme of "The Flying Dutchman," and while on his way to Dresden he passed near the castle of Wartburg, in the valley of Thuringia, whose legends inspired his well-known opera of "Tannhäuser." He next removed to Zurich, and about this time appeared "Lohengrin," his most popular opera. "Tristan and Isolde" was produced in 1856, and his comic opera, "Die Meistersinger von Nürnberg," three years later. In 1864 he received the patronage of King Louis of Bavaria, which enabled him to complete and perform his great work, "Der Ring der Nibelungen." He laid the foundation of the new theatre at Baireuth in 1872, and in 1875 the work was produced, and created a profound sensation all over the musical world. "Parsifal," his last opera, was first performed in 1882. His works have aroused great opposition, especially among conservative musicians, for the reason that he has set at defiance the conventional operatic forms, and in carrying out his theory of making the musical and dramatic elements of equal importance, and employing the former as the language of the latter in natural ways, has made musical declamation take the place of set melody, and swept away the customary arias, duets, quartets, and concerted numbers of the Italian school, to suit the dramatic exigencies of the situations. Besides his musical compositions, he enjoys almost equal fame as a littérateur, having written not only his own librettos, but four important works, — "Art and the Revolution," "The Art Work of the Future," "Opera and Drama," and "Judaism in Music." His music has made steady progress through the efforts of such advocates as Liszt, Von Bülow, and Richter in Germany, Pasdeloup in France, Hueffer in England, and Theodore Thomas in the United States. In 1870 he married Frau Cosima von Bülow, the daughter of Liszt, — an event which produced almost as much comment in social circles as his operas have in musical. He died during a visit to Venice, Feb. 13, 1883.

Love Feast of the Apostles.

"Das Liebesmahl der Apostel" ("The Love Feast of the Apostles"), a Biblical scene for male voices and orchestra, dedicated to Frau Charlotte Emilie Weinlig, the widow of the composer's old teacher, was written in 1843, the year after "Rienzi," and was first performed in the Frauen-Kirche in Dresden at the Men's Singing Festival, July 6 of that year.

The work opens with a full chorus of Disciples ("Gegrüsst seid, Bruder, in des Herren Namen"), who have gathered together for mutual help and strength to endure the persecutions with which they are afflicted. The movement flows on quietly, though marked by strong contrasts, for several measures, after which the chorus is divided, a second and third chorus taking up the two subjects, "Uns droht der Mächt'gen Hass," and "O fasst Vertrau'n," gradually accelerating and working up to a climax, and closing pianissimo ("Der Mächt'gen Späh'n verfolgt uns überall").

In the next number the Apostles enter (twelve bass voices) with a sonorous welcome ("Seid uns gegrüsst, ihr lieben Brüder"), reinforced by the

LOVE FEAST OF THE APOSTLES. 341

Disciples, pianissimo ("Wir sind versammelt im Namen Jesu Christi"), the united voices at last in powerful strains ("Allmächt'ger Vater, der du hast gemacht Himmel und Erd' und Alles was darin") imploring divine help and the sending of the Holy Ghost to comfort them. At its close voices on high are heard ("Seid getrost, ich bin euch nah, und mein Geist ist mit euch"). The Disciples reply with increasing vigor ("Welch Brausen erfüllt die Luft"). The Apostles encourage them to steadfast reliance upon the Spirit ("Klein müthige! Hört an was jetzt der Geist zu Künden uns gebeut"), and the work comes to a close with a massive chorale ("Denn ihm ist alle Herrlichkeit von Ewigkeit zu Ewigkeit"), worked up with overpowering dramatic force, particularly in the instrumentation. Though but a small composition compared with the masterpieces for the stage which followed it, it is peculiarly interesting in its suggestions of the composer's great dramatic power which was to find its fruition in the later works from his pen.

WEBER.

CARL MARIA VON WEBER was born Dec. 18, 1786, at Eutin, and may almost be said to have been born on the stage, as his father was at the head of a theatrical company, and the young Carl was carried in the train of the wandering troupe all over Germany. His first lessons were given to him by Henschkel, conductor of the orchestra of Duke Friedrich of Meiningen. At the age of fourteen he wrote his first opera, "Das Waldmädchen," which was performed several times during the year 1800. In 1801 appeared his two-act comic opera, "Peter Schmoll and his Neighbors," and during these two years he also frequently played in concerts with great success. He then studied with the Abbé Vogler, and in his eighteenth year was engaged for the conductorship of the Breslau opera. About this time appeared his first important opera, "Rubezahl." At the conclusion of his studies with Vogler he was made director of the opera at Prague. In 1816 he went to Berlin, where he was received with the highest marks of popular esteem, and thence to

Dresden as hofcapellmeister. This was the most brilliant period in his career. It was during this time that he married Caroline Brandt, the actress and singer, who had had a marked influence upon his musical progress, and to whom he dedicated his exquisite "Invitation to the Dance." The first great work of his life, " Der Freischütz," was written at this period. Three other important operas followed, — " Preciosa," " Euryanthe," the first performance of which took place in Vienna in 1823, and " Oberon," which he finished in London and brought out there. Weber's last days were spent in the latter city, and it was while making preparations to return to Germany, which he longed to see again, that he was stricken down with his final illness. On the 4th of June, 1826, he was visited by Sir George Smart, Moscheles, and other musicians who were eager to show him attention. He declined to have any one watch by his bedside, thanked them for their kindness, bade them good-by, and then turned to his friend Fürstenau, and said, "Now let me sleep." These were his last words. The next morning he was found dead in his bed. He has left a rich legacy of works besides his operas, — a large collection of songs, many cantatas (of which the "Jubilee" and "Kampf und Sieg" are the finest), some masses, of which that in E flat is the most beautiful, and several concertos, besides many brilliant rondos, polaccas, and marches for the piano.

Jubilee Cantata.

The "Jubilee Cantata" was written in 1818 to celebrate the fiftieth anniversary of the reign of King Friedrich August of Saxony. The King having expressed a desire that there should be a court concert on the day of the anniversary, September 20, Count Vitzthum commissioned Weber to write a grand jubilee cantata. The poet Friedrich Kind supplied the words. While engaged in its composition Weber was informed by friends that other arrangements were being made for the concert, and on the 12th of September the information was confirmed by a letter from the Count which informed him that notwithstanding his personal protests, the Jubilee Cantata was not to be given. The son in his biography of his father intimates that the change was the result of intrigues on the part of his Italian rivals, Morlacchi, Zingarelli, and Nicolini. The same authority says that the cantata was finally produced in the Neustadt church for the benefit of the destitute peasantry in the Hartz mountains, Weber himself conducting the performance, and that only the overture to the work, now famous the world over as the "Jubel," was played at the court concert. The best authorities, however, now believe that the Jubel overture is an entirely independent work, having no connection with the cantata. The text of the cantata, which commemorates many special events in the life of the King, being found unsuitable for general performance, a second text was subsequently written by Amadeus Wendt, under the title of " Ernte-Cantata " (" Harvest Cantata ") which is the one now in common use, although still another version was made under the name of " The Festival of Peace," by Hampdon Napier, which was used at a performance in London under the direction of the composer himself only a few days before his death.

The cantata is written for the four solo voices, chorus, and orchestra. It opens after a short allegro movement with a full jubilant chorus (" Your thankful Songs upraise "), the solo quartet joining in the middle part with chorus. The second number is a very expressive recitative and aria for tenor (" Happy Nation, still receiving "). The third is characterized by quiet beauty, and is very devotional in spirit. It begins with a soprano recitative and aria (" Yet not alone of Labor comes our Plenty "), leading up to a second recitative and aria (" The gracious Father hears us when we call "), which are very vivacious in style, closing with a tenor recitative (" The Air is mild and clear and grateful to the Reapers "). These prepare the way for a short but very powerful chorus (" Woe ! see the Storm-Clouds "). In the next number (" How fearful are the Terrors Nature brings ") the bass voice moralizes on the powers of Nature, followed by a plaintive strain for two sopranos, which leads up to a majestic prayer for chorus (" Lord Almighty, full of Mercy "). A bass recitative (" Lo, once our Prayer ") introduces a beautiful quartet and chorus of thanksgiving

("Wreathe into Garlands the Gold of the Harvest"). They are followed by a tenor recitative and soprano solo ("Soon noble Fruit by Toil was won"), and the work comes to a close with a stately chorus of praise ("Father, reigning in Thy Glory").

Kampf und Sieg.

In June, 1815, Weber arrived in Munich and during his stay made the acquaintance of Fraulein Wohlbrück, the singer, which led to an introduction to her father, who was both an actor and a poet. On the very day that he met Wohlbrück, the news came to Munich of the victory of the Allies at Waterloo, the whole city was decorated and illuminated, and a great crowd, Weber with them, went to St. Michael's Church to listen to a Te Deum. While there the idea of a grand cantata in commemoration of the victory came into his mind. On his return home he met Wohlbrück and communicated his purpose to him. The enthusiastic poet agreed to furnish the words. About the first of August the text was placed in Weber's hands, and he at once set it to music. It was first produced on the 22d of December at Prague, and made a profound impression by its stirring military character and vivid battle-descriptions.

The cantata is written for the four solo voices, chorus of sopranos, altos, two tenors, and basses and orchestra. A stirring orchestral introduction leads up to a people's chorus which describes the disappearance of dissensions heralding the approach of victory. No. 3 is a bass solo entitled "Faith," with a delightful violoncello accompaniment. In No. 4, Love (soprano) and Hope (tenor) join with Faith in a song full of feeling. No. 5 is a soldiers' chorus of an enthusiastic and martial character, while in the distance is heard the Austrian Grenadier's march mingling with it. In the next number the approach of the enemy is heard as the chorus closes with the majestic phrase, " Mit Gott sei unser Werk gethan." The lively march of the enemy comes nearer and nearer, interwoven with the next chorus, which is set to Körner's prayer " Wie auch die Hölle braust." Then follows the opening of the battle, with the roar of cannon, the shouts of the soldiers, and the cries of the wounded, through which is heard the French national air defiantly sounding. Another soldiers' chorus follows. It pictures the advance of the Prussian Jägers (" Ha ! welch ein Klang "), followed by the simple strains of " God save the King ! " In No. 9 the fight is renewed, the music reaching a pitch of almost ferocious energy, until the joyous cry is heard, " Hurrah ! Er flieht," and the triumphant march of victory emphasizes the exultant pæan, " Heil dir im Siegerkranz." The rest of the cantata is purely lyrical in style. Once more the voices of " Faith " and " Love " are heard, leading up to the final majestic chorus, " Herr Gott, Dich loben wir," accompanying a solo voice chanting the theme " Gieb und erhalte den Frieden der Welt."

WHITING.

GEORGE ELBRIDGE WHITING was born at Holliston, Mass., Sept. 14, 1842. He began the study of the piano at a very early age, but soon abandoned it for the organ. His progress was so rapid that at the age of thirteen he made his public appearance as a player. In 1857 he went to Hartford, Conn., where he had accepted a position in one of the churches, and while there organized the Beethoven Society. In 1862 he removed to Boston, but shortly afterwards went to England, where he studied the organ for a year with Best. On his return he was engaged as organist of St. Joseph's Church, Albany, N. Y., but his ambition soon took him to Europe again. This time he went to Berlin and finished his studies with Radecke and Haupt. He then returned to Albany and remained there three years, leaving that city to accept a position at the church of the Immaculate Conception, Boston. In 1874 he was appointed organist at the Music Hall, and was also for some time at the head of the organ department of the New England Conservatory of Music. In

1878 he was organist for the third Cincinnati May Festival, and in 1879 accepted a position in the College of Music in that city, at the same time taking charge of the organ in the Music Hall, with what success those who attended the May Festivals in that city will remember. He remained in Cincinnati three years and then returned to his old position in Boston. Mr. Whiting ranks in the first class of American organists, and has also been a prolific composer. Among his vocal works are a mass in C minor (1872); mass in F minor (1874); prologue to Longfellow's "Golden Legend" (1873); cantatas, "Dream Pictures" (1877), "The Tale of the Viking" (1880); a concert overture ("The Princess"); a great variety of organ music, including "The Organist," containing twelve pieces for that instrument, and "the First Six Months on the Organ," with twenty-five studies; several concertos, fantasies, and piano compositions, and a large number of songs.

The Tale of the Viking.

"The Tale of the Viking" was written in competition for the prize offered by the Cincinnati Musical Festival Association in 1879, and though unsuccessful, is still regarded as one of the most admirable and scholarly works yet produced in this country. The text of the cantata is Longfellow's "Skeleton in Armor," that weird and stirring story of the Viking, which the poet so ingeniously connected with the old mill at Newport.

The work comprises ten numbers, and is written for three solo voices (soprano, tenor, and barytone), chorus, and orchestra. A long but very expressive overture, full of the dramatic sentiment of the poem, prepares the way for the opening number, a short male chorus : —

>"'Speak! speak! thou fearful guest
>Who, with thy hollow breast
>Still in rude armor drest,
>   Comest to daunt me!
>Wrapt not in Eastern balms,
>But with thy fleshless palms
>Stretched, as if asking alms,
>   Why dost thou haunt me?'"

Next comes a powerful chorus for mixed voices ("Then from those cavernous Eyes"), which leads up to the opening of the Viking's story ("I was a Viking old"), a barytone solo, which is made very dramatic by the skilful division of the song between recitative and the melody. In the fourth number the male chorus continues the narrative ("But when I older grew"), describing in a vivacious and spirited manner the wild life of the marauders on the sea and their winter wassails as they told the Berserker legends over their cups of ale. In the fifth the soprano voice tells of the wooing of "The blue-eyed Maid" in an aria ("Once, as I told in Glee") remarkable for its varying shades of expression. At its close a brilliant march movement, very sonorous in style and highly colored, introduces a vigorous chorus ("Bright in her Father's Hall"), which describes the refusal of old Hildebrand to give his daughter's hand to the Viking. A dramatic solo for barytone ("She was a Prince's Child") pictures the flight of the dove with the sea-mew, which is followed by a chorus of extraordinary power as well as picturesqueness ("Scarce had I put to Sea"), vividly describing the pursuit, the encounter, and the Viking's escape with his bride. A graceful but pathetic romance for tenor ("There lived we many Years"), which relates her death, and burial beneath the tower, leads to the closing number, a soprano solo with a full stately chorus, admirably worked up, picturing the death of the Viking, who falls upon his spear, and ending in an exultant and powerful burst of harmony, set to the words:—

"' Thus, seamed with many scars,
Bursting these prison bars,
Up to its native stars
 My soul ascended;
There from the flowing bowl
Deep drinks the warrior's soul,
Skoal! to the Northland! skoal!' .
 Thus the tale ended."

APPENDIX.

HE following alphabetical list has been prepared to present the reader with the titles of the more important cantatas by well-known composers and the dates of their composition. To make an exhaustive catalogue of works of this class would be impossible, as a great number have been lost entirely, and hundreds of others are now only known by name; but the writer believes that those subjoined will provide musical students, as well as the general reader, with as complete a reference list as can be desired.

ADAM, ADOLPHE. Le Premiers Pas (1847); La Fête des Arts (1852); Chant de Victoire (1855); Birth of the Prince Imperial (1856).

ANDERTON, THOMAS. The Song of Deborah and Barak (1871); The Wreck of the Hesperus (1882); The Norman Baron (1884); Yuletide (1885).

ARNOLD, SAMUEL. Sennacherib (1774).

ASPA, EDWARD. The Gypsies (1870); Endymion (1875).

ASTORGA, EMANUELE. Quando penso (1706); Torne Aprile (1706); In questo core (1707); Dafni (1709).
BACH, JOHN SEBASTIAN. Two hundred and twenty-six sacred cantatas, of which the following are most commonly sung: Ich hatte viel Bekümmerniss; Festo Ascensionis Christi; Ein' Feste Burg (Reformation festival of 1717); Aus tiefer Noth schrei ich; Christ unser Herr zum Jordan kam; Ehre sei Gott in der Höhe (Christmas cantata); Gottes Zeit ist die allerbeste Zeit (mourning cantata); Lobe den Herrn (New Year's Day); O Ewigkeit, du Donnerwort; Gott ist mein König; Wie schön leucht uns der Morgenstern. Twenty-eight birthday, funeral, and secular cantatas: among them, Komische cantate, Kaffee cantate, Bauern oder Hochzeit's cantate.
BALFE, MICHAEL. Mazeppa (1862); The Page (?).
BARNBY, JOSEPH. Rebekah (1870).
BARNETT, JOHN FRANCIS. The Ancient Mariner (1867); Paradise and the Peri (1870); Lay of the Last Minstrel (1874); The Good Shepherd (1876); The Building of the Ship (1880).
BEETHOVEN, LUDWIG VON. Der Glorreiche Augenblick (1814); Meeresstille und glücklich Fahrt (1815).
BENDALL, WILFRED. Parizadeh (1870); The Lady of Shalott (1871).
BENEDICT, JULIUS. Undine (1860); Richard Cœur de Leon (1863); Legend of St. Cecilia (1866); Legend of St. Elizabeth (1867); St. Peter (1870); Graziella (1882).
BENNETT, WILLIAM STERNDALE. May Queen (1858); International Exhibition Ode (1862); Cambridge Installation Ode (1862).

BERLIOZ, HECTOR. Sardanaple (1830); Romeo and Juliet (dramatic symphony with solos and chorus) (1839); Damnation of Faust (dramatic scenes) (1846); L'Imperiale (1855); Le Cinq Mai (1857).
BISHOP, HENRY. The Seventh Day (1840).
BOITO, ARRIGO. Ode to Art (1880).
BRAHMS, JOHANNES. Rinaldo (1868); Rhapsodie (1870); Schicksalslied (1871); Triumphlied (1873); Gesang der Parzen (1877); Boadicea (1878).
BRIDGE, JOHN FREDERICK. Rock of Ages (1880); Boadicea (1880).
BRISTOW, GEORGE FREDERICK. Daniel (1876).
BRONSART, HANS VON. Christmarkt (1876).
BRUCH, MAX. Die Birken und die Erlen (1853); Jubilate-Amen (1856); Rinaldo (1858); Rorate Cœli (1861); Frithjof's Saga (1862); Salamis (1862); Die Flucht der heilige Familie (1863); Gesang der heiligen drei Könige (1864); Römischer Triumphgesang (1864); Römische Leichenfeier (1864); Schön Ellen (1869); Odysseus (1872); Arminius (1873); Normannenzug (1874); Song of the Bell (1876); Achilleus (1885).
BRÜLL, IGNAZ. Die Gesternähren (1875).
BUCK, DUDLEY. Forty-sixth Psalm (1872); Don Munio (1874); Centennial Cantata (1876); The Nun of Nidaros (1878); Golden Legend (1880); Voyage of Columbus (1885); Light of Asia (1886).
CALDICOTT, ALFRED JAMES. La Primavera (1880); The Widow of Nain (1881); Rhine Legend (1883); Queen of the May (1885).
CARISSIMI, GIACOMO. Jephthah (1660).
CHERUBINI, MARIE LUIGI. La Pubblica Felicità (1774); Amphion (1786); and seventeen others.
CIMEROSA, DOMENICO. La Nascita del Delfino (1786); and one hundred others.

CLAY, FREDERICK. The Knights of the Cross (1866); Lalla Rookh (1877).
CORDER, FREDERICK. The Cyclops (1880); The Bridal of Triermain (1886).
COSTA, MICHAEL. The Dream (1815); La Passione (1827).
COWEN, FREDERICK HYMEN. The Rose Maiden (1870); The Corsair (1876); St. Ursula (1881); The Sleeping Beauty (1885).
CUMMINGS, WILLIAM HAYMAN. The Fairy Ring (1873).
DAMROSCH, LEOPOLD. Ruth and Naomi (1870); Sulamith (1877).
DAVID, FÉLICIEN CÉSAR. The Desert (1844).
DVOŘÁK, ANTON. Patriotic Hymn (1880); The Spectre's Bride (1885).
ERDMANNSDORFER, MAX. Prinzessin Ilse (1870); Die Schneewittchen (1871).
FOOTE, ARTHUR. The Legend of Hiawatha (1879).
FOSTER, MYLES BIRKETT. The Bonnie Fishwives (1880).
FRY, WILLIAM HENRY. The Fall of Warsaw (1858).
GABRIEL, VIRGINIA. Dreamland (1870); Evangeline (1873).
GADE, NIELS WILHELM. Comala (1843); Spring Fantasie (1850); The Holy Night (1851); Erl King's Daughter (1852); Frühlingsbotschaft (1853); Kalamus (1853); Psyche (1856); Zion (1860); The Crusaders (1866).
GADSBY, HENRY ROBERT. Alice Brand (1870); Lord of the Isles (1880); Columbus (1881).
GARCIA, MANUEL. Endimione (1822).
GAUL, ALFRED ROBERT. Ruth (1881); The Holy City (1882).

GERNSHEIM, FRIEDRICH. Odin's Meeresritt (1860).
GILCHRIST, WILLIAM WALLACE. Forty-seventh Psalm (1882) ; The Rose (1886).
GLEASON, FREDERICK GRANT. God our Deliverer (1878); The Culprit Fay (1879) ; Praise of Harmony (1886).
GLOVER, FERDINAND. The Fire Worshippers (1857).
GLOVER, WILLIAM. The Corsair (1849).
GLOVER, WILLIAM HOWARD. Tam O'Shanter (1855).
GLUCK, CHRISTOPH WILLIBALD. Alexander's Feast (1753); De Profundis (1760) ; The Last Judgment (finished by Salieri) (1761).
GOETZ, HERMANN. By the Waters of Babylon (1874) ; Noenia (1875).
GOLDMARK, KARL. Frühling's Hymne (1876).
GOUNOD, CHARLES FRANÇOIS. Marie Stuart et Rizzio (1837); Daughters of Jerusalem (1838); Fernand (1839); À la Frontière (1870); Gallia (1871).
GRIEG, EDWARD. Land Kennung (1865).
HALÉVY, JACQUES FROMENTAL. Les Plages du Nil (1850) ; Italie (1850).
HAMERIK, ASGER. Friedenshymne (1868).
HANDEL, GEORGE FREDERICK. Passion (1704) ; twelve called " Hanover" (1711) ; seventy-nine written in Italy (1706–1712); Acis and Galatea (1720) ; Sei del cielo (1736) ; Alexander's Feast (1736) ; Ode on St. Cecilia's Day (1739) ; L' Allegro, il Penseroso, ed il Moderato (1740).
HATTON, JOHN LIPHOT. Robin Hood (1856).
HAUPTMANN, MORITZ. Herr, Herr! wende dich zum Gebet (1840); Die lustigen Musikanten (1842).
HAYDN, JOSEPH. Birthday of Prince Nicholas (1763) ; Applausus Musicus (1768) ; Die Erwahlung eines Kapellmeisters (1769) ; Ah! come il core mi pal-

pito (1783); Invocation of Neptune (1783); An die Freude (1786); Das Erndtefest (1786); Deutschland's Klage auf den Tod Friedrichs der Grossen (1787); Des Dichter's Geburtsfest (1787); Hier liegt Constantia (1787); Ariadne a Naxos (1792); Ombra del caro bene (1798); Der Versohnung's Tod (1809).

HEAP, C. SWINNERTON. The Maid of Astolat (1885).

HESSE, ADOLPH FRIEDRICH. Sei uns gnadig, Gott der gnaden (1831); Von Leiden ist mein Herz bedrängt (1832).

HILLER, FERDINAND. Die lustige Musikanten (1838); O, weint um Sie (1839); Morning of Palm Sunday (1839); Whitsuntide (1840); Israel's Siegesgesang (1841); Song of the Spirits over the Water (1842); Prometheus (1843); Rebecca (1843); The Night of the Nativity (1843); Heloise (1844); Loreley (1845); Die Nacht (1846); Ostermorgen (1850); Richard Löwenherz (1855); An das Vaterland (1861); Song of Victory (1871); Song of Heloise (1871); Nala und Damajanti (1871); Pentecost (1872); Prince Papagei (1872).

HIMMEL, FRIEDRICH HEINRICH. La Danza (1792); Hessan's Söhne und Prussien's Töchter (1797); Das Vertrauen auf Gott (1797); Funeral Cantata (1799).

HOFMANN, HEINRICH K. J. Deutschland's Erhebung (1874); Aschenbrödel (1875); Song of the Norns (1875); Melusina (1876); Cinderella (1879).

HUMMEL, JOHANN NEPOMUK. Diana ed Endimione (1818).

ISOUARD, NICOLO. Hebe (1813).

JACKSON, WILLIAM. Lycidas (1767); The Praise of Music (1770); The Year (1785).

JENSEN, ADOLF. Jephtha's Daughter (1864); Donald Caird ist wieder da (1875); The Feast of Adonis (1881).
KRUG, ARNOLD. Nomadenzug (1877); Sigurd (1882).
KÜCKEN, FRIEDRICH. Friedenshymne (1870).
KUHLAU, FRIEDRICH. Die Feier des Wohlwollens (1818).
LACHNER, FRANZ. Die vier Menschenalter (1843); Der Sturm (1845); Sixty-third Psalm (1849); Des Krieger's Gebet (1851); Siegesgesang (1852); Mozart Fest Cantate (1852); Sturmesmythe (1853); Bundeslied (1854); One Hundred and Fiftieth Psalm (1854).
LAHEE, HENRY. Building of the Ship (1869); The Blessing of the Children (1870).
LASSEN, EDWARD. Les Flamands sous van Arteveldt (1854); The Artists (1861); Fest Cantate (1874).
LEFÉBVRE, WÉLY LOUIS. Après le Victoire (1863).
LESLIE, HENRY DAVID. Judith (1858); Holyrood (1860); The Daughter of the Isles (1861).
LINDPAINTNER, PETER JOSEPH VON. Widow of Nain (1846).
LISZT, FRANZ. Prometheus (1850); Ave Maria (1851); Pater Noster (1852); Schiller Cantata (1859); Die Seligkeiten (arranged from " Christus ") (1863); Eighteenth Psalm (1867); Beethoven Festival Cantata (1870); Requiem (1870); One Hundred and Sixteenth Psalm (1873); The Bells of Strasburg (1874); An den heiligen Franziskus (1874); St. Cecilia (1875); Thirteenth Psalm (1877).
LLOYD, CHARLES HARFORD. Hero and Leander (1884); The Song of Balder (1885); Andromeda (1886).

MACFARREN, GEORGE ALEXANDER. Lenora (1852);
May Day (1857); The Soldier's Legacy (1857);
Christmas (1860); Songs in a Cornfield (1868);
The Lady of the Lake (1877); Outward Bound
(1877).

MACKENZIE, ALEXANDER CAMPBELL. The Bride
(1880); Jason (1882); Story of Sayid (1886).

MASSENET, JULES ÉMILE FRÉDÉRIC. David Rizzio
(1863); Paix et Liberté (1867); Mary Magdalen
(1873); Eve (1875); Narcisse (1877).

MENDELSSOHN, BARTHOLDY FELIX. Christe, du
Lamm Gottes (1827); Ach Gott von Himmel
(1827); Humboldt Fest Cantate (1828); Walpurgis
Night (1831); As the Hart pants (1838); Friedrich August Fest Cantate (1842); Lauda Sion
(1846); To the Sons of Art (1846).

MERCADANTE, SAVERIO. L'Unione delle belli Arte
(1818); The Seven Words (1821).

MEYERBEER, GIACOMO. Seven sacred Cantatas from
Klopstock (1810); God and Nature (1810); March
of the Bavarian Archers (1816); The Genius of
Music at the Grave of Beethoven (1830); Gutenberg Cantata (1836); Le Festa nella Corte di Ferrara (1843); Maria und ihr Genius (1851).

MOZART, WOLFGANG AMADEUS. Grabmusik (1767);
Davidde penitente (1783); Die Seele (1783); Die
Maurer freude (1785); La Betulia liberata (1786);
Eine Kleine Freimaurer Cantate (1791).

NEUKOMM, SIGISMOND. Napoleon's Midnight Review (1828); Easter Morning (1829).

OXENFORD, EDWARD. Crown of Roses (1886).

PACINI, GIOVANNI. Dante Centenary (1865).

PAER, FERDINAND. Bacco ed Ariadna (1804); La
Conversazione Armonica (1804); Il Trionfo della

chiesa Cattolica (1805); Europa in Creta (1806); Il S. Sepolcro (1815).

PAINE, JOHN KNOWLES. Œdipus (1881); Phœbus Arise (1882); The Nativity (1883); Realm of Fancy (1884).

PAINE, ROBERT P. From Death unto Life (1883); Great is the Lord (1884); The Lay of the Last Minstrel (1884); A Day with our Lord (1885).

PAISIELLO, GIOVANNI. Peleus (1763); Achille in Sciro (1783); Giunone Lucina (1784).

PARKER, JAMES C. D. Redemption Hymn (1877); The Blind King (1886).

PARKER, H. W. King Trojan (1885).

PATTISON, THOMAS MEE. The Ancient Mariner (1885); The Lay of the Last Minstrel (1885).

PEPUSCH, JOHN CHRISTOPHER. Alexis (1712).

PERGOLESI, GIOVANNI. Siciliana (1730); Euridice (1730).

PONCHIELLI, AMILCARE. Donizetti ed Mayr Cantata (1875).

PROUT, EBENEZER. Hereward (1878); Freedom (1880); Alfred (1881); Queen Aimée (1885).

RAFF, JOSEPH JOACHIM. Wachet auf (1865); Deutschland's Auferstehung (1865); Einer Entschlaffener (1876); One Hundred and Thirtieth Psalm, " De Profundis " (1878); Die Tageszeiten (1878).

RANDEGGER, ALBERT. Medea (1869); The One Hundred and Fiftieth Psalm (1872); Fridolin (1873); Saffo (1875).

REICHARDT, JOHANN FRIEDRICH. Trauer Cantate auf den Tod Friedrich (1786); La Danza (1790).

REINECKE, KARL. Ein geistliche Abendlied (1851); Schlachtlied (1852); Schneewittchen (1852); Salvum fac regem (1859); Weinachts (1861); Belshazzar (1863); Te Deum Laudamus (1870); Flucht der heilige Familie (1873); Dörnroschen (1875); Aschenbrödel (1877); Hakon Jarl (1877); Die wilden Schwäne (1881).

REISSIGER, KARL GOTTLIEB. Der Herr macht Alles wohl (1830).

REISSMANN, AUGUST. Drusus' Death (1870); Lorelei (1871).

RHEINBERGER, JOSEPH. Wasserfee (1867); Die Nacht (1868); Die tödte Braut (1873); Johannisnacht (1875); Klärchen auf Eberstein (1876); Christophorus (1880); Toggenburg (1880).

RIES, FERDINAND. Der Morgen (1835).

ROCKSTRO, WILLIAM SMYTH. The little Daughter of Jairus (1871); The Good Shepherd (1885).

RODE, THEODORE. Passion's Cantata (1864).

ROMBERG, ANDREAS. The Transient and the Eternal (1801); Lay of the Bell (1808).

ROSSINI, GIOACHINO. Didone abandonnata (1811); Eglo e Irene (1814); Teti e Peleo (1816); I pastori (1820); Cara patria (1820); La Riconoscenza (1821); Il pianto delle Muse (1823); La sacra Alleanza (1823); Il vero ommagio (1823); Joan of Arc (1859).

RUBINSTEIN, ANTON. E dunque vero (1865); Die Nixe (1866); The Morning (1868); Mignon (1869); Hecuba (1872); Hagar in the Wilderness (1872).

RYAN, DESMOND L. The Maid of Astolat (1886).

SAINT-SAENS, CHARLES CAMILLE. Les Noces de Prométhée (1867); Le Deluge (1876); Eighteenth Psalm (1877); Chanson d' Ancêtre (1878); La Lyre et la Harpe (1879); Hymn to Victor Hugo (1885).

APPENDIX. 363

SALAMAN, CHARLES KENSINGTON. Shakspeare Jubilee (1850).
SALIERI, ANTONIO. Le Dernier Jugement (1788); La Riconoscenza (1796).
SCARLATTI, ALESSANDRO. Povera pelegrina (1697).
SCHARWENKA, LUDWIG PHILIPP. Herbstfeier (1882); Sakuntala (1883).
SCHIRA, FRANCESCA. The Lord of Burleigh (1873).
SCHMITT, ALOYS. Die Wörter des Glaubens (1816); Die Huldigung der Tonkunst (1818); Die Hoffnung (1820).
SCHUBERT, FRANZ. Salieri's Jubilee (1815); Prometheus (1816); Cantata (Spendau) (1816); Glaube, Hoffnung und Liebe (1816); Der Frühlingsmorgen (1818); Vogl Cantata (1818); Die Allmacht (1820); Constitution's Lied (1822); À la belle Irene (1827); Miriam's Song (1828).
SCHUMANN, ROBERT. Mignon's Requiem (1849); Advent Hymn (1849); Pilgrimage of the Rose (1851); The King's Son (1851); The Singer's Curse (1852); The Page and the King's Daughter (1852); The Luck of Edenhall (1853).
SINGER, OTTO. Landing of the Pilgrims (1876); Festival Ode (1877).
SMART, HENRY. Bride of Dunkerron (1864); King René's Daughter (1871); The Fishermaidens (1871); Jacob (1873).
SPOHR, LOUIS. The Liberation of Germany (1814); Lord, Thou art great (1815); How lovely are Thy Dwellings (1815); Jehovah, Lord of Hosts (1820); The Lord's Prayer (1829); Hymn to the holy Cecilia (1856).
SPONTINI, GASPARD. Borussia (1826); Gott segne der König (1828).
STAINER, JOHN. The Daughter of Jairus (1878); St. Mary Magdalene (1883).

STANFORD, CHARLES VILLIERS. The Revenge (1880); God is our Hope (1881).
SULLIVAN, ARTHUR. Kenilworth (1864); On Shore and Sea (1871); The Martyr of Antioch (1875); The Golden Legend (1886).
SVENDSEN, JOHANN. Marriage Cantata (1873).
THOMAS, AMBROISE. Lesueur Cantata (1852); The Tyrol (1867); Carnival of Rome (1868); The Atlantic (1868); Sabbath Night (1869); Boieldieu Cantata (1875).
THOMAS, ARTHUR GORING. The Sun Worshippers (1881).
TSCHAIKOWSKY, PETER I. Coronation Cantata (1882).
VOLKMANN, FRIEDRICH R. To-night (1867); Sappho (1868).
WAGNER, RICHARD. New Year's (1834); Das Liebesmahl der Apostel (1843); Gelegensheit Cantate (1843).
WEBER, CARL MARIA VON. Der Ester Ton (1808); Kampf und Sieg (1815); Natur und Liebe (1818); Jubilee Cantata (1818).
WHITING, GEORGE ELBRIDGE. Dream Pictures (1877); Lenora (1879); Tale of the Viking (1880); Henry of Navarre (1885).
WINTER, PETER. Pigmalione; Piramo e Thisbe; Die verlassene Dido; Vortigerne; Hector; Inez de Castro; Henri IV.; Baiersche Lustbarkeit; Der Franz Lustgarten; Die Hochzeit des Figaro; Andromaque; Prague et Philomela; Timoteo; Die Erlösung des Menschen; Die Auferstehung Germania's Friedens; (all written between 1789 and 1793).
ZINGARELLI, NICOLO. Telemaco (1785); Eco (1802); Cantata Sacra (1829).

INDEX.

ACIS AND GALATEA, 27, 166.
Addison, 58, 59.
Advent Hymn, 27, 319.
Alexander's Feast, 27, 173.
American Cantatas, 28.
Antigone, 254.
Appendix, 353.
Ariadne, 198.
Arnold, Edwin, 117, 233.
As the Hart Pants, 262.
Auber, 66.

BACH, 22-25, 63, 308; life of, 29.
Balfe, 56; life of, 44.
Bassani, 18.
Beethoven, 20, 134, 135, 146, 250, 269, 314; life of, 48.
Bells of Strasburg, 221.
Benedict, 66, 128, 299; life of, 56.
Bennett, 27, 227, 332; life of, 62.
Berlioz, 27, 295; life of, 68.
Bononcini, 19, 164.
Brahms, 27, 135, 317; life of, 82.
Bridal of Triermain, 124.
Bride of Dunkerron, 328.
Bruch, 27; life of, 86.
Buck, 27, 28, 153, 156, 335; life of, 101.
Burney, 14, 16, 18.
Byron, 45, 70.

CALDARA, 19.
Cantata, origin of, 13; earlier form, 14; in France, 20; in Germany, 21; Church cantatas, 26-28; modern cantatas, 26-28.
Carissimi, 13, 14, 16.
Carlyle, 38, 39, 40.
Centennial Meditation of Columbia, 28, 106.
Cesti, 16.
Chandos Anthems, 26, 164, 167.
Chopin, 317.
Chorley, 58, 64, 210, 265, 332.
Choron, 15, 201.
Christmas, 228.
Christophorus, 304.
Comala, 27, 144.
Corder, life of, 123.
Cowen, 27; life of, 128.
Crusaders, 149.
Culprit Fay, 28, 157.

DAMNATION OF FAUST, 27, 74.
Dante, 198.
D'Astorga, 19.
Davidde Penitente, 274.
Donizetti, 59.
Don Munio, 27, 28, 103.
Dryden, 19, 58, 59, 170, 173, 175, 177, 178.

Drummond, 289.
Dvořák, life of, 134.

EIN' FESTE BURG, 38.
Erl King's Daughter, 147.
Exhibition Ode, 66.

FAIR ELLEN, 93.
Festa Ascensionis Christi, 37.
Foote, 28; life of, 140.
Forty-sixth Psalm, 28, 154.
Fridolin, 27, 299.
Frithjof's Saga, 27, 87.

GADE, 27, 295; life of, 143.
Gasparini, 17, 18.
George Sand, 216.
Gilchrist, 28; life of, 153.
Gleason, 28; life of, 156.
Glorious Moment, The, 53.
Gluck, 192.
Goethe, 54, 80, 86, 148, 248, 249, 251.
Golden Legend (Buck), 28, 109.
Golden Legend (Sullivan), 27, 335.
Gottes Zeit, 33.
Gounod, 78, 79.
Gutenberg Fest, 263.

HAMERIK, 28, 107, 109.
Handel, 19, 20, 25, 27, 32, 58, 59, 85; life of, 163.
Handel's Passion Cantata, 25.
Hanover Cantatas, 25.
Hatton, life of, 186.
Hawkins, 13, 16.
Haydn, 26, 48, 54, 250; life of, 191.
Heil der in Siegerkranz, 84.
Heine, 39.
Hiawatha, 28, 141.
Hiller, 27, 86, 123, 318; life of, 201.
Hofmann, 27; life of, 205.
Holyrood, 210.

ICH HATTE VIEL BEKUMMERNISS, 31.

Irving, 103, 114.
Italian Cantata writers, 16-20.

JUBILEE CANTATA, 344.
Jubilee Ode, 237.

KAMPF UND SIEG, 27, 346.
Keats, 288.
King René's Daughter, 330.
King Thamos, 270.
King Trojan, 28, 292.

L' ALLEGRO, 178.
Lamartine, 216.
Landing of the Pilgrims, 28, 325.
Lauda Sion, 265.
Lay of the Bell, 27, 309.
Legrenzi, 17.
Leslie, life of, 209.
Light of Asia, 27, 28, 117.
Liszt, 27, 82, 83, 324, 339, 340; life of, 215.
Lotti, 17, 19.
Longfellow, 110, 141, 221, 222, 335, 349.
Love Feast of the Apostles, 340.
Luther, 38, 39, 40, 42.

MACFARREN, 50, 52; life of, 226.
Mackenzie, life of, 232.
Marcello, 19.
Mary Magdalen, 242.
Masonic Cantatas, 276.
Massenet, life of, 241.
May Queen, 27, 64.
Mazeppa, 45.
Melusina, 27, 206.
Mendelssohn, 20, 27, 36, 40, 52, 62, 87, 134, 143, 161, 203, 206, 295, 307; life of, 246.
Meyerbeer, 41, 66.
Milton, 178, 179, 286.
Minstrel's Curse, 322.
Miriam's War Song, 314.
Mozart, 20, 48, 62, 134, 176, 250; life of, 268.

NATIVITY, THE, 28, 286.
Nicolai, 41.

INDEX.

ODYSSEUS, 27, 95.
Œdipus at Colonos, 259.
Œdipus Tyrannus, 28, 259, 281.
On Shore and Sea, 334.

PAGANINI, 70.
Paine, 28, 140; life of, 280.
Paisiello, 20.
Parker, H. W., 28; life of, 291.
Parker, J. C. D., 28; life of, 295.
Pergolesi, 20.
Phœbus, Arise, 28, 289.
Pilgrimage of the Rose, 321.
Pope, 170.
Porpora, 19, 164, 192.
Praise Song to Harmony, 28, 161.
Prometheus, 27, 217.

RAFF, 136.
Rákóczy March, 77.
Randegger, 27; life of, 298.
Realm of Fancy, 28, 288.
Redemption Hymn, 28, 296.
Rheinberger, 27, 291; life of, 303.
Robin Hood, 187.
Romberg, 27, 308.
Romeo and Juliet, 70.
Rosa Salvator, 17.
Rossi, 17.
Rossini, 44.
Rousseau, 20.
Ruins of Athens, 49.

SAINT-SAENS, 153.
Salamis, 92.
Salieri, 215, 313.
Sarti, 20.
Scarlatti, 18, 19.
Schiller, 299, 309.

Schubert, 27, 49, 148, 318; life of, 313.
Schumann, 27, 62, 82, 251, 295, 307, 315; life of, 317.
Scott, Walter, 124.
Seven Words, The, 194.
Shakspeare, 71, 75, 87, 227, 246, 254, 332.
Singer, 28, 109; life of, 324.
Sleeping Beauty, 27, 129.
Smart, life of, 327.
Song of Miriam, 27.
Song of Victory, 27, 203.
Spectre's Bride, 136.
Spring Fantasie, 146.
St. Cecilia, 57.
Story of Sayid, 233.
Strozzi, 13.
Sullivan, 27; life of, 332.

TALE OF THE VIKING, 28, 349.
Tennyson, 67.
Thomas, Ambroise, 241.
Thomas, Theodore, 102, 109, 153, 233, 281, 324, 333, 339.
Toggenburg, 27, 306.
Triumphlied, 27, 83.

UHLAND, 320, 322, 323.

VERDI, 66, 213.
Victor Hugo, 216.
Voyage of Columbus, 28, 114.

WAGNER, 41, 106, 127, 145, 149, 216; life of, 338.
Walpurgis Night, 27, 248, 262.
Weber, 27, 56, 251; life of, 342.
Whiting, 28, 153; life of, 348.

www.ingramcontent.com/pod-product-compliance
Lightning Source LLC
Chambersburg PA
CBHW020225240426
43672CB00006B/423